Proactivity is more than each one of us doing things. Proactivity is about communities at work making things happen. This book is a practical and evidence-based guide to proactivity at work in ever more agile and complex meso and macro environments. I recommend this book to all managers, leaders, coaches, and HR practitioners.

Professor Almuth McDowall, *Birkbeck, University of London*

Powering Workplace Proactivity is one of the most important books on workplace motivation to be published in recent years. Dr Joanne Gray has developed a highly accessible, evidence-based framework that anyone can use to better understand others and be more proactive. Filled with useful insights and tools, this book is essential for anyone who manages people or who helps teams be more effective.

Dr Hayley Lewis, *Managing Director, HALO Psychology*

A timely and comprehensive exploration of proactivity in the workplace with insightful, practical guidance. I welcomed the wide repertoire of relevant research evidence used to help us develop a better understanding of how individual, job, social, leadership, and organizational factors can enhance or inhibit proactivity. The mix of case studies, the PROACTIVE work design model, and other techniques make this book a useful toolkit for creating environments where proactive individuals can flourish.

Professor Kamal Birdi, *Head of the Institute of Work Psychology, Sheffield University*

I0095135

Powering Workplace Proactivity

Empowering, customizable, and backed by organizational research, this book introduces the PROACTIVE work design model and diagnostic tool to help organizations create optimal conditions for proactivity at work to flourish.

The pressures and expectations of 21st-century life have led to short-term, reactive behavior in the workplace, however, long-term business success relies on proactive behavior, which is self-directed, future-focused, and change-orientated. But proactivity does not occur in a vacuum – it is a complex, social process heavily affected by contextual and situational factors. With its distinct and flexible design model, this book solves the problem of "how" to create the optimal conditions for proactivity at work to flourish, and to drive sustainability and competitive advantage. And its diagnostic feature recognizes that readers are time-pressured and may already be doing some things well within their organizations, so it offers a solution to their problems without having to read the entire book before they can start making a difference. Uniquely, this book recognizes how important it is for leaders to shape the work environment and to be a positive role model to stimulate employee proactive behavior.

Intended as a practical resource, this book provides a range of evidence-based tools and techniques and includes insightful case studies that will be useful for leaders, managers, HR professionals, OD practitioners, and consultants who want to drive proactive behaviors within their organizations.

Joanne Gray, Chief Progressivist at The Progress Lab, is a business psychologist and EMCC-accredited coach who embodies proactivity. With over 25 years of diverse professional experience, including leading global teams in the consumer products industry, she has established herself as a "pracademic," combining academic insights with real-world expertise. By focusing on human motivation, she empowers individuals, teams, and leaders to unlock their full potential and achieve growth. She holds a Professional Doctorate in Occupational Psychology from Birkbeck, University of London, UK.

Powering Workplace Proactivity

How to Build a Future-Focused, Change-Oriented Culture

Joanne Gray

Routledge
Taylor & Francis Group

NEW YORK AND LONDON

Designed cover image: Getty

First published 2025
by Routledge
605 Third Avenue, New York, NY 10158

and by Routledge
4 Park Square, Milton Park, Abingdon, Oxon, OX14 4RN

Routledge is an imprint of the Taylor & Francis Group, an informa business

© 2025 Joanne Gray

ISBN: 9781032769783 (hbk)
ISBN: 9781032767352 (pbk)
ISBN: 9781003480693 (ebk)

DOI: 10.4324/9781003480693

Typeset in Sabon
by Newgen Publishing UK

To Mum, Dad, Dan & Esmee
For fuelling my Can-do, Reason-to, and Energized-to

Contents

Acknowledgments

"She believed she could, so she did" – an inspirational message on the front of a card I received to celebrate my graduation. I embarked on writing this book with self-belief. But just as it takes a village to raise a child, I've relied on a community of supporters who've helped make it happen; my heartfelt gratitude goes out to every one of them.

This journey began when I presented my PROACTIVE work design framework to Helenor Rogers, who urged me to bring this knowledge to the world. A coaching conversation with Jane Stewart sparked the idea of this book, and I'm deeply grateful to Barry Carpenter for seeing its potential and connecting me with the wonderful team at Routledge. I wanted to make this book a practical resource by including case studies of exemplars in business who are doing great work to power proactivity. I am grateful for the time trailblazers from Avon, Harris Creative, Southern Co-op, Timpson's, and Virgin Money have afforded me. Thank you to all of my research participants for sharing their perspectives and experiences, and to the brilliant academics whose work has shaped my thinking, Sharon Parker's dedication to advancing the proactivity literature is truly remarkable. With special thanks to Rob Sayers-Brown and Zoe Nwosu for imparting your knowledge and entrusting me to give voice to your research participants, and Almuth McDowall for such wisdom and guidance around neurodiversity. I am indebted to Harriet Gill and Jo Price for such dedication as critique partners in reviewing the entire book, chapter by chapter. And a note of gratitude to beta readers Elaine Berry, Abbey Cullen, and Nicola Jopling.

Practical support and guidance have been enablers, but I could not have done this without the emotional support of my wonderful family – they have helped me to be energized to the very end. And to all of my friends who have been there for me, though I can't mention each of you by name, your kindness, and cheerleading have meant the world to me.

Part I

Proactivity at Work

Introduction

The Inspiration for This Book

The world of work has undergone seismic shifts in recent decades due to a perfect storm of globalization, technological advancements, economic forces, demographic changes, and environmental concerns. A willingness to adapt and challenge the status quo are important qualities for employees in this dynamic environment. Being proactive and using one's initiative are increasingly sought-after characteristics at work, featuring in over 40% of all job postings on Indeed.com.[1] Unsurprising, given the abundance of research extolling the benefits of this workplace behavior, proactive actions are undoubtedly useful during organizational change and to gain competitive advantage.

Having a proactive personality and recognizing that it doesn't always lead to positive outcomes sparked my curiosity to delve further into this topic as part of my studies. The conclusion of my thesis, *A Multifaceted Examination of Proactivity at Work*, is that proactivity is a complex phenomenon. It is an individual behavior that is heavily influenced by others and the context within which the individual is operating. I chose the name *Powering Workplace Proactivity* for this book because I wanted to explicitly acknowledge how power and influence are so deeply ingrained in acts of proactivity at work. Whether executives recognize the role of power and influence in their organization or not, the reality is most organizations operate by distributing decision-making authority, and these structures inevitably provide a power base for individuals, particularly when vying for scarce resources. This book is premised on the idea that organizations are inherently political structures, but we shouldn't see that as a negative; we should see it as an opportunity to distribute power and to encourage greater collaboration and cooperation through positive influence and building strong relationships, to make empowering and engaging workplaces.

Using my initiative and challenging the status quo has been my way of being for as long as I can remember. I smile wryly when thinking back to

DOI: 10.4324/9781003480693-2

a failed proactive experience early on in high school when I tried to pro-actively initiate a change in uniform policy. It was back in the late 80s, and the height of fashion for culottes, an item of clothing that looked like a skirt but were trousers. Culottes gave you the freedom to play around acrobatically at break time without fear of exposing your underwear! So, it seemed logical to me that the head of school should be open to adding culottes to the approved uniform list, even back then it seemed so binary to me that girls were expected to wear skirts and boys wear trousers. On reflection, I was ahead of my time and my inexperience meant that my proactivity was enacted like a bull in a china shop! I lacked any kind of political skill or situational judgment and relied solely on personal appeal to influence the decision. And when that didn't work, I became cantan-kerous, so unsurprisingly the existing uniform policy remained firmly in place for the duration of my school years. But we live and learn, I can take comfort that 20 years after that episode I was able to proactively influence the workwear policy of a previous employer, by introducing a smart casual dress code. It was certainly a lot easier to make that happen when in a pos-ition of power and seniority.

This leads me back to the critical role of context and culture. Proactivity does not operate in a vacuum. It is a social endeavor that relies on an environment that is conducive to empowering self-directed behaviors and open to new ideas and constructive challenges. As my childhood example demonstrated, when leadership is set on maintaining the status quo, even the most proactive individual will become stifled, and in the workplace that has a range of pernicious consequences. I firmly believe that the envir-onment significantly influences outcomes related to proactivity. After all, if a flower doesn't bloom, you adjust the environment in which it grows, not the flower itself. *Powering Workplace Proactivity* spotlights the import-ance of creating the optimal workplace environment for proactive behav-iors to flourish not flounder. Throughout this book, I draw on a body of organizational research, including my doctoral studies to provide some of the latest evidence-based thinking. Research has informed the core concept of this book: my nine-dimensional PROACTIVE work design framework and diagnostic tool, aimed at shaping work contexts to encourage employ-ees to be more proactive within their organizations. To provide practical value, I share activities and resources that I have used with clients, and where possible I offer insights from exemplars in business who are demon-strating best practices in the areas I will be discussing.

How to Use This Book

Chapters 1 and 2 act as scene-setters, clarifying proactivity at work, and highlighting its importance in a world of work often described as volatile, uncertain, complex, and ambiguous (VUCA). I share insights into the motivational factors driving us to be proactive, or not. I intend to offer solutions in the areas that are most relevant to you, without the need to read the entire book cover to cover. You are already likely to be doing some things well within your organization, therefore it is more helpful to prioritize the areas of the PROACTIVE work design framework that are going to make a genuine difference. So, Chapter 3 provides an opportunity to reflect on your organization to see how it shapes up, the diagnostic tool should help guide the focus areas for intervention development specific to your organization.

Part II, Chapters 4–12 break down the PROACTIVE work design framework, with the acronym representing the importance of creating **P**sychological safety; clarifying **R**ole and remit expectations; establishing a sense of **O**rganizational fairness; promoting **A**utonomy; reinforcing the role of explicit **C**ommunication; valuing the **T**ime investment; recognizing the need for **I**nfluencing skills; appreciating the role of **V**alues and motivation, and acknowledging the **E**nergy and effort involved in being proactive at work. In each of these chapters, I demonstrate the importance of each of the concepts and their associated outcomes. I highlight some of the pitfalls when each of these conditions for proactivity are not met; and share some tools, techniques, and case studies from pioneering organizations to help inform the design of organizational interventions. At the end of each chapter, I provide space for you to pause and reflect and encourage you to capture your thoughts and set some proactive goals, which I call *Implementation Intentions*.

Part III invites you to consider some of the elements of the PROACTIVE work design framework through different lenses, namely from the perspectives of employees from historically under-recognized groups, older workers, and employees identifying as neurodivergent. Fairness and equality sit at the heart of my values; as an advocate for equitable experiences at work, I will share some insights that may help you shape PROACTIVE interventions with inclusivity in mind. Given the complexity and variation across individual experiences, these chapters are intended to provide food for thought, dispel myths, and raise some important questions. I do hope this will spark some proactive thinking and action on your part to support a diverse workforce.

Before exploring proactivity at work in-depth, I'd encourage you to reflect for a moment and consider your personal preferences towards this type of behavior at work. Are you the type of person who searches for a solution straight away when something goes wrong, or is your occupational maxim let's wait and see? As we'll discover throughout this book, being proactive at work involves taking some level of interpersonal risk, and that comes more naturally to some than others. Creating the optimal environment for everyone to feel confident in being self-directed is vitally important. This book identifies nine ingredients for proactivity to flourish, in essence, it's about creating a culture that values learning and growth, builds a sense of inclusivity, and empowers employees to be their best. And while there's a recipe for creating a future-focused, change-oriented workplace, this is not a check-box exercise; organizations are dynamic places, and as such ongoing effort and attention are required to create and sustain a culture of proactivity.

Reference

1. Indeed.com (2024) Job search results from the UK site of Indeed.com. Accessed on 29 February 2024.

Chapter 1

What Is Proactivity at Work and Why Is It Important?

This chapter is a deep dive into proactivity at work, an increasingly important behavior in navigating complex, dynamic, and uncertain workplaces. Different forms of proactive behavior are explained and explored, to show how individuals can be proactive at work. The consequences of being proactive are then brought to life, reminding us that it's a double-edged sword, with the potential for both positive and negative outcomes. I'll conclude by emphasizing proactivity as a social process, whereby contextual, situational, and relational factors can act to help or hinder its effectiveness.

The Growing Importance of Proactivity at Work

A global pandemic and subsequent economic crises have had a significant impact on how we work. Increased pressures and expectations across various life domains (personal, family, work) have culminated in employees experiencing higher job demands and feeling excessively busy which leads to short-term, reactive behavior. However, busyness and firefighting at work are not a healthy state of being for organizations that want to remain competitive and sustainable. Performance, innovation, and long-term business success rely on proactive behavior which is self-directed, future-focused, and change-orientated. Being proactive typically means being one step ahead, it involves taking initiative to make things happen rather than waiting for things to happen. Whether it's pre-empting an issue and fixing it before it becomes a problem or seeing an opportunity and capitalizing on it for competitive advantage. Being proactive does not imply doing more work or taking on more responsibility, it is about leaning into change and being prepared to do things differently, without being asked to do so.

Proactivity at work can be personality driven or it can be developed as a learned behavior. Individuals with a proactive personality are often

DOI: 10.4324/9781003480693-3

Table 1.1 Different Forms of Proactive Behavior

Categorization	Description	Forms of Proactive Behaviors
Proactive person-environment fit (P-E fit)	Setting proactive goals to achieve greater congruence between one's personal attributes and that of the internal work environment	• Career initiative • Personal initiative • Job crafting • Negotiating personalized work arrangements • Feedback seeking
Proactive work behaviors (PWB)	Behaviors intended to improve the internal organizational environment	• Speaking up • Taking charge (e.g., to improve ways of working) • Proactive problem solving • Innovative behavior • Safety proactivity
Proactive strategic behaviors (PSB)	Behaviors aimed at initiating change to improve the organization's strategy	• Issue-selling (directed upwards to Senior stakeholders) • Strategic scanning (e.g., identifying market opportunities)

Source: Adapted from Ref. [2].

defined as being "relatively unconstrained by situational forces, and who effects environmental change."[1] Values such as an openness to changes, a preference toward learning goals, and a strong future orientation are commonly associated with having a proactive personality. From a behavioral perspective, we can categorize different forms of proactive behavior into three different areas: *proactive person-environment fit (P-E fit)*; *proactive work behavior (PWB)*; and *proactive strategic behavior (PSB)*. Each varies in the type of outcome the individual aims to bring about. Drawing on the works of Sharon Parker and Catherine Collins, Table 1.1 provides a summary of the categorization of proactive behaviors and a short description of each of the forms of proactivity and associated concepts. We will delve into these different forms throughout this book.

Outcomes of Proactive Behavior

It is becoming increasingly important for employees to think beyond their job description in initiating and activating change at work. There is general agreement in organizational research that proactive behavior can contribute to personal, team, and organizational effectiveness and is particularly useful during organizational change. Studies have demonstrated that taking charge behaviors based on improving processes can enhance organizational adaptability and long-term success.[3] When proactive behaviors are encouraged and welcomed by supervisors and co-workers, they tend to induce positive emotions, such as pride and accomplishment. Proactivity can stimulate the *flow experience*, in which a person is so immersed in their work they experience a pleasant state of consciousness and may lose track of time.[4]

Person-Environment Fit Proactive Behavior

Let's first consider person-environment fit (PE-fit) forms of proactivity and associated outcomes. This form of proactivity is primarily concerned with initiating changes that enable a greater fit between oneself and the work environment. Studies exploring this form of proactivity have spotlighted its relationship to career development, networking, performance, engagement, and career success. Proactive individuals are more likely to engage in behaviors such as career planning, self-improvement, and seeking out mentors and support, which in turn contributes to career development and progression.[5] Mass hybrid working has amplified the value of proactive behavior, such that it is considered one of the core competencies for individuals balancing home and office work. In an article setting out the implications of hybrid working, organizational behavior experts Mark Mortenson and Martine Haas coined the phrase *"hybridity competence."* They suggest that employees who can think and act adaptably are better able to navigate complex environments and are more likely to take initiative in asking for resources. By contrast, employees lacking these skills will be disadvantaged and may struggle with hybrid or remote working.[6] Job crafting is also an interesting form of PE-fit proactive behavior, and a form explored further in this book, particularly in relation to motivating older workers, in Chapter 14. Job crafting is where employees independently modify aspects of their jobs to create a better match to their skills and personal interests. An example of this could be where an employee who is passionate about fairness and equality, puts themself forward to engage in diversity, equality, and inclusion initiatives at work. Or it might be an employee who is proficient in a piece of software and wants to take on a new challenge, so proactively takes on the role of software superuser. Research into job crafting suggests this form of proactive behavior allows employees to make work more engaging and meaningful.[7] Distinct from job crafting, but with some parallels, is the notion of proactively negotiating personalized work arrangements, such as an employee requesting compressed hours to facilitate caring responsibilities; or requesting support for personal development, for example, enrolling in a program of study. On the positive side, if personalized arrangements are negotiated, it can improve motivation and retention. However, there are some pitfalls, for example, some employees may feel a sense of obligation or reciprocity towards their organization, and put more effort and hours in at work, which can be detrimental to work-family balance.[8]

Proactive Work Behaviors – Speaking Up

Proactive work behaviors (PWB) can occur at every level of the organization. Whether it's an individual improving how they carry out their tasks, team-related activities, or suggesting company-wide practice improvements. Research suggests that *speaking up* and *taking charge* are the most prominent forms of proactive behavior at work. Perhaps unsurprisingly, numerous organizational scandals and reports of unethical behavior have necessitated the move toward "speak up" cultures. A speak-up culture is where employees are encouraged to speak their minds and raise concerns without being branded a troublemaker or being judged negatively by others. There are countless articles online extolling the benefits of creating a speak-up culture, a quick search on Google using the term "speak-up culture" revealed more than one billion results! The business case for organizations is that safety in speaking up nurtures a sense of inclusivity, while also protecting against reputational, financial, and legal risks. However, while this proactive behavior may be perceived as a business imperative, the psychological mechanisms involved in activating it are complex. This can be explained by how speaking up is observed by others, it is often perceived to be challenging, confrontational, and potentially damaging to the organization. In Chapter 4, I will unpack some of the considerations around creating psychological safety which is a key ingredient in creating speak-up cultures.

Proactive Work Behaviors – Taking Charge and Innovative Behavior

Let's now consider *taking charge* as another common form of proactive work behavior. Taking charge tends to happen when individuals identify suboptimal ways of working and focus on improving processes, procedures, or policies. Studies exploring this form of proactive behavior highlight the value it provides in enhancing organizational effectiveness. That's because it's often not possible for leaders and managers to fully appreciate or foresee the challenges associated with role-related activities. My research highlighted a link between taking charge and innovative behavior, often in identifying sub-optimal processes and procedures, employees come up with a better way of doing things. It is this "better way" that could be described as proactive innovative behavior. Once the idea has been hatched, taking charge follows to bring that idea to fruition. That said, proactive innovative behavior can also relate to creative idea generation that extends beyond process improvement; whether that be the search for new goods/services or finding novel ways to extend the use of existing products, they all contribute to improving organizational outcomes. In most industries, innovation is the lifeblood of an organization and an imperative to remain relevant and competitive. But as we'll see in Chapter 5, there is a fine line between the extent to which individuals believe they can drive innovation and take charge and the expectation to operate within their "remit." Taking charge also carries risks concerning how others perceive the intent behind this behavior. Influential thinker and organizational psychologist Adam Grant carried out two studies to demonstrate this. The first among managers and their direct supervisors across professional sectors, and the second among firefighters and their platoon supervisors. His findings suggested that when supervisors assumed individuals' motivation to be proactive was guided by self-interest and not in the interest of others, it could negatively impact performance ratings.[9] In Chapter 8, we will explore the role of communicating with intent and creating a culture of positive interpretations whereby building "negative narratives" around the intentions, words, and actions of proactive employees are avoided.

Proactive Work Behaviors – Safety Proactivity

Another form of proactive work behavior that is high on the agendas of organizations, governments, and regulators is *safety proactivity*. This form of proactive behavior is concerned with prioritizing workplace health and safety. It is rooted in the assumption that employees will take a proactive role in promoting safety at work. While training employees on risks and hazards is important to minimize safety-related issues, the key to success lies in creating a culture of safety that relies on self-initiated, change-oriented behaviors. Safety proactivity can be motivated by a desire to promote changes in approaches to improve safety standards, for example, by suggesting new ideas or taking charge; or it can be driven by a desire to protect against undesirable behavior and may come in the form of whistleblowing or raising concerns with supervisors. Either way, higher safety proactivity is associated with lower occupational risks and accident rates and a happier more productive workforce.[10] A case study often cited as an exemplar in championing safety proactivity is Alcoa, a major producer of Aluminum based in the United States. Back in the late 1980s, then-CEO Paul O'Neill came into an organization in a state of decline, some of which was due to ineffective processes. The turnaround of the business is attributed to O'Neill's fixation on championing safety and a culture of accountability that relies on proactive behavior. The results speak for themselves, over O'Neill's tenure, Alcoa dropped from 1.86 lost workdays to injury per 100 workers to 0.2, and by 2012, the rate had fallen to 0.125.[11] And the reduction in workday rate directly correlated with an increase in market value. Today, the organization describes itself as a values-based company, with 85% of employees recommending it as a good place to work.[12]

Proactive Strategic Behaviors

The final category of proactivity at work encompasses *strategic proactive behaviors*, these are aimed at initiating change to improve the organization's strategy and contribute to long-term sustainability. This set of behaviors includes strategic scanning, which involves identifying market opportunities, and what is described as issue-selling, which has some parallels with speaking up. The key difference in these forms of proactivity is that they are specifically directed upward to senior stakeholders within an organization. Interestingly, having a proactive personality does not necessarily drive individuals to engage in proactive strategic behaviors.[13] In my research among older workers, I found that this form of proactivity was often associated with one's job role. For example, if they held senior positions or in roles involving future thinking, planning, and change, such as business transformation, they'd be more inclined to engage in proactive strategic behavior. For most of my research participants, this form of proactivity was considered "outside" of their role and remit. What was revealing, was for those who did engage in this type of proactivity, there were some extremely negative consequences associated with it, specifically when their proactivity had been "stifled" by senior stakeholders. I heard several stories of individuals who felt frustrated and powerless when their strategic proposals were not given any airtime by their bosses; despite their job role involving strategy generation they were not being allowed to proactively put strategies forward, which seemed to worsen the situation. In these instances, for some individuals, the frustration fueled an impetus to be more proactive and persistent, while for others it led to disengagement and in some cases rebellious behavior, such as bad-mouthing the boss.

The Proactivity Paradox

I imagine you are now starting to see the double-edged nature of proactivity at work. On the one hand, there's lots of evidence highlighting the benefits of this type of behavior, yet on the other hand, in certain circumstances, it can lead to negative consequences for both employees and the organization. There is also an interesting paradox when it comes to energy levels and proactivity. In some instances, proactivity can be sparked when we feel overworked and are running low on energy. This can happen when we feel under pressure with high work demands, leading us to respond with personal initiative to find better ways of working or doing a task differently. Yet, other studies have also shown that being proactive requires energy, particularly if it involves having to negotiate with skeptical stakeholders, and if we are not adequately recuperating at the end of each day, then we are less likely to be proactive on subsequent days.[14] In 2018, a group of researchers from Australia conducted an illuminating study into the consequences of proactive behavior relating to work outcomes and well-being. Their findings concluded that there are two distinct pathways through which proactivity at work impacts employee well-being.[15] The first is an energy-generating pathway whereby proactive behavior boosts end-of-workday vitality, supporting the idea that when proactive endeavors go well, it generates feelings of pride and accomplishment. The second is a strain pathway that leads to feelings of anxiety, which can result in rumination outside of work that impairs our ability to recover and recuperate in readiness for our next workday. Regarding the strain pathway, according to this study's findings, feelings of anxiety were associated with how supervisors responded to mistakes and the perceived level of support they provided. In other words, when proactive employees' actions are met with punitive reactions, there is a potential for the strain pathway to be experienced. Negative reactions to an individual's proactivity are also particularly evident across the organizational research looking at proactive voice and taking charge, with studies highlighting how proactive individuals can be negatively judged by their supervisors and co-workers. These studies highlight the double-edged nature of proactivity at work, where on one side it can be praised and rewarded, but on the other side, it can be met with suspicion and opposition. Chapter 12 explores the proactivity-energy relationship further and provides insights into how to minimize the effects of energy depletion.

Without a doubt, proactivity at work is a complex phenomenon. One thing is clear – the vital role of a supportive organization and empowering leadership behaviors to enable this future-focused, change-oriented behavior to flourish and maximize the positive outcomes it can provide.

Key Takeaways

- Proactive behavior at work is becoming increasingly important as the world of work becomes more complex, dynamic, and uncertain.

- Whilst being proactive comes more naturally to some, it can be learned by all.
- Proactivity comes in different shapes and forms, each with different outcomes.
- Proactivity can be described as double-edged; experiences and outcomes of being proactive at work can be both positive and negative.
- Proactivity at work does not operate in a vacuum, it is a highly social process, whereby contextual, situational, and relational factors can act to help or hinder its effectiveness.

Reflective Questions

- What forms of proactivity are most prominent in your organization? Why might that be?
- Are employees who are naturally less inclined to be proactive within your organization being disadvantaged? If so, how could you address that?
- How open are your senior stakeholders to employee strategic proactive behavior – is this form of proactivity fully embraced or met with resistance? If so, what are the consequences of that?

My Implementation Intentions

Jot down in this space any actions you will take in response to the reflective questions.

References

1. Bateman, T. S., & Crant, J. M. (1993). The proactive component of organizational behavior: A measure and correlates. *Journal of Organizational Behavior*, 14(2), 103–118.
2. Parker, S. K., & Collins, C. G. (2010). Taking stock: Integrating and differentiating multiple proactive behaviors. *Journal of Management*, 36(3), 633–662.
3. Parker, S. K., & Collins, C. G. (2010). Taking stock: Integrating and differentiating multiple proactive behaviors. *Journal of Management*, 36(3), 633–662.
4. Csikszentmihalyi, M. (2000). Happiness, flow, and economic equality. *American Psychologist*, 55(10), 1163–1164.
5. Seibert, S. E., Kraimer, M. L., & Crant, J. M. (2001). What do proactive people do? A longitudinal model linking proactive personality and career success. *Personnel Psychology*, 54(4), 845–874.
6. Mortenson, M., & Haas, M. (2021). Making the hybrid workplace fair. *Harvard Business Review*, 99(3), 68–75.
7. Tims, M., Bakker, A. B., & Derks, D. (2013). The impact of job crafting on job demands, job resources, and well-being. *Journal of Occupational Health Psychology*, 18(2), 230.
8. Hornung, S., Rousseau, D. M., & Glaser, J. (2008). Creating flexible work arrangements through idiosyncratic deals. *Journal of Applied Psychology*, 93(3), 655.
9. Grant, A. M., & Ashford, S. J. (2008). The dynamics of proactivity at work. *Research in Organizational Behavior*, 28, 3–34.
10. Crant, J. M., Hu, J., & Jiang, K. (2016). *Proactive personality: A twenty-year review*. In *Proactivity at work* (pp. 211–243). Taylor & Francis.
11. Curcuruto, M., & Griffin, M. A. (2016). *Safety proactivity in the workplace. In Proactivity at work: Making things happen in organizations (p. 105)*. Taylor & Francis.
12. Baer, D. (2014). Business insider. www.businessinsider.com/how-changing-one-habit-quintupled-alcoas-income-2014-4?r=US&IR=T
13. Glassdoor Overviews. Accessed on 11th December 2023. Available at Glassdoor.com
14. Sonnentag, S. (2003). Recovery, work engagement, and proactive behavior: A new look at the interface between nonwork and work. *Journal of Applied Psychology*, 88(3), 518.
15. Cangiano, F., Parker, S. K., & Yeo, G. B. (2019). Does daily proactivity affect well-being? The moderating role of punitive supervision. *Journal of Organizational Behavior*, 40(1), 59–72.

Chapter 2

Proactive Motivation

In this chapter, I introduce the proactive motivation model, including the phases of determining and striving toward proactive goals and the motivational states fueling proactive behavior at work. I go on to explore how our personality, values, and personal experiences play a role in influencing our proactive motivation. Before going on to consider the role of leadership, and specifically how empowering leadership behaviors and a supportive organizational culture help to stimulate proactive behaviors. This chapter concludes by introducing the concept of *Wise Proactivity*, which encourages intentional behaviors that mitigate the risk of proactivity causing chaos.

Proactivity Processes

To create the conditions for proactivity to flourish, it is important to understand the processes involved and the role of proactive motivation. With a deeper understanding of the process, the influencing factors and the outcomes become easier to grasp. Let's start with a model of proactive goal generation and goal striving, as shown in Figure 2.1, which encompasses four distinct phases.[1]

The proactivity process starts with perceiving a problem or opportunity and imagining a solution, this is called the *envisioning* phase. Let's bring this to life with an example that encompasses proactive innovative behavior and taking charge. Imagine you work in operations for a retail chain, and you're experiencing a challenge with staff shortages in some stores which is impacting opening hours and negatively hitting sales. You are also aware that in other stores there are employees keen to work additional hours, so you envision a solution whereby employees work across several different stores rather than being assigned to one specific store. Once the proactive goal has been derived, the next phase is *planning*, so deciding on appropriate actions. In this example, it

DOI: 10.4324/9781003480693-4

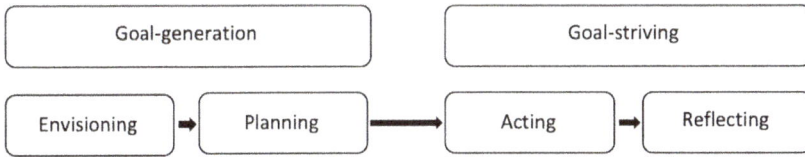

Figure 2.1 The Proactive Goal-Generation and Goal-Striving Process.
Source: Adapted from Ref. [1].

might include speaking to colleagues who work in stores to gauge their interest and openness to your idea; it may involve information gathering from colleagues in other departments, such as HR to understand any people-related implications and speaking to IT to understand if additional tech support may be needed. Once insights have been garnered, building a business case and proposal would usually follow. Assuming the project gets the green light, the next phase is *acting*, so engaging in the proactive goal, implementing the plan to bring about that different future, and making the change happen. In this example, the *acting* phase is likely to involve cross-collaboration across multiple functions within the organization to ensure the smooth implementation of the project plan. No doubt there will be the need to influence and negotiate with colleagues and stakeholders during this phase, given it involves a considerable change to existing ways of working. Finally, the *reflecting* phase, could be done formally by getting the project team together and doing a "lessons learned" on what went well and what could have been done differently, or it may be done in a more self-reflective manner. Either way, the aim is to evaluate the outcomes to inform future proactive endeavors. This process can be applied to any form of proactive behavior, essentially individuals will generate and strive towards various proactive goals, some will lead to successful outcomes, some will not. Now let's turn to where the motivation for setting and striving towards proactive goals comes from in the first place.

A team of leading proactivity researchers, led by Sharon Parker, developed a useful model premised on the idea that proactive action is stimulated by three distinct motivational states.[2] To achieve proactive goals, we need to feel confident in our ability to achieve them, we need to feel motivated to spur us into action and we need to feel optimistic so that we won't fall at the first hurdle, as shown in Figure 2.2. The *Can-do* motivational states arise from feelings of self-efficacy, which is our perception that we have the required abilities and skills and can overcome potential obstacles. We also feel a sense of control and don't feel worried about the

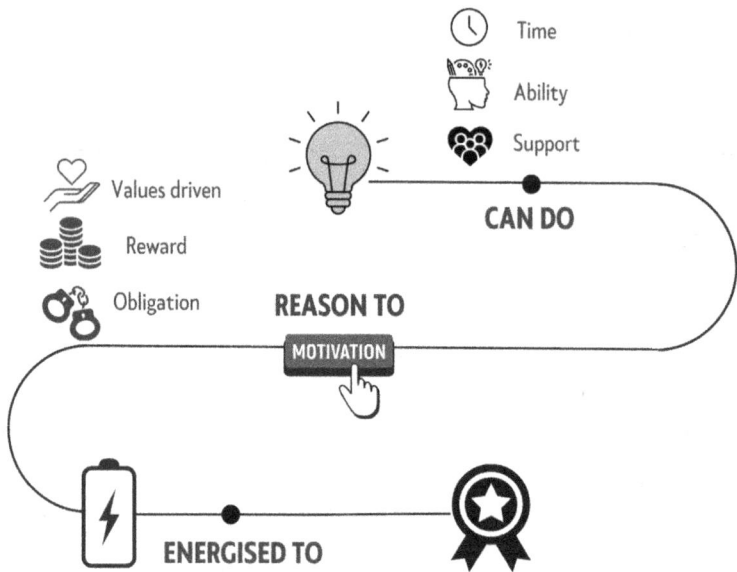

Figure 2.2 The Proactive Motivation Process.
Source: Adapted from Ref. [2].

associated risks of taking proactive action. The *Reason-to* motivational state relates to why someone is proactive and is strongly associated with our utility judgments (e.g. it's worth it) and our sense of autonomy. Interestingly, research suggests that proactive goals driven by external rewards, such as recognition, may be more difficult to sustain when faced with challenges. Similarly, if we are doing something proactively because we feel we ought to (e.g., people-pleasing), this might also hinder our ability to follow through to the *acting* phase. When we feel a sense of obligation, we are more likely to fall at the first hurdle or make excuses for not sustaining and attaining the proactive goal. The *Energized-to* motivational state relates to feeling positively energized, when emotions are positive, we are more likely to set proactive goals and stick with them. Feeling optimistic is evidenced to help us overcome obstacles when we are faced with challenges. When I'm working with coaching clients, who find themselves procrastinating and putting off proactive goals, I often discover that a lack of energy is at the root cause. In which case, I ask "What would it take to make you feel more optimistic?" Or I suggest, they spend some time recuperating and re-building energy levels and then re-embark on their proactive goal striving.

Factors Influencing Proactivity

Individual Factors

We've considered the processes involved in motivating proactivity, let's turn to some of the factors influencing our proactive experiences which can be attributed to individual differences, leadership behaviors, and the organizational culture. At an individual level, there is extensive research exploring the role of personality traits in shaping proactive behavior; a proactive personality and conscientiousness are believed to be important for initiating proactive goals. Another concept in psychology known as *core self-evaluations* (CSE) has also been associated with proactive behavior at work.[3] CSE is made up of self-esteem (confidence and satisfaction in oneself), self-efficacy (belief in one's abilities), locus of control (the degree to which people believe that they have control over the outcome of events), and emotional stability (the ability to balance emotions under stress). A desire for control as a personality preference has also been identified as potentially important. As highlighted in Chapter 1, future-oriented thinking, being open to change, valuing independent thinking, and having a preference toward learning goals rather than performance goals are also associated with being proactive. Delving deeper, it has been suggested that individuals with a high learning goal orientation are more likely to engage in proactive feedback-seeking, as it is perceived as less risky, and they are more likely to persist in the event of setbacks. Whereas those who are performance goal-orientated are less likely to engage in proactive goals because there may be a higher fear of failure.[4]

Contextual Factors

There are several factors relating to leadership and organizational culture that influence proactivity at work, for example, Psychological Safety, which is explored further in Chapter 4. The relationship between psychological safety and proactivity cannot be underestimated. Individuals are far less likely to engage in proactive behavior where perceptions of psychological safety are low as the costs of speaking up are deemed too high. If employees are expected to raise concerns and drive innovative behavior, feeling safe is a prerequisite. Beyond this, consideration should be given to the decision-making discretion provided by managers and leaders. In my research, the notion of "permission" cropped up repeatedly; when individuals believe they can carry out a broader range of tasks than specified in their job description, they are more likely to be proactive. Ideas around permission, role, and remit will be explored in Chapter 5; highlighting the importance of providing role clarity whilst also providing a sense of role breadth that allows for contributions beyond what is formally expected. Similarly, organizational fairness is critical in creating the right conditions for proactivity to flourish and will be discussed in Chapter 6. Negative consequences of proactive behavior are highly dependent on how the organization is perceived by its employees. When the workplace is perceived as unfair negative outcomes can unfold when proactivity is enacted. Leadership styles also influence outcomes of proactivity, empowering and inclusive leadership styles that create a sense of autonomy and trust are associated with higher levels of proactive behavior.[5] Like fairness, perceptions around autonomy can activate a reward or threat response in the human brain, which either drives us towards being proactive or forces us to shy away.[6] Supportive leadership behaviors are equally important, being proactive at work can be exhausting, particularly if it involves high levels of stakeholder influence and negotiation, which will be explored further in Chapter 10. Punitive leadership behaviors, the antithesis of supportive leadership will be discussed in Chapter 12, where I'll highlight the potential for proactivity to deplete energy when employees fear being blamed or shamed by their supervisor for taking personal initiative.

Being Wise with Our Proactivity

I'd like to conclude this chapter by drawing on another concept that I think is particularly helpful. This is the notion of *Wise Proactivity*,[7] which reminds us that setting proactive goals is rarely done in isolation from others. While there are many positive outcomes associated with proactivity at work, widespread proactivity may destabilize organizational structures and create chaos! In Chapter 8, I'll outline the benefits of being more explicit in communicating the forms of proactivity that are valued by the organization to have a more coordinated approach to self-directed behaviors. In the meantime, there are questions I try to reflect on before I go all guns blazing on my next proactive goal and I encourage my coaching clients to do the same. The first question is "Do I even need to be proactive here, and is it appropriate to the situation and current context?" By reflecting on this question, I am drawing on my situational awareness skills and reminding myself that not every situation requires a proactive response. The second question I ask is "Am I the right person for this and/or is it right for me?" This draws on my self-awareness skills and puts into question my *Can-do* and *Reason-to*. I'm also demonstrating self-compassion by recognizing that I might not be *Energized-to* in this instance either. The third question I ask is "What is the impact on others and are my reasons for being proactive well intended?" Here I'm thinking beyond myself, drawing on social awareness and emotional intelligence to consider those around me. If we can consider those three questions and feel confident in our responses, it's likely our proactive behavior will be positively received by others.

Key Takeaways

- When determining and striving toward proactive goals we navigate four distinct phases: envisioning, planning, acting, and reflecting/learning.
- Three motivational states determine proactive behavior: *"Can-do,"* *"Reason-to,"* and *"Energized-to."*
- Our personality, values, and personal experiences play a role in influencing our proactive motivation.
- Empowering leadership behaviors and a supportive organizational culture help fuel proactive behaviors.
- Widespread proactivity may destabilize organizational structures and create chaos; to mitigate this risk the adoption of *Wise Proactivity* is encouraged.

Reflective Questions

- What support might be helpful at each of the four stages of proactive goal generation and goal-striving?
- What factors are influencing the *"Can-do,"* *"Reason-to,"* and *"Energized-to"* motivational states within your organization?

My Implementation Intentions

Jot down in this space any actions you will take in response to the reflective questions.

References

1. Bindl, U. K., & Parker, S. K. (2009). *Investigating self-regulatory elements of proactivity at work*. In Working paper. Institute of Work Psychology, University of Sheffield.
2. Parker, S. K., Bindl, U. K., & Strauss, K. (2010). Making things happen: A model of proactive motivation. *Journal of Management, 36*(4), 827–856.
3. Judge, T. A., Erez, A., Bono, J. E., & Thoresen, C. J. (2003). The core self-evaluations scale: Development of a measure. *Personnel Psychology, 56*(2), 303–331.
4. Porath, C. L., & Bateman, T. S. (2006). Self-regulation: From goal orientation to job performance. *Journal of Applied Psychology, 91*(1), 185.
5. Pieterse, A. N., Van Knippenberg, D., Schippers, M., & Stam, D. (2010). Transformational and transactional leadership and innovative behavior: The moderating role of psychological empowerment. *Journal of Organizational Behavior, 31*(4), 609–623.
6. Rock, D. (2009). Managing with the brain in mind. *Strategy+Business*. Retrieved from www.strategy-business.com/article/09306
7. Parker, S. K., Wang, Y., & Liao, J. (2019). When is proactivity wise? A review of factors that influence the individual outcomes of proactive behavior. *Annual Review of Organizational Psychology and Organizational Behavior, 6*, 221–248.

Chapter 3

How Does Your Organization Shape Up?

Before diving into the PROACTIVE work design framework in Part II, why not take 5–10 minutes to see how your organization shapes up in creating the conditions for proactivity to flourish? Figure 3.1 is a short diagnostic tool that will help guide you to the priority chapters, ensuring you focus on the areas that will be most beneficial for you and your organization. Please rate the following statements based on your observations within your organization. If you work for a large organization, please consider answering the following questions based on your perspective of your team or the teams you work closely with. This will provide insights specific to your immediate work environment. Some questions may be challenging to answer as they refer to the general experience within the organization. Since you can only speak from your perspective, and may not know exactly how others feel, please use your best judgment based on your observations and interactions.

Scoring Instructions

For each section, there are three statements, please follow these steps:

1 Rate your response to each statement in the section.
2 Assign the following points based on your answer:
   • You always observe the statement = 5 points
   • You often observe it = 4 points
   • You sometimes observe = 3 points
   • You rarely observe it = 2 points
   • You never observe it = 1 point
3 To calculate your score for each section, add up the points for all three statements in the section. This total is your score for that section. Repeat this process for each section of the survey.

DOI: 10.4324/9781003480693-5

QUESTIONS:	RATING SCALE:				
	1. Never	2. Rarely	3. Sometimes	4. Often	5. Always
Employees can openly express their opinions and share concerns, without fear of any negative consequences	○	○	○	○	○
Leaders in the organization are open to hearing improvement ideas	○	○	○	○	○
Relationships in the organization are depicted by high levels of trust and respect	○	○	○	○	○
Add your scores for this section (Chapter 4):					
Employees understand how much authority they can exercise	○	○	○	○	○
Employees are encouraged to broaden their knowledge and abilities in areas that go beyond the technical requirements of their role	○	○	○	○	○
Employees are encouraged to get involved with cross-functional activities	○	○	○	○	○
Add your scores for this section (Chapter 5):					
Employees are fairly rewarded for the work they do	○	○	○	○	○
Managers in the organization communicate decisions in a kind and considerate manner	○	○	○	○	○
Most employees here would say they are treated fairly	○	○	○	○	○
Add your scores for this section (Chapter 6):					
Micro-management is not a common practice here	○	○	○	○	○
Employees have some control over what they are supposed to accomplish	○	○	○	○	○
Employees are generally allowed to decide how to get their work done	○	○	○	○	○
Add your scores for this section (Chapter 7):					

Figure 3.1 The Powering Workplace Proactivity Diagnostic Tool.

Source: Created by the author.

QUESTIONS:	RATING SCALE:				
	1. Never	2. Rarely	3. Sometimes	4. Often	5. Always
Managers here generally think the best of their employees, trusting in their abilities and intentions					
Co-workers here make time for one another, prioritizing collaboration and mutual support to ensure everyone succeeds					
Employees are generally not suspicious of the intentions of others; we have an atmosphere of trust and openness					
Add your scores for this section (Chapter 8):					
Urgent, last-minute requests tend to be the exception rather than the norm here					
When it comes to change-related projects, the organization values individuals making time for thoughtful analysis, planning, and learning from lessons					
Established processes and ways of working exist to enable individuals to effectively prioritise their tasks and make the best use of their time at work					
Add your scores for this section (Chapter 9):					
Employees in our organization are generally skilled in navigating organizational politics					
When new starters join, there is a robust onboarding programme to enable them to develop a depth of knowledge about the job and the organization					
Employees here generally feel comfortable raising issues with top-level management					
Add your scores for this section (Chapter 10):					
Employees in our organization understand each other's values and how that drives their work behaviors					
There's a recognition in our organization that different individuals are motivated by different things, and that's ok					
Leaders in our organization are generally good at understanding the motivational drivers of their team members					
Add your scores for this section (Chapter 11):					

Figure 3.1 (Continued)

QUESTIONS:	RATING SCALE:				
	1. Never	2. Rarely	3. Sometimes	4. Often	5. Always
There is good awareness in our organization about the factors that deplete and energize employees at work	◯	◯	◯	◯	◯
In this organization, it is easy to take initiative without facing significant barriers, such as complex approval processes, or internal conflict	◯	◯	◯	◯	◯
Overall, employees in our organization demonstrate high levels of positive energy and enthusiasm in their work	◯	◯	◯	◯	◯
Add your scores for this section (Chapter 12):					

Figure 3.1 (Continued)

Interpreting the Scoring System

Upon completing the diagnostic, you should have a total score for each section. These scores are designed to guide you on which chapters of the book will be most beneficial for you to read. Here's how to interpret your scores:

Score 9 or Below: This suggests that the chapter is highly recommended for you. It offers detailed information and guidance crucial for enhancing effectiveness, stimulating proactivity, and contributing to individual, team, and organizational success.

Score 10–12: A score in this range indicates that your organization is already embracing many of the key factors discussed in the topic. However, you may still find valuable hints and tips in the chapter. Reviewing it could provide additional insights to further enhance practices and drive effectiveness at all levels.

Score 13–15: If you score within this range, the chapter may offer some informative content, but it is likely not essential for you. You already have a strong grasp of the topic, and reading this chapter is optional based on your interest and available time.

Use this scoring system to tailor your reading journey and focus on the chapters that will provide the most value to you. Happy reading!

Part II

PROACTIVE Work Design Model

Chapter 4

Psychological Safety

This chapter provides an in-depth exploration of psychological safety and its vital role in stimulating proactivity at work, particularly speaking up, innovative behavior, and proactive safety behavior. I'll explore the telltale signs of a psychologically safe workplace and, just as importantly, how to recognize when one is not. I introduce the idea of *deep rules* in organizations and then go on to highlight the key ingredients for building psychological safety: trust, interpersonal relationships, and inclusive leadership. I'll conclude by introducing several frameworks for building a "speak up" environment and ideas for developing the skills to be more proficient in building psychological safety.

What Is Psychological Safety?

Psychological safety was first introduced in the 1960s but popularized in the late 1990s by Amy Edmondson, a prominent Organizational Psychologist. Our interest in it has exploded in recent years; in January 2024 alone over 500 LinkedIn posts talked about psychological safety. Psychological safety – the belief that one feels safe to speak up and express oneself without fear of judgment or humiliation, is one of the strongest predictors of creativity, team effectiveness, and performance at work.[1] Yet, there is an inherent connection between our perceptions of what is and isn't safe and our past experiences that contribute to the complexities of creating psychological safety. Some of this can be explained by childhood experiences; as a child, the fear of punishment for getting things "wrong" often leads us to withhold truths. For many individuals, this tendency persists into adulthood, particularly when faced with an environment that feels psychologically "unsafe."

Edmondson's research on psychological safety began with her examination of teamwork in healthcare settings.[2] During her fieldwork, she observed the critical role of communication and collaboration among

DOI: 10.4324/9781003480693-7

healthcare professionals to ensure patient safety. However, she noticed that in some instances, team members were hesitant to speak up about potential issues or mistakes due to a fear of reprisal, particularly from more senior members of the medical team. One of the key moments in Edmondson's research was the study of medical errors in hospitals. Contrary to initial expectations, she discovered that errors in medical teams were less about individual incompetence or negligence, but more about systemic factors that contributed to mistakes. Ironically, the teams that appeared to be functioning better were those that reported more mistakes. Yet, she soon discovered, it wasn't that the other teams were making fewer mistakes, they simply weren't discussing them, or worse weren't reporting them. This highlighted the importance of creating an environment where team members felt safe to report errors, voice concerns, and engage in open communication without fear of blame or punishment. The term *psychological safety* was coined to describe the shared belief within a team that it is safe to take interpersonal risks, such as asking questions, admitting mistakes, or proposing innovative ideas. In psychologically safe environments, individuals feel confident that their contributions will be valued and that they won't face negative consequences for speaking up. Since her early work in healthcare settings, the concept has gained widespread recognition as a critical factor in promoting effective teamwork, innovation, and learning within organizations. Psychological safety is a business imperative, associated with improved performance and results.

Spotting the Signs: High vs. Low Psychological Safety

The concept of *impression management* can be used to explain why we might hold back on proactivity when we perceive low levels of psychological safety. Impression management, also known as *self-presentation*, refers to the conscious or subconscious process by which individuals attempt to control or influence the perceptions others have of them, essentially to fit in. It involves the strategic use of verbal and nonverbal communication, behaviors, and other cues to create a particular image or impression in the eyes of others. If people don't want to appear ignorant, they won't proactively ask questions; if individuals fear being perceived as incompetent, they won't speak up and admit to mistakes; if employees fear coming across as negative, they will be less likely to challenge the status quo.[3]

In environments depicting high levels of psychological safety, you would observe employees who openly admit mistakes and ask for help. You'd experience a culture of feedback where employees are willing to give and receive constructive feedback without taking it personally. You'd be likely to see active listening in practice, where co-workers show empathy and understanding of one another and seek to understand first and foremost. Whereas in environments depicting low levels of psychological safety, you would more likely encounter a competitive or hostile environment in which criticism, shaming, and belittling are commonplace. In these types of environments, you might observe those in power dominating conversations and having a silencing effect on others.

As someone who is naturally proactive and generally confident in expressing my voice and speaking up, I have not been immune to the effects of low psychological safety during my career. I have experienced numerous situations at work where I have felt silenced due to a complete lack of psychological safety. For example, in my early career, working as a marketing executive for a venture-capitalist-owned consumer goods company, I recall our dreaded "Monday meetings," which brought together commercial functions to discuss performance and approve new initiatives. For me, these meetings epitomized low psychological safety. Egotistical behavior took center stage as certain individuals dominated discussions and dismissed opposing viewpoints, resulting in attendees often holding back in expressing their opinions. Senior leaders followed a mantra that discouraged raising issues and bringing problems, employees who did so were not perceived positively. Later in my career, I worked for an organization whose CEO had a reputation for being "shouty." Their reputation preceded them so much that new employees were warned not to get on the wrong side of them, which resulted in employees not speaking up for fear of being on the receiving end of aggressive behavior. These types of leadership behaviors contribute to organizational norms, as such, toxic behavior trickles down and becomes accepted. It was in this same organization that I witnessed workplace bullying by a senior leader, yet I did not feel compelled to speak up, which I regret to this day. While I recall feeling profoundly uncomfortable, I can only surmise that I remained silent for fear of repercussions. Needless to say, this experience contributed to my decision to leave that organization.

In interviewing participants for my research, I heard similar stories and experiences to mine. I coined the phrase *stifled proactivity* to describe attempts to proactively speak up, take charge, or offer innovative ideas that are shut down or "silenced" by others (usually superiors). For the most part, *stifled proactivity* occurs because individuals fear their concerns being trivialized or not taken seriously, which risks making them feel foolish. In other cases, they feared their concerns being undermined and unduly questioned, which culminated in feelings of hopelessness and frustration. For some, the fear of being branded a troublemaker and being punished was at the heart of their decision to remain silent. Over time, there is a risk that these feelings chip away at self-esteem and self-confidence, so individuals hold back on speaking up to protect themselves and their self-concept.

Deep Rules in Organizations

The feeling of being silenced can be explained by the concept of *deep rules*, a phenomenon introduced by Jim Detert, Professor of Business Administration at The University of Virginia. He suggests that even if work environments feel "safe," we must not forget the hidden power of *deep rules*.[4] He describes *deep rules* as an unwritten understanding of what can and can't be said in organizations. These unwritten rules are often bound up in power structures, and if they go unchecked, then most of what gets said simply won't challenge the status quo. One of the biggest issues with *deep rules* is they can prevent meaningful conversations from happening, those conversations that could genuinely improve organizational functioning. In other words, employees are more likely to self-censor on topics they deem "out of bounds." A great example of this can be seen in responses to hybrid and remote working. While there is no conclusive evidence to support policies mandating a minimum number of on-site working days, many employers are nonetheless adopting such policies. When employees raise genuine concerns, it is not uncommon to be met with threats of being fired. I recently worked with a group of managers from an organization that had implemented a policy requiring employees to work three days a week from the office. The decision sparked widespread outrage among this group, who felt they had proven their ability to work effectively from home and felt compromised in enforcing such a universal policy, regardless of circumstances. Despite being extremely vocal in sharing their dissatisfaction with me, no one was willing to speak up or raise their concerns publicly for fear of repercussions. If there is a genuine appetite to build psychological safety, leaders in organizations also need to open up and acknowledge the idea of *deep rules* and be prepared to get the root cause of organizational issues. Later in this chapter, I'll offer some advice on how to start getting under the surface and promote a culture of open communication, regardless of rank and power.

Proactivity and Psychological Safety

If we view psychological safety as the key to facilitating organizational change, learning, and engagement,[5] it's clear to see how it relates to proactivity at work which is premised on future-focused, change-oriented behavior. Being proactive is often associated with interpersonal risk, particularly if it is undervalued in the organization and elicits disapproval from others. That said, it has been suggested that proactive individuals who have strong social networks and generally get along easily with others, tend to be less sensitive to perceptions of low psychological safety. In other words, they are more likely to speak up regardless of whether the environment feels safe, or not.[6] While that may be true for some, my research demonstrated that even the most gregarious proactive employees would hold back in raising issues if they believed they would be received with hostility. A fascinating insight from my research relates to how employees describe experiences of speaking up at work, which is often laden with the language of warfare. Idioms such as "being shot down," "putting your head above the parapet," and "sticking to your guns" were repeatedly used, reinforcing the interpersonal risk and the fear of negative consequences. Psychologically safe workplaces alleviate those interpersonal risks, so employees feel more comfortable in contributing ideas and concerns for the benefit of the organization. You may have heard of Google's Project Aristotle, a research project carried out between 2012 and 2014 to identify the key factors of high-performing teams, unsurprisingly one of the most significant findings that emerged was the importance of psychological safety. This was also borne out by Edmondson's research.

Let's now delve into some fascinating insights from psychological and organizational research relating to different forms of proactivity and the role of psychological safety.

Speaking Up

A wealth of studies highlights the critical role of psychological safety in influencing an individual's decision to proactively speak up. It also serves as the linchpin driving positive outcomes, including heightened levels of work engagement.[7] Two recent studies explore the relationship between light-heartedness and speaking up, which relies on psychological safety. The first of these studies looked at leader humor and found employees whose leader used humor in their interactions perceived higher levels of psychological safety, which in turn increased speaking up.[8] Similarly, researchers in China found that workplace fun enhances speaking up, and again, this was associated with psychological safety. These findings suggest organizations might want to explore ways to create fun to promote a feeling of psychological safety (albeit not in a forced way – no one likes forced fun!). This, in turn, can increase speaking-up behaviors and make the workplace a more engaging place to be.[9] A simple search online for "how to make more fun" reveals an array of websites offering suggestions, but from my experience, asking the question of your team and getting them to come up with some ideas is preferable.

Innovative Behavior

Imagine cultivating an environment where team members not only feel encouraged but also empowered to voice their ideas – it's in these conditions that transformation happens. Creativity and proactive innovative behavior are more likely to flourish when employees perceive high levels of psychological safety. Driving innovation by its very nature means operating in novel, uncertain territory, so again carries risk. Speaking up, questioning, and providing solutions are key components of creativity and innovation. When psychological safety is low, employees are more likely to deploy defensive strategies and less likely to offer up new ideas.[10] Researchers from Nebraska University conducted a study that showed inclusive leadership was positively associated with psychological safety, which in turn engenders employee involvement in creative problem-solving and idea generation.[11] We'll explore the role of inclusive leadership later, but needless to say, employees are more likely to share innovative ideas when they perceive the environment to be safe. In Chapter 9, I introduce the *CLEAR IDEAS model*, an evidence-based framework for developing new ideas to boost innovation among employees.

Proactive Safety Behavior

The final proactive behavior we'll explore relates to proactive safety behavior, which can include whistleblowing. Back in the 1970s, behaviorist theorists suggested that when employees experienced a lack of safety or some form of deterioration in their organization, it would motivate them to take action to repair the situation.[12] But, over the decades, swathes of research have challenged this assumption. In her illuminating book *Wilful Blindness*, Margaret Heffernan presents the dangers associated with whistleblowing, a proactive safety behavior. She argues that whistleblowers often face significant risks, including retaliation, ostracization, and career repercussions. Heffernan highlights how organizations may exhibit a culture of wilful blindness, where individuals turn a blind eye to unethical or unsafe behavior. She emphasizes the importance of cultivating a culture that encourages transparency and accountability, rather than punishing those who speak out. Overall, Heffernan's insights shed light on the complexities and challenges whistleblowers encounter when exposing wrongdoing within organizations.[13] Examples of this include Lukasz Krupski, a former Tesla employee, who raised concerns about safety issues at the company's manufacturing plant. He claimed that his warnings regarding safety hazards, such as faulty equipment and inadequate training, were repeatedly ignored by Tesla management. Krupski alleged that these safety concerns posed serious risks to employees' well-being. Despite his efforts to address the issues internally, Krupski felt marginalized and ultimately left the company.[14] In the end, Tesla subsequently recalled millions of its cars over safety concerns. Similarly, Rosalind Ranson, a medical director on the Isle of Man during the pandemic, experienced months of humiliation after raising concerns that policymakers were misleading the public and not following the advice of medical experts. An employment tribunal found evidence supporting her claims, shedding light on a troubling environment whereby speaking up was met with resistance.[15] Cases like this reinforce the importance of listening to employee concerns and prioritizing safety in the workplace. One way to address this is through an approach known as *blameless reporting*, whereby employees are actively encouraged to speak up about problems or safety concerns, to pre-empt potential issues. This workplace policy promises that reporting will not be penalized and will be welcomed. Some organizations go so far as to say that employees would be reprimanded for not reporting issues in a timely fashion. In her book *Right Kind Of Wrong*, Amy Edmondson advocates this approach but reinforces the importance of psychological safety as an enabler for *blameless reporting*.[16]

Ingredients for Creating Psychological Safety

We've established that psychological safety is vital for stimulating proactive behaviors at work, so we now consider how to create and nurture a psychologically safe work environment. The diagram in Figure 4.1 shows the dynamic trio of trust, interpersonal relationships, and inclusive leadership. Individually, they hold their significance, but together, they form the foundation of psychological safety in the workplace. Trust is imperative for helping individuals feel secure in being themselves and expressing their opinions. Interpersonal relationships create connections that promote collaboration and open communication. Meanwhile, inclusive leadership acts as the guiding force, ensuring that every voice is heard and valued. As we explore these ingredients of trust, interpersonal relationships, and inclusive leadership, we'll uncover how these come together to create psychological safety, the catalyst for proactive behaviors at work.

Trust

Amy Edmondson notes that while there are characteristics shared by both trust and psychological safety, they are different concepts. Trust is the willingness to be vulnerable and give others the benefit of the doubt. While psychological safety is the extent to which you believe others will give you

Figure 4.1 Ingredients for Psychological Safety.
Source: Created by the author.

the benefit of the doubt when taking risks.[17] Feeling psychologically safe depends on feeling trusted by those around you. Trust is the foundation upon which psychological safety is built because individuals must trust that their colleagues and superiors won't use their vulnerabilities against them. When there's mutual trust, people are more willing to be open and honest, promoting an atmosphere of psychological safety. In their seminal work, Roger Mayer, David Schoorman, and James Davis distinguished scholars in the field of organizational behavior developed the *Three Component Model of Trust*. This model identifies *ability*, *benevolence*, and *integrity* as the three key elements that influence trust in organizational settings.[18] More recently, researchers from Germany, have extended the taxonomy of trust to include *transparency* and *predictability*. So, when the following conditions exist, high levels of trust are likely to emerge:

- Confidence in our colleagues' *abilities*.
- Care and *kindness* are demonstrated by reciprocal respect.
- *Integrity* is shown through good moral judgment.
- *Transparency* is demonstrated by information sharing and openness.
- Team members follow through on commitments consistently and *predictably*.

An interesting finding from that recent study was that both the drivers and outcomes of team trust did not differ significantly from face-to-face to virtual team interactions.[19] We can therefore conclude that when there are high levels of trust, behaviors associated with psychological safety such as owning up to mistakes, sharing confidential information, and asking for help are more likely to ensue.

Interpersonal Relationships

Positive interpersonal relationships depicted by high levels of trust have been identified as a precursor to psychological safety.[20] Human beings are social creatures, wired to seek connection and belonging. *Social Instinct* by Nichola Raihani explores the fascinating intricacies of human social behavior and our evolutionary roots to explain how we live and shape our societies. Raihani emphasizes the importance of trust and cooperation in fostering successful social relationships and collective action. She discusses how factors such as *reputation*, *reciprocity*, and *social norms* influence our willingness to cooperate with others.[21] Expanding on biological and evolutionary theory, the neuroscience of trust is also intriguing, it reinforces *reciprocity* or *exchange* by highlighting the power of stimulating oxytocin (the love hormone) to reduce our fear of trusting others. When we show vulnerability and ask for help, it taps into our human impulse to cooperate, which also stimulates oxytocin production in others, creating a virtuous circle.[22] We often worry that asking for help will make others question our ability, where it can actually help strengthen trusting relationships.

The COVID-19 pandemic emphasized the value of social connectedness in the workplace like never before. As remote work became the norm, leaders recognized the need to create a sense of belonging and camaraderie among team members, particularly in virtual settings. Efforts were made to create "social moments," such as virtual coffee mornings and weekly check-ins, to maintain motivation and morale. Post-pandemic, some of these initiatives waned, it's important leaders remember the enduring value of nurturing social connectedness in the workplace for both the well-being of employees and the performance of their teams. In essence, social connectedness is a "need to have," not a "nice to have." This reminds us that intentional action is required to sustain a feeling of belonging and connectedness at work.

Reinforcing interdependence in work design is also helpful in building social connectedness within and across teams, by promoting collaboration, open communication, shared accountability, and collective success. I often use the jigsaw analogy to bring the idea of interdependency in organizations to life – just as puzzle pieces rely on neighboring pieces to fit and hold their place, individuals within an organization are interconnected.

Those closest to us, whether in roles, departments, or business units have a greater impact on our work, but ultimately every piece is essential in making the organization function as a whole. I encourage leaders to reinforce the value of interdependency to help break down workplace silos. I've seen this done well in the past when the organization I worked for convened monthly "lunch and learn" all-staff meetings. These bite-size learning sessions were hosted by a different functional department each month, to share information on their purpose, roles, responsibilities, and pinch-points across the year. In doing so, interdependencies became more evident, and it was clearer to see how each function relied on other functions in the organization to get things done. Empathy between departments grew, for example, we discovered the last three days of the month were stressful for our Finance team, so the Marketing team gave Finance colleagues a wide berth and held off sending non-urgent requests in these periods. Finding ways to build and strengthen interpersonal relationships at work should not be considered as less of a priority, an over-emphasis on task orientation at the expense of nurturing relationships has significant consequences for individuals, teams, and the functioning of organizations. If you want employees to perform well at work, they need to feel well, positive relationships at work significantly contribute to well-being.

Inclusive Leadership

The third foundation of psychological safety is inclusive leadership, which promotes proactive behaviors such as speaking up and taking charge. The behaviors of an inclusive leader who strives for excellence, not perfection, are most helpful in creating an environment that is not averse to risk or fear of failure. Amy Edmondson and her colleague Ingrid Nembhard developed the concept of *Inclusive Leadership*,[23] premised on valuing the contributions every employee has to offer. They highlighted the importance of understanding the unique needs of team members and encouraging them to work independently and participate in decision-making. Fairness is at the heart of inclusive leadership, in that employees are recognized and valued for bringing diverse perspectives and are treated fairly in diverse contexts. A tolerance of failures is also a key feature of this approach to leadership, but again, being comfortable with failure does not mean operating with low standards and excusing avoidable mistakes. It is about recognizing that in uncertain times when navigating unchartered territories, it is highly possible we won't always make the right decisions, but we will certainly learn from these experiences. This is where the distinction between *preventable* and *productive failures* can be made, the former can and should be avoided, and the latter helps us learn and move forward. Proactivity will flourish in an organizational environment that has a tolerance for *productive failures*, whereby employees are given "permission" to be innovative, to try new ways of doing things, and to experiment and learn. But when there are perceptions of there being a "right" or "wrong" way, concerns around the consequences of getting it wrong will be more prevalent, and proactivity will be stifled.

Approaches for Building Psychological Safety

Despite the wealth of research on psychological safety and its importance, there is much less in the way of research exploring the efficacy of interventions designed to enhance psychological safety. That said, there are several principles for building psychological safety from prominent thought leaders. In this section, I'll share two simple approaches for building psychological safety and tackling the challenges associated with *deep rules*. I'll then outline ways to facilitate meetings or group projects with psychological safety in mind. To conclude, I reflect on the essential skills leaders need to become adept at creating psychological safety and introduce a novel way to develop those skills.

Three Steps to Psychological Safety

To create a speak-up culture and enable candor, Amy Edmondson encourages leaders and managers to demonstrate vulnerability and experiment.[24] This involves bringing questions to group discussions rather than feeling like they need to have all of the answers. It also means being prepared to empower others to make sense of what is being said rather than directing the conversation laden with your own assumptions. These three steps to building psychological safety are helpful when bringing individuals together to contribute ideas:

i   **Frame the Challenge and Situation**: position any work-related dilemma or challenge as a learning problem that needs everyone's voices, making time for questions and concerns and giving permission to experiment with suggestions and ideas. Demonstrate humility and vulnerability by openly acknowledging that you don't have all the answers.

   Conversation starter: "We haven't done this before, so I'm going to need everyone's input."

ii **Encourage Active Participation**: make it 100% clear that everyone's voices are welcome, demonstrate curiosity, and look out for what's not being said (unspoken concerns) – remember we don't know what we don't know.

   Connection prompt: "You look concerned, is there something on your mind?"

When asking such a question, it is important to use the power of the pause to allow a considered response.

iii **Respond with Empathy**: make speaking up a positive experience for everyone, even if you don't like what you are hearing – remember not to take things personally. Try to avoid responding defensively or introducing personal judgments – instead, show gratitude and move forward constructively.

Thoughtful response: "I'm grateful for you raising this, that took some courage."

These three actions should be carried out in multiple ways at every opportunity, keeping in mind that your choice of words should be authentic to you but be empathic to the needs of others. I've heard some horror stories of managers wanting to create psychological safety but, in their attempts to do so, shut down conversations by being too liberal in using "Why" responses. For example, when inviting contributions to improve a process, if a colleague offers up some thoughts on the underlying issues, rather than saying, "Why do you think that?" change it to "I'd like to understand your perspective, could you tell me more?" Also, be mindful of the context, for example, if the team has experienced low psychological safety previously, it may take some time to rebuild it.

Tackling Deep Rules

Creating a speak-up culture that gets to the heart of organizational issues requires those in power to take the lead to make employees feel safe in breaking *deep rules*. Inspired by the work of Jim Detert,[25] here are some ideas and conversation prompts for challenging *deep rules*. Not forgetting psychological safety needs to be established in the first instance before trying to encourage employees to break the unwritten rules.

• **Breaking the Silence**: people in power must take the lead in creating a space where employees feel safe to break *deep rules*. To break the silence, employees need to feel that they have permission, and the conversation starter needs to focus on exploring what is normally kept unsaid:

Conversation starter: "What might we talk about if we decided to tackle the topics we typically avoid."

To boost psychological safety, and to make it feel less intimidating, you could ask everyone to write down the unspoken topics anonymously on a slip of paper and redistribute them for someone else to read aloud. Once the topics have surfaced, there is an opportunity to openly discuss how to collaboratively address the issue(s).

- **Address the Contradictions**: another conversation starter for addressing unspoken topics is to invite everyone to reflect on examples where there is a mismatch between what the organization claims to value and prioritize but acts differently. For example, where an organization claims to put diversity, equality, and inclusion center-stage but neglects to ensure that a pool of candidates for a job vacancy includes individuals from a variety of backgrounds. This prompt can help to reveal the organizations' contradictions:

  Conversation starter: "What differences do you notice between the values or goals the organization promotes and the way things are actually done day-to-day?"

  An easy way to capture contradictions is to take a piece of paper, draw a line down the middle, and label one side "Says" and the other "Does." Then, go through example by example, writing down what the organization claims in the first column and what actually happens in the second.

- **Identifying Inequities**: fairness issues in organizations often go unchecked; I discuss the associated consequences in Chapter 6. For now, it's helpful to consider how to uncover fairness issues that are associated with *deep rules* and how to change that. The *Who, What, Why* approach can be used to good effect, start by drawing the three columns on a whiteboard or sheet of paper. First, invite everyone to think of the different groups or individuals in the organization and write them down in the *Who* column. Next, ask them to discuss the challenges, barriers, or unfair treatment these groups might face in the organization, placing these ideas in the *What's Unfair* column. For each inequity, ask the group to brainstorm the root causes and capture these in the *Why* column. This activity opens up the conversation, providing a structured way to talk about inequity gaps and determine where action can be taken.

While employees will appreciate being listened to, they will also expect a response. Opening up these topics of unspoken rules, contradictions, and inequities requires a plan to engage constructively with what is discussed. It's important to be prepared for what comes next and manage expectations around how these issues might be addressed and escalated for discussion within the organization. And as the adage says, "There is only one way to eat an elephant: a bite at a time." Recognizing that messy, challenging problems are often best-tackled bit by bit.

Let's now turn to some examples of evidence-based practices that enhance perceptions of psychological safety in group work. The first intervention is a way of working that encourages learning and adapting using reflective practice. While the second can be utilized by team or project leaders as a framework for group projects (Boxes 4.1–4.3).

These ideas are aimed at provoking thinking and sparking creativity in designing your own workplace approaches to enhance psychological safety, they are not intended as a direct copy and paste. No one organization is the same, context matters and so one-size-fits-all approaches are best avoided. That said, taking some of the guiding principles and ideas and adapting them to reflect the environment you are operating in, can be beneficial. Encouraging participation and involving team members in the development of interventions to meet their needs is strongly advised, by taking a co-design approach, employees will feel more motivated and committed to the initiatives, which will inevitably influence the outcomes in a positive direction.

Box 4.1 Holistic Facilitation

Donna Brown and Brendan McCormack from Ulster University developed a method to create psychologically safe spaces using holistic facilitation, to assist teams in exploring and improving their practice.[26] Holistic facilitation is premised on helping employees uncover their potential and bring about positive change by giving them space to collectively reflect. This requires a deliberate, conscious, collaborative process that allows individuals in a team to openly discuss what is happening in practice and to step back and question habitual behaviors and actions. This intervention works well with smaller groups, reflective sessions tend to take no longer than 1.5 hours. In these sessions, team members are invited to reflect on questions, such as:

   i "What are some of the challenges you are facing?"
  ii "How might you do things differently?"

This intervention can be carried out in-house or by an external facilitator, either way, it does require well-honed facilitation skills. A simple online search using "reflective practice questions" will provide a host of resources with additional reflective practice prompts.

Box 4.2   Group Work – CENTRE Tool

The next approach can be utilized by team or project leaders as a framework when initiating group work. Douglas Cave and colleagues from the University of British Columbia created a method of developing agreed principles and processes to improve group work and to create psychological safety and cohesion.[27] Originally intended to reduce the risk of interpersonal conflict within clinical teams, the approach has proven to have appeal outside of clinical settings. The development of the CENTRE tool is premised on the assumption that group work is often entrenched in unspoken rules, norms, and agreements, which have the potential to create conflict when misunderstandings or confusion arise due to the lack of universal understanding. The tool is intended to act as a "team contract" to agree on how the group wants to work together, with more explicit intention. The mnemonic CENTRE encompasses:

- **Confidentiality** – highlighting the importance of individuals only sharing their own experiences outside of team meetings and not talking about the experiences of others, based on the idea that "it's not your story to share" and therefore not your place to disclose without the consent of the person it relates to.
- **Equal Airtime** – reminds leaders/facilitators who are managing team discussions to ensure all voices are heard, and that dominant voices don't overshadow others and as a group. Everyone is encouraged to self-monitor and be aware of how much "space" they take up in the conversations.
- **Nonjudgmental Listening** – is premised on the idea that everyone should trust what someone says as that person's genuine experience, whether you agree, disagree, or find it relatable or nonrelatable, it is that person's truth. This form of listening also requires giving the speaker undivided attention, so switching off distractions and being fully present.
- **Timelines** – this simply refers to respecting and adhering to agreed timings of meetings, for example, arriving and finishing on time and completing tasks within agreed deadlines.
- **Right to Pass** – while participation is encouraged by all, there is a recognition that some individuals are more reflective and may not be ready to participate when they are invited to speak, in which case the leader/facilitator should return to that person again later in the meeting.

- **Engaged** – every participant is encouraged to be fully engaged and is invited to consider what distractions might be getting in the way of their engagement and to try to switch off the distractions.

When using this approach, it is recommended that there is some participative group discussion in advance of adopting the guidelines, so that everyone can raise questions or make suggestions to improve them. As with most good approaches, I'd always recommend tailoring them to the group you are working with.

Box 4.3   Leadership Skills for Building Psychological Safety

As highlighted throughout this chapter, there are some core skills leaders must develop to be equipped to build psychological safety. With this in mind, Ronald Dufresne, of St Joseph's University in Philadelphia, designed a leadership development program to develop these skills. His workshops used improvisational comedy to build the capabilities to help navigate the complexities of the modern business environment.[28] While I appreciate the idea of role-play and improvisation can be anxiety-inducing or even cringeworthy for some, bear with me on this. The program aimed at enhancing self-awareness, emotional intelligence, and perspective-taking, utilizes "improv" to encourage listening and build confidence in dealing with the discomfort of "not knowing" and making mistakes. All of which form the armory of a leader equipped to create psychologically safe work environments. Before attending the workshop, participants are invited to watch a short video to explain the principles of improv, which include an outline of the "Yes, and" approach – a core element of improv that relies on accepting what the other person has offered/suggested and building on it, aimed at increasing interpersonal skills. The importance of listening and failing is also highlighted in the pre-brief. The workshops are co-facilitated by members of an improvisation group, skilled in this art form. The workshop comprises a series of different improv games, each followed by a debriefing to reflect on the leadership lessons illuminated. Lessons are typically centered around allowing ourselves to fail, being fully present, attentive listening, taking the perspectives of others, and collaborating. While Dufresne also acknowledges that this form of interactive education can take participants out of their comfort zone and might cause anxiety for some, this seemed to be overcome once the activities commenced. That said, an opt-out approach to this novel form of training and development would be advised, and bringing in experienced facilitators to deliver this kind of training is essential. As part of my research for this book, I enrolled in an improv taster session to experience these types of activities for myself. I quickly overcame the initial awkwardness and allowed myself to be in the moment. Overall, I found the experience uplifting, liberating, and thought-provoking and would highly recommend it.

Psychological Safety: Everyone Plays a Role

While organizational climate and leadership styles drive psychological safety, developing and nurturing it is the responsibility of everyone. Systemic change requires activities to happen at each level of the organization. For that reason, I've mapped out some recommendations for individuals, teams, managers/leaders, and the organization, as shown in Table 4.1.

Key Takeaways

- Proactive behaviors in the form of speaking up, taking charge, innovative behavior, and safety proactivity rely on psychological safety.
- A workplace that cultivates psychological safety is likely to create an environment conducive to the success of both proactive individuals, who naturally take initiative and those who may lean towards a more passive approach. This inclusive atmosphere contributes to innovation, adaptability, and positive organizational outcomes.
- Creating psychological safety requires ongoing effort, intentional action is essential to nurture the crucial elements of trust, interpersonal relationships, and inclusive leadership.
- Policies and processes can assist in building psychological safety, for example, blameless reporting encourages safety proactivity.
- A participatory approach to designing interventions to build psychological safety is recommended, drawing on the ideas outlined in this chapter, but tailoring to the needs of the group to enhance commitment and motivation.

Table 4.1 Practical Recommendations Overview

Level	Recommendations
Individual	Psychological safety relies on individuals being open to doing things differently, experimenting, and learning, which requires a high learning orientation. Engaging in personal development, seeking learning opportunities, and working with a coach or mentor can provide invaluable support in developing a learning-orientated mindset.
Team-group	One of the ways to develop high-quality interpersonal relationships is to amplify the importance of interdependency within and between teams. Team meetings provide opportunities to learn, share, and exchange information; cross-functional working groups broaden perspectives and ensure expertise is drawn from across the organization, while special interest or community groups strengthen networks and provide support.
Manager/ Leader	Inclusive leaders encourage their team members to bring their unique selves to work and actively encourage the sharing of different perspectives. In creating a culture of learning, it's important to embrace the "joy of not knowing," remain curious, and encourage everyone to engage in *productive failure* – remember "think like a scientist." Leaders and managers also need to be open to receiving "bad news" and/or hearing perspectives that might not align with their own. It is crucial to act when employees voice genuine concerns, as they expect a response. Asking people to speak up is pointless if it leads to no concrete outcomes.
Organization	The importance of a supportive and trusting culture, where everyone feels valued, empowered, and encouraged to learn and grow is key. When thinking about work design, the importance of creating role clarity, autonomy, and reinforcing interdependency is paramount – these factors rely on clearly defined processes and employee-focused policies, that are effectively communicated throughout the organization, and fully understood by managers and leaders.

Reflective Questions

- What signs are you spotting in your organization concerning high or low levels of psychological safety?
- What do you perceive has been the driver for high or low levels of psychological safety in your organization?
- What would better promote or enable psychological safety in your organization?

My Implementation Intentions

Jot down in this space any actions you will take in response to the reflective questions.

References

1. Frazier, M. L., Fainshmidt, S., Klinger, R. L., Pezeshkan, A., & Vracheva, V. (2017). Psychological safety: A meta-analytic review and extension. *Personnel Psychology*, 70(1), 113–165.
2. Edmondson, A. (1999). Psychological safety and learning behavior in work teams. *Administrative Science Quarterly*, 44(2), 350–383.
3. Edmondson, A. C. (2018). *The fearless organization: Creating psychological safety in the workplace for learning, innovation, and growth.* John Wiley & Sons.
4. Detert, J. (2024, October 14). *What you still can't say at work.* MIT Sloan Management Review. https://sloanreview.mit.edu/article/what-you-still-cant-say-at-work/
5. Frazier, M. L., Fainshmidt, S., Klinger, R. L., Pezeshkan, A., & Vracheva, V. (2017). Psychological safety: A meta-analytic review and extension. *Personnel Psychology*, 70(1), 113–165.
6. Wu, C. H., & Li, W. D. (2016). Individual differences in proactivity: A developmental perspective. *In Proactivity at work* (pp. 244–275). Routledge.
7. Ge, Y. (2020). Psychological safety, employee voice, and work engagement. *Social Behavior and Personality: An International Journal*, 48(3), 1–7.
8. Potipiroon, W., & Ford, M. T. (2021). Does leader humor influence employee voice? The mediating role of psychological safety and the moderating role of team humor. *Journal of Leadership & Organizational Studies*, 28(4), 415–428
9. Yang, G., & Wang, L. (2020), Workplace fun and voice behavior: The mediating role of psychological safety. *Social Behavior and Personality: An International Journal*, 48(11), 1–8.

10. Rank, J., Pace, V. L., & Frese, M. (2004). Three avenues for future research on creativity, innovation, and initiative. *Applied Psychology*, 53(4), 518–528.
11. Carmeli, A., Reiter-Palmon, R., & Ziv, E. (2010). Inclusive leadership and employee involvement in creative tasks in the workplace: The mediating role of psychological safety. *Creativity Research Journal*, 22(3), 250–260.
12. Hirschman, A. O. (1972). *Exit, voice, and loyalty: Responses to decline in firms, organizations, and states.* Harvard University Press.
13. Heffernan, M. (2011). *Wilful blindness: Why we ignore the obvious.* Simon and Schuster.
14. BBC News. (2023, December 5). *Ex-Tesla employee casts doubt on car safety.* BBC. www.bbc.co.uk/news/technology-67591311
15. BBC News. (2023, December 5). Humiliated Covid whistleblower says boss tried to 'break' her. BBC. www.bbc.co.uk/news/health-67565498
16. Edmondson, A. C. (2023). *Right kind of wrong: The science of failing well.* Simon and Schuster.
17. Edmondson, A. C., & Lei, Z. (2014). Psychological safety: The history, renaissance, and future of an interpersonal construct. *Annual Review of Organizational Psychology and Organizational Behavior* , 1(1), 23–43.
18. Mayer, R. C., Davis, J. H., & Schoorman, F. D. (1995). An integrative model of organizational trust. *Academy of Management Review*, 20(3), 709–734.
19. Breuer, C., Hüffmeier, J., Hibben, F., & Hertel, G. (2020). Trust in teams: A taxonomy of perceived trustworthiness factors and risk-taking behaviors in face-to-face and virtual teams. *Human Relations*, 73(1), 3–34.
20. Kahn, W. A. (1990). Psychological conditions of personal engagement and disengagement at work. *Academy of Management Journal*, 33(4), 692–724.
21. Raihani, N. (2021). *The social instinct: How cooperation shaped the world.* Random House.
22. Zak, P. J., Stanton, A. A., & Ahmadi, S. (2007). Oxytocin increases generosity in humans. *PloS One*, 2(11), e1128.
23. Nembhard, I. M., & Edmondson, A. C. (2006). Making it safe: The effects of leader inclusiveness and professional status on psychological safety and improvement efforts in health care teams. *Journal of Organizational Behavior: The International Journal of Industrial, Occupational and Organizational Psychology and Behavior,* 27(7), 941–966.
24. Edmondson, A. C. (2023). *Right kind of wrong: The science of failing well.* Simon and Schuster.
25. Detert, J. (2021). *Choosing courage: The everyday guide to being brave at work.* Harvard Business Press.
26. Brown, D., & McCormack, B. (2016). Exploring psychological safety as a component of facilitation within the Promoting Action on Research Implementation in Health Services framework. *Journal of Clinical Nursing*, 25(19–20), 2921–2932.
27. Cave, D., Pearson, H., Whitehead, P., & Rahim-Jamal, S. (2016). CENTRE: Creating psychological safety in groups. *The Clinical Teacher*, 13(6), 427–431.
28. Dufresne, R. L. (2020). Using improvisation to develop leadership for a volatile world. *Journal of Leadership Education*, 19(4), 123–133.

Chapter 5

Role and Remit

In navigating complex and dynamic workplaces, employees are often expected to think and act beyond their prescribed job description. Simply going through the motions of assigned tasks doesn't cut it (unless, of course, the job requires adherence to strict legal or regulatory guidelines). Instead, organizational success hinges on nurturing adaptable and proactive employees who embrace diverse roles and take initiative. This Chapter draws on role-related and job design theories[1] to explain how proactivity can be stimulated by an employee's understanding of their role and by the expectations of their supervisor. Leadership characteristics and behaviors that promote employee proactivity will also be explored to accompany the role-related considerations. In concluding this chapter, I highlight the importance of recruiting for proactivity with specificity and intention to garner benefits, such as retention and engagement.

Three important role-related theories influence proactivity at work. The first relates to an individual's confidence in their ability to initiate tasks that go beyond the technical boundaries of their job. I will refer to this as *role breadth confidence* (the academic term is *role breadth self-efficacy*,[2] but I've chosen what I believe to be a more accessible term). Distinct from this is what I am calling *role breadth remit* (the original academic term is *flexible role orientation*[3]), this relates to a perception of greater levels of ownership and having "permission" to go beyond one's formal job description. Neither of these concepts is necessarily about "going the extra mile" and engaging in discretionary extra-role behaviors. Instead, they are centered around perceptions of being able to step outside of what is formally expected within a role, which influences one's *can-do* motivational state.[4] The third concept is *role clarity*, which is premised on minimizing ambiguity associated with one's role responsibilities and goals.[5] We will explore how these can be used effectively to stimulate proactive behaviors such as taking charge, speaking up, proactive problem solving, and innovative behavior.

DOI: 10.4324/9781003480693-8

Role Breadth Confidence

Simply put, *role breadth confidence* is about individuals feeling comfortable in engaging in activities they wouldn't normally do. For example, I had a coachee who valued equality and diversity and had lived experience of depression and anxiety. This motivated them to proactively get involved in their organization's employee network group (ENG) that supported mental well-being at work. Involvement in ENGs wasn't in their job description, yet they knew their experience and confidence in this area could be useful in supporting those struggling with mental health challenges, and they valued the opportunity to "give back" to others. In part, it was a perception of *role breadth confidence* that sparked their *can-do* motivational state to proactively becoming a mental health first aider, which they then crafted into their job role. When individuals are high in *role breadth confidence*, they see opportunities in their environment more readily and have greater confidence in enacting proactivity. Whereas those low in *role breadth confidence* are less sure of their ability to perform tasks outside of their prescribed role and will then hold back on taking initiative.

The good news is that *role breadth confidence* can be enhanced. An intervention study at a glass manufacturing company in the UK, conducted

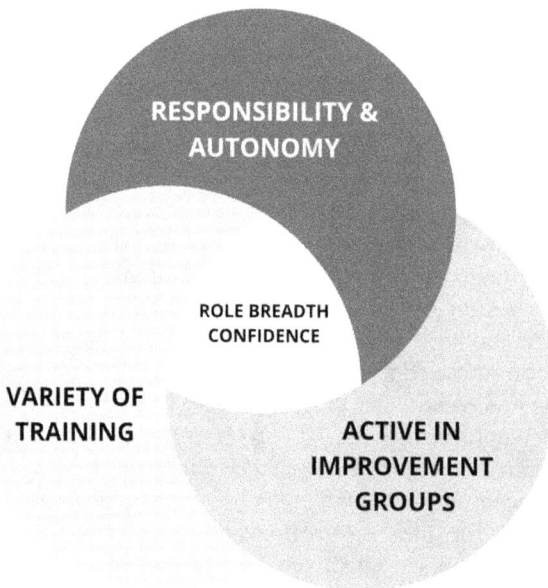

Figure 5.1 Three Vital Components of Role Breadth Confidence.
Source: Created by the author.

by Carolyn Axtell and Sharon Parker, highlighted three pivotal factors for enhancing this vital driver of proactivity.[6] The diagram in Figure 5.1 shows the importance of responsibility and autonomy, active involvement in improvement groups, and a variety of training.

Responsibility and Autonomy

We'll delve into autonomy more in Chapter 7, but in the meantime, it's important to reinforce the value of giving employees responsibility and greater decision-making latitude to enhance feelings of accountability. For clarity, increasing responsibility is not the same as role expansion; it is not about asking individuals to do more work but asking that they do more of their work without seeking their supervisor's input or approval. To avoid chaos and confusion, this requires a conscious effort by managers and leaders in re-distributing power and control, clarifying expectations, and effectively communicating them. The importance of clarifying expectations is brought to life in *Wilful Blindness* by Margaret Heffernan. In this book, she shares a case study of Unilever in Nigeria, where middle managers and senior leaders convened to enhance communication and decision-making.[7] During the event, middle managers were tasked with presenting a challenging issue to senior leadership, while senior leaders considered the best approach for receiving such matters. Interestingly, the methods employed by middle managers didn't match senior leaders' expectations, reflecting common misunderstandings in real-world scenarios where assumptions are common, yet expectations are vague. This underlines the importance of clearly defining protocols for decision-relevant issues and ensuring ongoing alignment with expectations. Some practical ways to provide clarity around decision-making latitude include creating standard operating procedures (SOPs) outlining who has the authority to make specific decisions in various situations, developing and communicating a written policy that clearly outlines the financial sign-off limits for different levels of authority within the organization; and utilizing technology solutions such as decision-support systems or workflow automation tools to streamline decision-making processes. In Chapter 6, I describe how Southern Coop reaches business-critical decisions using a *Compass* tool; this is another practical example of how to create alignment and clarity of expectations.

Improvement Groups

The second vital ingredient to boost *role breadth confidence* over the long term is active membership in improvement groups. Employee improvement groups offer significant value by developing foundational skills and encouraging participation in structured problem-solving activities. The initial mastery gained from partaking in such groups can then empower individuals to become more self-directed in their ongoing learning and problem-solving endeavors. Improvement groups can also bring employees from across the organization together, encouraging cross-functional working and emphasizing interdependency, which was highlighted in Chapter 4 as an important factor in nurturing interpersonal relationships and psychological safety. I've been working with an innovative food company in the Middle East that has recently launched an improvement group focused on empowering team members in foundational roles. This initiative provides opportunities for them to lead projects that align with the company's growth goals, creating a collaborative and proactive culture. The program has been thoughtfully structured, featuring leadership team sponsors to guide and support participants. It includes a clear initiative selection process and a regular cadence of meetings to ensure ongoing progress and alignment with the organization's objectives. If you are looking to kick-start a similar program within your organization, this five-step approach to cultivating workplace enhancements through active employee improvement groups provides some suggestions and a road map:[8]

i **Preparation:** In setting up improvement groups, inviting participation is preferable over enforced participation, this will ensure greater levels of commitment and motivation towards the initiative. It is also important to develop a framework for internal communications, setting out expected outcomes and the employees' roles in proposing and initiating improvements.

ii **Screening:** This stage requires data analysis, whether that be a survey, risk assessment, or SWOT analysis, to establish the key issues and opportunities and to enable staff to provide feedback on what needs to be improved.

iii **Action Planning:** At this stage, it's advisable to run a workshop with the improvement group to determine an action plan and priorities based on the outputs of the screening stage. Each task within the action plan should have clearly defined objectives, outcomes, deadlines, and accountability.

iv **Implementation:** At this stage, it is important to ensure the improvements are being implemented as planned, a workshop to review the action plan should be convened, and at this point, the improvement group should begin to cascade some of their responsibilities to others, this will promote greater participation and engagement across the organization and will reduce the burden placed on individual members of the group.

v **Evaluation:** When considering measures for evaluation, it is important to look at proximal changes, such as working conditions and/or procedures, and distal changes, such as turnover or employee engagement. Evaluation outputs should inform future objectives and actions, to ensure time and resources are being invested in activities that are going to make a difference.

For an improvement group to succeed, it's essential that participants feel truly empowered. Setting clear expectations and ensuring alignment with leadership will be critical to maintaining momentum and giving employees the bandwidth to drive meaningful change.

Variety of Training

The third component in building *role breadth confidence* is providing employees with a broad range of training in a range of skills that go beyond technical job role requirements. The expanded competency and skills gained from such a variety of training bolster employees' confidence across various proactive behaviors. For example, enhancing interpersonal skills through training helps in negotiation and influencing others, crucial for garnering support for proactive initiatives. Similarly, preventative maintenance or health and safety training is useful in building competence in acting before problems arise and stimulating safety proactivity.

In England, while the overall participation of adults in employer-sponsored training has remained relatively consistent over time, there has been a notable decline in the average number of training days per employee, dropping by 19% since 2011.[9] While in the United States, larger companies increased their investment in staff training between 2017 and 2020, investments in training time have been decreasing since then.[10] This trend may stem from uncertainty surrounding the returns on training investment, prompting CEOs and CFOs to revisit their training and development budgets. No doubt, individuals and firms may not fully consider the comprehensive benefits of training when making investment decisions. This speaks to a popular meme that reflects the importance of investing in employee development and growth to retain talent within an organization:

The CFO asks the HR Director, "What happens if we invest in developing our people and then they leave us?"
The HR Director responds : "What happens if we don't, and they stay?"

McKinsey underscores the importance of investing in enhancing employees' knowledge, skills, and abilities through their study, which examines the relationship between people development practices and the financial performance of 1,800 large companies across 15 countries.[11] Coined *People + Performance Winners*, the firms that have consistent financial performance and the ability to retain and attract talent even in challenging times, are those who emphasized people development. What makes *People + Performance Winners* superior to other firms is their ability to drive a results-orientated culture through an emphasis on bottom-up innovation, in other words, proactive innovative behavior across the organization. While training and development is an investment for organizations, there are opportunities for skills development that require time and effort rather than a monetary budget. The three E's approach to learning and development helps highlight the different components organizations can tap into to create comprehensive learning and development experiences that support employee growth and skill development:

- **Education:** refers to providing employees with the knowledge and information they need to perform their roles effectively. This typically includes formal training sessions, workshops, online courses, or educational resources. To truly maximize training budgets, encouraging individual learners to share their newly gained knowledge with others within the organization can be incredibly beneficial. This practice not only encourages greater levels of collaboration but also helps to build a stronger collective knowledge base, benefitting the entire organization.

- **Experience:** refers to the practical application of knowledge and skills gained through education. It involves opportunities for employees to put their learning into practice, whether through on-the-job experiences or projects. To maximize the impact of training, it is crucial to consider how learners will apply new skills in real-world scenarios and actively commit to implementing them. Line managers play a key role in encouraging this focus on application, supporting their team members to translate the insights from training into meaningful action within the organization.

- **Exposure:** refers to providing employees with opportunities to learn from others and gain insights from different perspectives. This may include mentoring, job shadowing, cross-functional projects, or exposure to senior leaders and experts within the organization. Again, making the most of learning from others requires line managers to create an environment that emphasizes the value of shared knowledge, creating a culture of openness that enhances the impact of learning across the team. Exposure only leads to growth if we actively learn from it.

As we've seen, there are several practical considerations for developing *role breadth confidence*. I've already touched on the important role of supervisors, managers, and leaders, but let's move on to consider that more fully.

Leader Emotional Intelligence

The role of leader characteristics and how they contribute to encouraging proactive behaviors at work is a recurring theme throughout this book. A recent study highlights the powerful combination of a leader's emotional intelligence together with an individual's *role breadth confidence* to stimulate proactive behavior.[12] The study of employees in a customs clearing company in Zimbabwe suggests that emotionally intelligent leaders treat employees with respect, which is motivating and engaging for them. This respectful approach encourages employees to take interpersonal risks associated with being proactive. There are some parallels between emotional intelligence and the characteristics of *Inclusive Leaders*, which were introduced in the previous chapter. Leaders who recognize and respond to the emotional needs of their employees are more likely to evoke positive behaviors in them. This is also reinforced in a study by consultancy Ernst & Young, which found over 80% of the 1,000 employees surveyed believed that receiving empathy from their supervisor positively impacts various aspects of their work life.[13] This includes morale, efficiency, creativity, innovation, job satisfaction, collaboration, and productivity. Interestingly, a boost in employee well-being also appears to correlate with increased company revenue and decreased staff turnover rates. The good news is that it is possible to develop greater levels of emotional intelligence. It all starts with building self-awareness and being able to recognize emotions and emotional responses in oneself. My go-to recommendation for anyone looking to develop emotional intelligence is to explore the work of Marc Brackett, a professor at Yale University who has developed the RULER approach to help understand and master emotions.[14]

Role Breadth Remit

Having provided an in-depth exploration of *role breadth confidence*, we turn our attention to *role breadth remit*. As a reminder, this concept is premised on the perception that employees can step outside of what is formally expected within their role. Organizations wanting to drive proactivity at work should avoid viewing it as a discretionary "going the extra mile" type of behavior but instead see it as the responsibility of every employee. When perceptions of *role breadth remit* are high, employees will define their roles more broadly and have a greater sense of ownership to engage in proactive activities that go beyond their formal job description, that's because they see it as being a critical part of their role. This idea of psychological ownership can be brought to life by considering proactive safety behavior. Individuals perceiving low levels of *role breadth remit* will narrowly engage in safety proactivity by correctly using equipment and following formal processes and procedures. Whereas those high in *role breadth remit* will take a broader approach, they are more likely to raise concerns about the quality of the processes and offer suggestions for improving them. In the latter case, there is a greater degree of personal responsibility and engagement in truly proactive behavior. Like *role breadth confidence*, HR and leadership practices can enhance *role breadth remit*, again relating to job design, knowledge acquisition, and leaders' characteristics.

Job Design

Job design practices can be used to boost *role breadth remit*. In their work on designing SMART teamwork, Sharon Parker and Caroline Knight emphasize the value of promoting stimulating work.[21] They suggest stimulating work can be created when tasks are complex and require teams to collectively problem-solve. Engaging in this form of work is motivating for employees because it tends to be more varied, interesting, meaningful, and challenging. In highly stimulating roles, individuals are more likely to:

- Use a diverse range of skills and abilities to accomplish tasks
- Perform various tasks to reach their objectives
- Employ innovative thinking to devise solutions to challenges

Advice to managers and leaders wanting to add more stimulation to job roles is to be more alert to non-routine situations occurring and use these as opportunities to bring teams together to work and learn through complexity. Checking in regularly with employees to understand if they feel sufficiently challenged by the tasks they are working on and that there is enough variety in their roles is also advisable. We'll return to other insights from the SMART work design framework when we come to the importance of Autonomy (Chapter 7).

Leader Attributes

There are two interesting leader attributes associated with driving improvement-related proactivity that relate to *role breadth remit*. The first focuses on a leader's felt responsibility for change, and the second points to how effective they are in providing access to the resources required to bring about change. Leaders who are high on *felt responsibility for constructive change*[15] focus not only on task accomplishment but have a strong desire to solve problems and improve work; they define performance with a continuous improvement mindset. As such, they are more likely to reward proactivity amongst their team, compared to leaders who are low in this attribute and who are more likely to regard proactivity, such as taking charge, as confrontational.[16] Taking a behavioral reinforcement perspective, if employees are rewarded and recognized by their supervisor for being proactive at work, they are more likely to continue to demonstrate proactivity. Whereas, if they perceive proactive behavior to be disallowed or "not welcomed," they are more likely to dial down this behavior. This reminds me of the quote, "You are a product of your environment," attributed to the late businessman and philanthropist William Clement Stone.

Transformational Leadership

At the risk of introducing yet another leadership framework, attributes of transformational leaders can be useful in understanding how to strengthen *role breadth remit*. Transformational leaders transcend their self-interest for the good of the group or organization. According to the theory, two dimensions of transformational leadership relate to this idea of *felt responsibility for change*. The first relates to *inspirational motivation*, whereby leaders put forth a compelling vision and communicate with optimism about the achievement of future-orientated goals. The second relates to *intellectual stimulation* and encouraging risk-taking behaviors, stepping outside of one's comfort zone to challenge the status quo.[17] Again, the good news is that transformational leadership skills can be learned and developed, but does require a commitment and dedication to growth and self-improvement, and starts with developing greater self-awareness. Studies have also highlighted that transformational leaders can be found at any level of the organization and are relevant to different types of situations across different cultural settings, making this leadership approach highly applicable.[18]

While the right leadership behaviors are critical in driving *role breadth remit*, of equal importance are the actions of leaders. Specifically, actions related to providing access to resources, e.g., time, budget, and people. A study of over 5,000 employees in a restaurant chain in the United States found that when employees were proactively offering improvement-orientated ideas but met with managers who were unwilling or unable to respond with adequate resources, it resulted in employees being demotivated and a higher turnover of staff.[19] It is imperative that managers and leaders provide appropriate and adequate access to resources to support proactive change-oriented behavior. You may know the oft-quoted saying: "You can give a person a fish, and they will come back hungry again tomorrow, teach them to fish, and you feed them for a lifetime," which reinforces the value of teaching skills and empowering others. In referring to this quote in a recent workshop, I was inspired by the response of one of the leaders who said, "In addition to teaching them how to fish, you'll need to give them the fishing rod." This spoke to the importance of providing the right resources to set individuals up for success. The proactivity research shows that when organizations have a culture where employees feel their contributions are valued and are supported by encouraging managers, it improves both team dynamics and boosts individual well-being.[20]

Role Clarity

The final role-related consideration driving proactivity is *role clarity*,[22] which reinforces the importance of employees having a clear understanding of their role within the team. Role clarity can be broken down into:

- **Goal Clarity** – this is the "what" and the "why" of the role, it helps employees understand the purpose of their role and the associated responsibilities.
- **Process Clarity** – this is the "how" of the role, it helps employees understand the processes involved in achieving their goals.

Role clarity is one of the major factors associated with workplace well-being, it is well documented that when there's ambiguity around the "what, why, and how" of our job roles, we are more likely to experience work-related stress.[23] So, while the previous section highlighted the value in enhancing *role breadth confidence* and providing *role breadth remit*, it is important to strike a balance between providing *role clarity* while encouraging proactive behaviors that go beyond one's technical job description. Proactive behaviors aligned with organizational goals should be encouraged, rewarded, and recognized, which means there needs to be a clear line of sight from individual and team-level goals (role clarity) to the organization's strategic priorities. A classic example of this is the story of the NASA janitor in 1962. When President John F. Kennedy asked the janitor what he was doing, the janitor apparently replied, "I'm helping put a man on the moon." This anecdote illustrates how understanding the broader purpose of one's work can inspire dedication and a sense of shared purpose, ultimately driving the organization toward its objectives. In a similar vein, in Chapter 7, the Timpson case study highlights the company's drive to "affect someone's day positively," and values employees' proactivity in engaging in acts of kindness and community support.

An interesting study conducted in China explored factors stimulating proactive innovative behavior, in which the researchers found that creativity can be enhanced amongst proactive people when there are high levels of *role clarity*.[24] This reinforced the importance of innovation as the responsibility of everyone rather than "extra work." The study is premised on the idea that *role clarity* allows employees to leverage *domain knowledge*, which is the foundation knowledge in a specific field of work. When teams come together and share their *domain knowledge*, they combine knowledge bases and bring different perspectives, thereby enabling more complex reasoning which generates more creative ideas. Essentially, the integration of knowledge from different fields is where innovation comes from.[25] Again, this speaks to the importance of ensuring employees are appropriately trained and given opportunities to build knowledge and competence. With the pace of change, that also means ensuring experienced employees keep abreast of changes in their areas of work. From a practical perspective, managers should review the team and organization's knowledge resources regularly, particularly if there has been team turnover. Promoting a learning culture and emphasizing the value of investing in developing employees across the lifespan is critical in sustaining vital domain knowledge within organizations.

Rising to Expectations

Another interesting finding from this study was that creative behavior can be enhanced further amongst proactive people when high levels of *role clarity* are also accompanied by high creativity expectations from their leader. There is a phenomenon in psychology called the *Pygmalion effect*,[26] which suggests that high expectations lead to improved performance and low expectations lead to lesser performance. Under this Pygmalion effect, employees will adapt to the situation, so if their supervisor is signaling high expectations for creative behaviors, employees are more likely to respond by generating and offering up new ideas. So, in addition to encouraging leaders to build responsibility for constructive change and to be equipped to allocate appropriate resources, leaders could enhance their communications to convey the value of creativity to encourage idea generation within their organization. A word of caution, however, in signaling creativity expectations, leaders need to avoid giving the impression that this is "expected of you," which has the potential to challenge one's free will and lead to demotivation and negative behaviors. It's also important to recognize that being creative uses requires cognitive energy, so leaders who are actively encouraging proactive innovative behaviors need to ensure their employees are replenishing their resources and adequately recuperating.[27] We'll explore the importance of energy depletion and recharging in Chapter 12.

Be Careful What You Wish For

In this final section, I'd like to draw on some insights from my research that highlight the importance of being specific when asking employees to be proactive and that starts with recruitment. A search of UK jobs using the job search engine Indeed.com revealed that 41% of all jobs advertised included proactivity (proactive, self-starter, self-directed, initiative) as a desired competency across a variety of different job functions from sales assistant, customer service, operations, HR, marketing roles to manufacturing technicians.[28] I coined a theme from my interviews: "Be careful what you wish for," and that's a warning aimed at organizations demanding proactive characteristics. In my interviews, for individuals identifying as having a proactive personality, there was a recurring story of joining organizations during their career where self-initiated behaviors were referenced in job profiles, but in practice, there was no scope to be proactive, which influenced their decision to leave the organization. One of my participants described feeling like "You were doing things with just two hands tied behind your back at all times," while another suggested that in the organization they joined, everything they suggested "fell on stony ground." If proactive people don't like the situation, they will find a way to change it, so if you bring proactive people into your organization but don't enable them to exercise any self-direction, they will inevitably find another job. Additionally, my research revealed how surprised participants were to discover the variety of different forms of proactive behavior at work. Many had assumed being proactive simply meant taking charge and speaking up; for some, they associated it with volunteering to take on extra responsibilities, which technically isn't proactive behavior. There is value in organizations being more explicit in how they want their employees to be proactive, communicating what forms of proactive behavior are aligned with the organizational goals, and rewarding and recognizing those. If you want to be a more innovative organization, you might want to encourage speaking up and proactive innovative behavior. If you want to improve your approach to health and safety, an emphasis on speaking up, taking charge, and proactive safety behavior will be beneficial. If you want to improve retention and motivation, you may want to consider promoting career initiative, feedback-seeking, and job-crafting behaviors. This comes back down to providing *role clarity* and being explicit in managing expectations with employees.

As a final word of caution, it is also important to acknowledge the potential pitfalls of proactivity in isolation of other skills and behaviors. For example, individual-level innovative behavior without business savviness can lead to misalignment; speaking up without situational awareness can undermine one's credibility and damage relations; taking charge without strong interpersonal skills can negatively impact team dynamics. As I've already mentioned and will continue to highlight throughout this book, proactivity does not occur in a vacuum; it is deeply entangled with social interactions and contextual considerations. Hence, a need for organizations to clarify which types of proactive behaviors are valued and to set expectations for how employees should best demonstrate them. By communicating clear expectations, we pave the way for our expectations to be met.

Key Takeaways

- To engage in proactivity at work, employees need to have confidence in their ability to initiate tasks that go beyond their job description and a perception that they have "permission" to do so.
- Investing in learning and development to build knowledge, skills, and abilities is key to enhancing an individual's confidence in being more self-directed at work.
- Leader's characteristics and behaviors play a vital role in stimulating and stifling proactivity at work. Emotionally intelligent leaders and those motivated by continuous improvement send signals to employees that proactive behavior is valued within the organization, which in turn creates a virtuous circle of proactivity.
- If organizations want to promote the expression of proactive behavior at work, they must provide employees with clarity about which forms of proactivity align with the organization's objectives.

Reflective Questions

- Among role breadth confidence, role breadth remit, and role clarity, which aspect requires the most attention in your organization?
- Do all employees have equal access to opportunities for enhancing domain knowledge and receiving broader training throughout their careers?
- How are expectations regarding valued proactive behaviors being communicated?

My Implementation Intentions

Jot down in this space any actions you will take in response to the reflective questions.

References

1. Anglin, A. H., Kincaid, P. A., Short, J. C., & Allen, D. G. (2022). Role theory perspectives: Past, present, and future applications of role theories in management research. *Journal of Management, 48*(6), 1469–1502.
2. Parker, S. K. (1998). Enhancing role breadth self-efficacy: The roles of job enrichment and other organizational interventions. *Journal of Applied Psychology*, 83(6), 835.
3. Parker, S. K., Wall, T. D., & Jackson, P. R. (1997). "That's not my job": Developing flexible employee work orientations. *Academy of Management Journal*, 40(4), 899–929.
4. Parker, S. (2000). From passive to proactive motivation: The importance of flexible role orientations and role breadth self-efficacy. *Applied Psychology*, 49(3), 447–469.
5. Sawyer, J. E. (1992). Goal and process clarity: Specification of multiple constructs of role ambiguity and a structural equation model of their antecedents and consequences. *Journal of Applied Psychology*, 77(2), 130–142.
6. Axtell, C. M., & Parker, S. K. (2003). Promoting role breadth self-efficacy through involvement, work redesign and training. *Human Relations, 56*(1), 113–131.
7. Heffernan, M. (2011). *Wilful blindness: Why we ignore the obvious*. Simon and Schuster.
8. Nielsen, K., Randall, R. & Albertsen, K. (2007). Participants' appraisals of process issues and the effects of stress management interventions. *Journal of Organizational Behavior: The International Journal of Industrial, Occupational and Organizational Psychology and Behavior*, 28(6), 793–810.
9. Institute for Fiscal Studies. (2023). *Investment in training and skills*. Retrieved from https://ifs.org.uk/publications/investment-training-and-skills
10. Statista. (2023). Hours of training per employee in the U.S. by company size 2021. Statista. Retrieved from www.statista.com/statistics/795813/hours-of-training-per-employee-by-company-size-us/
11. Madgavkar, A., Schaninger, B., Maor, D., White, O., Smit, S., Samandari, H., Woetzel, L., Carlin, D., & Chockalingam, K. (2023). Performance through people: Transforming human capital into competitive advantage. *McKinsey Global Institute*.
12. Choeni, P., Babalola, S. S., & Nwanzu, C. L. (2023). The effect of leader's emotional intelligence and role-breadth self-efficacy on proactive behavior at work. *International Journal of Business Science and Applied Management*, 18(1), 63_75.
13. Ernst & Young LLP. (2023). *Empathy in business survey 2023*. www.ey.com/en_us/consulting/authentic-empathy
14. Brackett, M. (2019). *Permission to Feel: Unlock the power of emotions to help yourself and your children thrive*. Hachette UK.
15. Morrison, E. W., & Phelps, C. C. (1999). Taking charge at work: Extrarole efforts to initiate workplace change. *Academy of Management Journal*, 42(4), 403–419.

16. Fuller, B., Marler, L. E., Hester, K., & Otondo, R. F. (2015). Leader reactions to follower proactive behavior: Giving credit when credit is due. *Human Relations*, 68(6), 879–898.

17. Judge, T. A., & Piccolo, R. F. (2004). Transformational and transactional leadership: A meta-analytic test of their relative validity. *Journal of Applied Psychology,* 89(5), 755.

18. Abrell, C., Rowold, J., Weibler, J., & Moenninghoff, M. (2011). Evaluation of a long-term transformational leadership development program. *German Journal of Human Resource Management*, 25(3), 205–224.

19. McClean, E. J., Burris, E. R., & Detert, J. R. (2013). When does voice lead to exit? It depends on leadership. *Academy of Management Journal*, 56(2), 525–548.

20. Zhang, M. J., Law, K. S., & Wang, L. (2021). The risks and benefits of initiating change at work: Social consequences for proactive employees who take charge. *Personnel Psychology,* 74(4), 721–750.

21. Parker, S. K., & Knight, C. (2024). The SMART model of work design: A higher order structure to help see the wood from the trees. *Human Resource Management*, 63(2), 265–291.

22. Sawyer, J. E. (1992). Goal and process clarity: Specification of multiple constructs of role ambiguity and a structural equation model of their antecedents and consequences. *Journal of Applied Psychology*, 77(2), 130.

23. Health & Safety Executive. (2017). *Management Standards Framework*. Health & Safety Executive.

24. Wang, X., Wang, M., & Xu, F. (2022). Domain knowledge and role clarity moderate the relationship between proactive personality and employee radical creativity. *Social Behavior and Personality: An International Journal*, 50(7), 1–11.

25. Gong, Y., Huang, J. C., & Farh, J. L. (2009). Employee learning orientation, transformational leadership, and employee creativity: The mediating role of employee creative self-efficacy. *Academy of Management Journal*, 52(4), 765–778.

26. Rosenthal, R. (1987). Pygmalion effects: Existence, magnitude, and social importance. *Educational Researcher*, 16(9), 37–40.

27. Shalley, C. E., Gilson, L. L., & Blum, T. C. (2009). Interactive effects of growth need strength, work context, and job complexity on self-reported creative performance. *Academy of Management Journal*, 52(3), 489–505.

28. Indeed. (2024, February 29). Job search results. Retrieved from https://www.indeed.com/

Chapter 6

Organizational Fairness

This chapter brings to the fore how perceptions of unfairness can nega-tively influence our desire to be proactive at work. Proactive motivation and fairness perceptions are examined through the lens of rewards and recognition, distribution of resources, moral standards, and effective com-munication. Fairness risks associated with proactivity are explored to emphasize the importance of creating equitable outcomes for all. Once more, the significance of leadership characteristics is highlighted, stressing that driving proactivity lies in a blend of fairness and supportive leadership behaviors. This combination creates a virtuous circle that starts with build-ing trust, which leads to increased commitment and identification with the organization, which stimulates proactive action. The chapter concludes with a case study from Southern Coop, showcasing their "Compass" approach to fair decision-making.

The Origins of Fairness

Fairness is a fascinating concept; it is often considered innate in humans because it emerges early in development and appears to be present across cultures. Evolutionary psychologists suggest that fairness may have evolved as an adaptive trait. In social species like humans, cooperation and fairness can promote group cohesion and survival. Individuals who are perceived as fair are more likely to be trusted and cooperated with, leading to bet-ter outcomes for the group.[1] As such, fairness may have been favored by natural selection over time. Developmental psychologists highlight how fairness plays a crucial role in child development as children begin to navigate social interactions, learn about relationships, and develop their understanding of right and wrong.[2] At a young age, I recall my daughter sharing her Haribo with friends, counting out and allocating them with such precision to ensure they were fairly distributed. That sense of fairness continues to develop as children grow and interact more with their peers

DOI: 10.4324/9781003480693-9

and begin to compare themselves to others. They may feel that certain situations are unfair if they perceive that others are receiving preferential treatment or if they feel they are not receiving their fair share of resources or attention. This tendency to judge perceptions of fairness by comparing ourselves with others is the basis of one of the most influential theories of motivation, known as *Equity Theory*.[3] I use it to explain why, now, as a parent of a teenager, fairness discussions in our house revolve around my daughter's sense of the injustice of not being allowed to have her phone in her room at night, where her friends are.

Fairness in Organizations

Bringing this to an organizational perspective, David Rock, a neuroscientist and organizational leadership expert, suggests that fairness is a critical component of creating a positive work environment and fostering employee engagement and productivity. Fairness is closely linked to the brain's reward system, and when individuals perceive fairness, their brains release dopamine, a neurotransmitter associated with feelings of pleasure and reward.[4] This neurological response reinforces positive behaviors and attitudes, contributing to a more affirmative and productive work environment. Along with many other researchers, Rock argues that when employees perceive their workplace as fair, they are more likely to trust their leaders, feel motivated, and collaborate effectively with their colleagues.

Fairness in organizations can be broken down into four components[5]:

- **Distributive Fairness**: the extent to which leaders and managers encourage fairness through equitable allocation of rewards and responsibilities.
- **Procedural Fairness**: refers to how leaders and managers accurately and consistently apply organizational policies, without bias.
- **Informational Fairness**: is concerned with how procedures are explained and communicated, to ensure employees are provided with open and timely information.
- **Interactional Fairness**: describes how respectful and considerate leaders and managers are in their communications with employees.

In a study of managers across various industries in the United States, 95% of participants believed fairness was an important consideration in their management approach, with most of them attributing it to keeping employees motivated and building positive relationships.[6] Results of this study support prior research that suggests managers tend to perceive fairness in a narrower scope compared to their employees, primarily emphasizing distributive fairness. Interestingly, managers tend to demonstrate greater fairness toward individuals they feel more positively about and that they trust.[7] All four aspects of fairness must be considered and offered to everyone to create a truly fair and equitable workplace.

Spotting the Signs: High v. Low Organizational Fairness

Employees in teams with a low procedural fairness climate tend to be more fearful about taking interpersonal personal risks associated with proactive behavior. Whereas employees in teams with a high procedural justice climate perceive their workplace to be a fair, open, and just environment, which stimulates greater feelings of commitment and identification toward their organization. This results in employees behaving more proactively, such as making improvement suggestions, because they don't fear being treated badly.[8] In environments depicting high levels of organizational fairness, when it comes to processes and procedures, you'd expect to see:

  i   Consistency among managers in applying rules and regulations.
 ii   Objectivity and a lack of bias in decision-making.
iii   The provision of adequate information and explanation.

Leaders are likely to be perceived as fair if they are seen to distribute resources equitably, whether that be access to personal development, training, flexible working arrangements, or career progression. Judgments of fair treatment from one's supervisor play a significant role in influencing employees' attitudes and behaviors; employees are more likely to engage in activities that are beneficial for the organization when they believe they are being treated fairly.[9] On the flip side, leaders displaying arrogant or belittling behaviors, for example, making derogatory remarks, are likely to signal low levels of interactional fairness and trust, which will inhibit employees' motivation to engage in proactive behavior.

Proactivity and Organizational Fairness

Developing a culture of fairness is vital in powering workplace proactivity. When employees perceive their organizations to be fair, they are more likely to behave proactively for the good of the organization.[10]

Proactive Innovative Behavior

The relationship between fairness and proactive innovative behavior has been widely researched, revealing some compelling insights. Survey results from public health organizations in the Netherlands indicated that proactive individuals who exhibit innovative behaviors expect to be rewarded for their efforts. So, when perceptions of *distributive and procedural fairness* were low, it resulted in uncertainty and ambiguity over rewards, which induced feelings of stress.[11] The importance of a fair contribution-reward ratio is echoed in these findings, which reinforces the notion of distributive fairness. When the efforts for being proactive are "fairly" rewarded, it is more likely to stimulate greater feelings of commitment to the organization, as proactive individuals will feel like their organization values their contribution. In another study conducted within the pharmaceutical industry in Indonesia, a different set of implications were highlighted. In this study, researchers found that proactive innovative behavior was associated with conflict with co-workers when perceptions of distributive fairness were low.[12] This was explained by highlighting how innovative ideas proposed by proactive employees might act to destabilize established routines and norms, which can bemuse and frustrate other colleagues, resulting in tension and conflict. We'll explore this further in Chapter 10 when discussing peer reactions to proactivity and the role of influence. Essentially, when there is a strong perception of fairness, proactive individuals are more likely to feel a sense of attachment toward their organization. This, in turn, motivates them to minimize conflicts by engaging colleagues more fully before attempting to implement proactive ideas.

Proactive Voice – Speaking Up

Perceptions of fairness also influence an individual's propensity to proactively speak up at work. A proactive voice is the expression of ideas, opinions, and concerns that are shared to improve the organization. At the opposite end of the spectrum is silence, whereby individuals withhold or suppress useful information, as a response to perceptions of injustice. Employees choose silence when they believe speaking up is not worth the effort and/or they fear reprisals or retaliation.[13] Silence can be contagious and pervasive in organizations, leaving employees feeling helpless, and culminating in withdrawal, disengagement, absenteeism, and increased turnover.[14] Some of the common issues that employees tend to remain silent on at work, include[15]:

- Concerns around co-workers' or supervisors' performance.
- Concerns regarding organizational processes or performance.
- Conversations about pay and pay inequity.

Jerald Greenberg was a renowned organizational psychologist and pioneering figure in the field of organizational justice, he coined the *voice effect,* which refers to the influence that giving employees a voice or input has on their perceptions of fairness and their subsequent reactions.[16] The *voice effect* suggests that when employees perceive the decision-making process as fair, due to their ability to voice their opinions, they are more likely to accept the outcome and exhibit higher levels of job satisfaction, engagement, and organizational commitment. Conversely, when employees feel their voices are not heard or considered, it can lead to feelings of injustice, decreased morale, and potentially negative behaviors – much like a virtuous circle versus a vicious circle. However, organizations must walk the talk, which means having systems in place to promote a proactive voice. Open-door policies and suggestion boxes can exacerbate perceptions of unfairness if individuals' efforts to speak up are not taken seriously. Effective systems to convey fairness and promote a proactive voice should[17]:

1 Create a psychologically safe environment (as outlined in Chapter 4).
2 Demonstrate credibility by using objective, nonbiased approaches.
3 Be accessible – easy to use and understand.
4 Provide timely and appropriate feedback and responses.

Studies specifically exploring the relationship between *interpersonal fairness* and speaking up have started to emerge. Unsurprisingly, being treated with respect by one's supervisor influences our propensity to speak up. In the same vein, perceptions of interpersonal unfairness in the form of social undermining, in other words being treated with contempt or being rejected by co-workers or supervisors, have the propensity to promote silence.[18]

Proactive Personality

This leads us to consider some of the implications of perceived *informational* and *interactional unfairness* and how it relates to proactive personalities. Individuals with a proactive personality associate fairness with maintaining high moral standards. I can relate to this; I often talk about my "fairness barometer" and how aware I am of my emotions rising when I perceive an injustice. It is not uncommon that when faced with an unjust workplace, proactive individuals demonstrate greater levels of frustration and react more negatively, which may lead to counterproductive work behaviors in the form of making disparaging remarks, expressing cynicism, and absenteeism. "Deontic anger" [19] has been used to describe this reaction, describing counter-productive work behaviors, I prefer the term "impish behavior," described by one of my research participants in their response to unfair situations at work. Either way, the outcomes are unlikely to be positive. During another interview, a research participant described a situation where their manager strongly expressed political beliefs during a meeting, dismissing and belittling those with differing political viewpoints. They believed their manager had crossed a line, appearing unprofessional and unfair, which sparked fury and frustration in them, and their anger was evident as they recounted their story. In another example, a participant had been working hard on what they'd been told was a high-priority strategic evaluation. They worked proactively to get a report finalized by the deadline, which involved extra effort. However, they later found out that the senior leadership team had not reviewed the proposals and had decided to move the goalposts, rendering the work obsolete. The response from the leadership team was perceived as unfair, as their efforts and hard work were disregarded without any discussion. In both cases, these experiences sparked feelings of frustration and disappointment in the proactive individuals, which impacted their motivation and levels of engagement.

Interestingly, individuals with a high proactive personality score, but limited organizational political skills and low situational awareness, are more likely to perceive their work environment as unfair. This is because they may struggle to interpret constraints from others' perspectives.[20] We'll explore the importance of political skill and situational judgment effectiveness in contributing to positive experiences of proactivity in Chapter 11. Ultimately perceptions of unfairness will vary from individual to individual, they are inherently complex and can be guided by our previous work-related experiences.[21] But, recognizing and responding to sensitivities toward (un)fairness is undoubtedly a managerial imperative.

When Proactivity Fuels Unfairness

We've uncovered how perceptions of injustice can affect our proactivity, let's turn to how proactivity can fuel unfairness. You may be wondering why, in a book designed to power proactivity, I'm sharing insights about proactive behavior being a threat to fairness. I want the insights from this book to stimulate proactivity at work across the workforce, so it's important to consider those who are predisposed to proactivity, as well as those who are not. Some of the fairness pitfalls I'll describe have the potential to disadvantage the latter, while simultaneously increasing unfairness perceptions for everyone. So, it's important managers and leaders are aware of some of these potential risks to mitigate them. Revisiting the notion of co-worker envy that was touched on earlier; damage to relationships within teams has also been highlighted as a potential pitfall of proactivity. It's not uncommon for supervisors who value action and achievement to show favoritism toward proactive members of the team.

In such cases, co-worker envy comes from a perception that proactive individuals unfairly receive favorable treatment at work and are provided greater access to resources.[22] I recently facilitated a series of workshops on goal setting, and when I asked how they knew if an individual was ready for a stretch goal (e.g. a development opportunity), the unanimous response was "They'd ask for it." This tells me that either everyone in that organization has a proactive personality, or opportunities to stretch and grow are being (unfairly) allocated to individuals who are more confident in speaking up, meaning some individuals are missing out. Managers can display a tendency to assign opportunities to the "usual suspects" in the team, those they know they can rely on, those they know who will "just get on with it," but this can put fairness perceptions at risk. Opportunities should not be allocated only to those who shout the loudest.

Hybrid working (flexible arrangements combining remote/office work) is another ripe area for creating disparities among team members. I am a strong advocate of hybrid working and its associated benefits for employees and organizations if managed intentionally and deliberately. However, it is concerning that hybrid working tends to favor proactive individuals who have developed what's been coined *hybrid competency*.[23] It's been suggested hybrid working rewards individuals who can think and act adaptably, can coordinate complex, dynamic environments, and are proactive in asking for, finding out about, and claiming resources. In contrast, less proactive individuals are more likely to experience lower confidence in being self-directed and asking for resources. Arguably those individuals who have a more passive disposition may be more likely to be most negatively affected by hybrid working due to lower levels of visibility and a higher propensity for them to go undetected by their managers, fuelling feelings of unfairness.

Leadership Characteristics

A culture of fairness relies on respectful leaders who value equality. As we already discovered in Chapter 4, inclusive leaders provide support, encourage employees to speak up, and value their contributions, thereby enhancing a sense of psychological safety. Inclusive leaders also demonstrate fairness via openness, availability, and accessibility when interacting with their colleagues, which reinforces perceptions of organizational fairness. Inclusive leaders not only provide emotional support to increase employee trust but also inspire employees who are less proactive to take initiative, which touches on the pitfalls identified earlier.[24] Behaviours associated with transformational leadership have also been identified in promoting perceptions of fairness and especially driving proactive innovative behavior. These include articulating a compelling vision; developing employees through coaching and mentoring; encouraging creative thinking; demonstrating honesty and respect in their interactions; and consistently adhering to policies, procedures, and regulations.[25] Fairness perceptions can be further enhanced by managers who advocate for issues raised by their team members and who effectively influence the decisions of senior leaders. This simple gesture underscores the value placed on employees' ideas. On the flip side, abusive or disrespectful behaviors from leaders signal a hostile environment, in which case employees will not feel safe to express themselves freely, leading to silence.

Practical Recommendations

To embed perceptions of organizational fairness, it is important to consider activities across the entire employee journey. Table 6.1 draws on insights shared within this chapter to provide some practical recommendations across various stages of the employee experience.

This chapter concludes with a case study from Southern Co-op, showcasing their approach to bringing fairness, one of their core values to life.

Table 6.1 Organizational Fairness Initiatives

Selection and assessment	Rewards and recognition
Recruit leaders with strong moral identity, by assessing candidates' values, ethics, and integrity during the recruitment process.	Provide clarity around how employees' contribution is rewarded and recognized. Make pay-related information accessible to employees through various channels.
Use behavioral-based interview questions to unearth how candidates handled ethical challenges in previous roles to gauge their moral reasoning and decision-making abilities.	Use external benchmarking to determine salaries to establish fair and competitive compensation practices that align with market standards and promote pay equity.
Clearly communicate your organization's values and ethical standards during the recruitment process and assess candidates' alignment to them.	Implement a peer recognition program where employees can nominate colleagues for their proactive contributions, to boost team cohesion.
Utilize psychometric tools in conjunction with other assessment methods. Personality assessments that identify potential 'derailers' e.g. negative behaviors that manifest under pressure, can be useful to determine 'organizational fit'.	Ensure that promotion and advancement opportunities are based on merit, skills, and qualifications.

(Continued)

Table 6.1 (Continued)

Training and development	Organizational approaches
Ensure managers and leaders are adequately trained on organizational policies and provide 'refreshers' to keep knowledge up to date. Be careful not to fall into the 'too much information' trap, provide managers with the tools they need to keep abreast of policy changes without it becoming onerous.	Consider integrating fairness as a core value within your organization, fostering an environment where every decision and action reflects equitable treatment, transparency, and integrity.
Develop awareness around cognitive biases in decision-making and share strategies for how to make objective decisions.	Implement Diversity, Equity, and Inclusion (DEI) initiatives, including Employee Network Groups (ENGs), within your organization. ENGs can provide support, networking opportunities, and advocacy for underrepresented groups.
Invest in interpersonal skills training for managers and leaders, to enhance their ability to communicate effectively, build relationships, resolve conflicts, lead with empathy, and engage and motivate their teams.	Hold regular 'Listening Groups' to make employees feel like their voices and ideas are valued.
	Establish fair and impartial processes for resolving conflicts and disputes in the workplace, ensuring issues are addressed promptly and equitably.
Ensure development opportunities are available to all and not reserved for 'top talent' or solely early career employees.	Take a non-biased, participative approach to determining the parameters around hybrid working arrangements, so that it works for individuals, the team, and the organization overall. Effectively communicate the rationale around hybrid working policies.

Box 6.1   Case Study

Southern Co-op's Commitment to Fairness – A Blueprint for Success

Established in 1873, Southern Co-op is an independent Co-operative operating across the south of England, running convenience food stores, funeral homes, crematoria, natural/woodland burial grounds, and a Starbucks coffee franchise. The member-owned organization has over 4,000 colleagues, and its purpose is simple: "working together for the benefit of our communities." Southern Co-op prides itself on a fresh, fair approach that underscores all its operations. Their strategic plan, known as "Our Plan," embodies their commitment to transparency and fairness, setting the stage for their initiatives and the organizational culture.

Fairness at Southern Co-op

Southern Co-op has embedded fairness into the core of its operations through several well-defined processes. This includes both internal mechanisms and the involvement of specialists to ensure objectivity. Fairness permeates every stage of the employee journey, from recruitment and onboarding to ongoing colleague experiences. At the recruitment stage, Southern Co-op ensures that its processes are equitable, with interview protocols designed to minimize bias. The onboarding process is comprehensive, aiming to integrate new employees smoothly and equitably into the cooperative. Regarding remuneration, salaries at Southern Co-op are benchmarked using external positioning, and job profiles are graded to ensure competitive and fair compensation. This systematic approach ensures that all employees receive fair pay reflective of their roles and the market standards.

Southern Co-op goes beyond mere compliance with regulations, proactively addressing issues such as the gender pay gap, modern slavery, and ethical supply chain practices. Their voluntary participation in initiatives to drive best practices across their sectors showcases their commitment to fairness. In April 2021, Southern Co-op introduced the "Compass," a decision-making tool designed to consider the broader implications of business decisions. Initially used for large procurement or sensitive decisions, it has since been expanded to various business, product, and personnel decisions. The Compass evaluates decisions across multiple factors, including brand, people, members/customers, community, commercial impact, and sustainability. When using the Compass to reflect on the best decision, colleagues are encouraged to gather information across the different factors by talking to one another and being open to diverse perspectives.

Impact and Results

The introduction of the Compass tool has had a significant positive impact on Southern Co-op's operations. It has driven accountability and necessitated collaboration across different functions, promoting quality conversations and breaking down silos. The Compass has enabled employees to have a shared language to raise concerns, while heightening awareness about responsible business practices and looking at opportunities through multiple lenses. It has also proven instrumental in crafting position statements, ensuring that the reasoning behind decisions is thoroughly considered and communicated both internally and externally. The success and effectiveness of the Compass have led other independent cooperatives to adopt this tool, highlighting its value in fostering fairness and transparency. By promoting a culture of fairness, Southern Co-op has strengthened its organizational integrity and enhanced its reputation in the industry.

Advice to Other Organizations

Southern Co-op's People & Sustainability Director shares that "the real value of the Compass lies in its ability to drive accountability for decisions while requiring collaboration and cooperation across functions. It brings about quality conversations and helps to remove silos within our organization."

For other organizations looking to implement similar initiatives, they offer several pieces of advice. To maintain its effectiveness, they suggest any approach needs regular reviews to ensure it remains relevant and fit for purpose. This helps prevent a regression into old habits – but to do that, colleagues must see the value in using the Compass. Proper training is also necessary to ensure that colleagues understand how to effectively use the Compass and appreciate its value beyond just a procedural requirement. The board's emphasis on the importance of such tools is vital, their support ensures that the tool is taken seriously and integrated into the organizational culture. Additionally, from a pragmatic perspective, it is acknowledged that not every decision may require a full Compass assessment, and it's essential to maintain proportionality.

Southern Co-op's commitment to fairness is evident through its strategic initiatives and the successful implementation of the Compass tool. By fostering a culture of transparency and fairness, Southern Co-op not only enhances internal operations but also sets a benchmark for other cooperatives. Their proactive stance on regulatory issues and dedication to equitable practices exemplify how fairness can be a driving force for responsible and sustainable business growth.

Key Takeaways

- Perceived fairness is crucial for organizations in fostering trust, engagement, commitment, and stimulating proactivity among employees.
- Leaders and managers play a critical role in demonstrating fairness, across the four dimensions of distributive, procedural, informational, and interpersonal fairness.
- When perceptions of unfairness prevail, proactive individuals may respond unfavorably, leading to negative outcomes for the organization.
- If not managed effectively, proactivity can itself fuel perceptions of unfairness, managers and leaders need to be aware of the pitfalls to ensure an inclusive approach is taken to the distribution of resources.
- A range of activities can be implemented across the entire employee journey to enhance perceptions of organizational fairness.

Reflective Questions

- In your organization, which of the four components of organizational fairness do you identify as an opportunity for improvement?
- What's your biggest takeaway from reading this chapter?
- What three things would you like to see more of in your organization?

My Implementation Intentions

Jot down in this space any actions you will take in response to the reflective questions.

References

1. Gintis, H., Henrich, J., Bowles, S., Boyd, R., & Fehr, E. (2008). Strong reciprocity and the roots of human morality. *Social Justice Research*, 21, 241–253.
2. Rakoczy, H., Kaufmann, M., & Lohse, K. (2016). Young children understand the normative force of standards of equal resource distribution. *Journal of Experimental Child Psychology*, 150, 396–403.
3. Rock, D. (2009). *Managing with the brain in mind*. Strategy + Business.
4. Adams, J. S. (1965). Inequity in social exchange. *In Advances in experimental social psychology* (Vol. 2, pp. 267–299). Academic Press.
5. Colquitt, J. A. (2001). On the dimensionality of organizational justice: A construct validation of a measure. *Journal of Applied Psychology*, 86(3), 386.
6. Long, C. P. (2016). Mapping the main roads to fairness: Examining the managerial context of fairness promotion. *Journal of Business Ethics*, 137(4), 757–783.
7. Seppälä, T., Lipponen, J., Pirttilä-Backman, A. M., & Lipsanen, J. (2012). A trust-focused model of leaders' fairness enactment. *Journal of Personnel Psychology*, 11(1), 20–30.
8. Tangirala, S., & Ramanujam, R. (2008). Employee silence on critical work issues: The cross level effects of procedural justice climate. *Personnel Psychology*, 61(1), 37–68.
9. Molina, A., & O'Shea, D. (2020). Mindful emotion regulation, savouring and proactive behaviour: The role of supervisor justice. *Applied Psychology*, 69(1), 148–175.
10. Li, N., Liang, J., & Crant, J. M. (2010). The role of proactive personality in job satisfaction and organizational citizenship behavior: A relational perspective. *Journal of Applied Psychology*, 95(2), 395.
11. Janssen, O. (2004). How fairness perceptions make innovative behavior more or less stressful. *Journal of Organizational Behavior*, 25(2), 201–215.
12. Shih, H. A., & Susanto, E. (2011). *Is innovative behavior really good for the firm? Innovative work behavior, conflict with coworkers and turnover intention: Moderating roles of perceived distributive fairness*, 22(2), 111–130. International Journal of Conflict Management.
13. Milliken, F. J., Morrison, E. W., & Hewlin, P. F. (2003). An exploratory study of employee silence: Issues that employees don't communicate upward and why. *Journal of Management Studies*, 40(6), 1453–1476.
14. Brinsfield, C. T., Edwards, M. S., & Greenberg, J. (2009). Voice and silence in organizations: Historical review and current conceptualizations. *Voice and Silence in Organizations*, 1, 34.
15. Harlos, K. P. (2001). When organizational voice systems fail: More on the deaf-ear syndrome and frustration effects. *The Journal of Applied Behavioral Science*, 37(3), 324–342.
16. Greenberg, J., & Folger, R. (1983). Procedural justice, participation, and the fair process effect in groups and organizations. *In Basic group processes* (pp. 235–256). Springer New York.

17. Harlos, K. P. (2001). When organizational voice systems fail: More on the deaf-ear syndrome and frustration effects. *The Journal of Applied Behavioral Science*, 37(3), 324–342.
18. Jung, H. S., & Yoon, H. H. (2019). The effects of social undermining on employee voice and silence and on organizational deviant behaviors in the hotel industry. *Journal of Service Theory and Practice*, 29(2), 213–231.
19. Li, N., Liang, J., & Crant, J. M. (2010). The role of proactive personality in job satisfaction and organizational citizenship behavior: A relational perspective. *Journal of Applied Psychology,* 95(2), 395.
20. Chan, D. (2006). Interactive effects of situational judgment effectiveness and proactive personality on work perceptions and work outcomes. *Journal of Applied Psychology*, 91(2), 475.
21. Jordan, S. L., Palmer, J. C., Daniels, S. R., Hochwarter, W. A., Perrewé, P. L., & Ferris, G. R. (2022). Subjectivity in fairness perceptions: How heuristics and self-efficacy shape the fairness expectations and perceptions of organisational newcomers. *Applied Psychology*, 71(1), 103–128.
22. Sun, J., Li, W. D., Li, Y., Liden, R. C., Li, S., & Zhang, X. (2021). Unintended consequences of being proactive? Linking proactive personality to co-worker envy, helping, and undermining, and the moderating role of prosocial motivation. *Journal of Applied Psychology*, 106(2), 250.
23. Mortensen, M., & Haas, M. (2021). Making the hybrid workplace fair. *Harvard Business Review*, 24. Retrieved from https://hbr.org/2021/02/making-the-hybrid-workplace-fair
24. Chang, P. C., Ma, G., & Lin, Y. Y. (2022). *Inclusive leadership and employee proactive behavior: A cross-level moderated mediation model,* 15. Psychology Research and Behavior Management, 1797–1808.
25. Khaola, P. P., & Oni, F. A. (2020). The influence of school principals' leadership behaviour and act of fairness on innovative work behaviours amongst teachers. *SA Journal of Human Resource Management*, 18, 8.

Chapter 7

Autonomy

The focus of this chapter is one of our basic psychological needs: autonomy. I'll demonstrate the importance of providing employees with a sense of freedom to make their own choices at work, to fuel proactivity. Drawing on self-determination theory (SDT), one of the most influential models of motivation, I'll explain why autonomy-supportive environments stimulate happy, healthy employees who are more committed to driving improvements that benefit the organization. The role of empowering leadership is explored, along with practical job design techniques that increase autonomy perceptions. The chapter concludes by sharing a case study from Timpson, showcasing their upside management approach.

The Power of Autonomy

Back in the days of wacky psychological experiments, often involving the use of animals to understand human behavior, a study of dogs enduring a series of shocks revealed some intriguing findings. The dogs in Martin Seligman's study faced situations where they had no control over the outcome. They learned a hard lesson: their efforts seemed pointless, and they resigned themselves to their fate. This phenomenon is known as *learned helplessness* and is associated with emotions such as apathy, despair, and unhappiness.[1] But there's another side to this story: the power of autonomy, which empowers us to take control of our lives. Autonomy is the freedom and ability to make our own choices and decisions and to take responsibility for them. In Seligman's research, autonomy emerges as the hero. Those who possess it believe in their ability to steer their lives in the direction they choose instead of feeling helpless.

In an organizational context, autonomy involves acting of one's own volition at work, it provides us with a sense of self-determination in decision-making, experiencing choice, and taking action. At the core of autonomy is the employee's desire to have options and feel in charge of their tasks.

DOI: 10.4324/9781003480693-10

When not granted autonomy, there is a propensity to experience learned helplessness, in this state, employees may lose their motivation to act, believing they lack control over their situation. The consequences of a lack of autonomy run deep in that a lack of control over one's work is a major cause of stress at work.[2] Professional services firm PwC published a report highlighting five imperatives for organizations to thrive, one of which is the provision of greater autonomy for employees. According to their survey of more than 1,200 businesses across 79 countries, 70% of companies say creating worker autonomy is important for the future. Yet only 45% agreed that their employees currently have a high degree of autonomy over how they work. The report encourages organizations to close the gap between rhetoric and reality.[3]

Unleashing Motivation through Psychological Needs

Before exploring the relationship between autonomy and proactivity, one must understand how autonomy influences motivation. One of the most influential theories to explain motivation at work is *Self-Determination Theory* (SDT).[4] At the heart of SDT is the notion that different things in our environment at work, like how our job is set up, or how our managers treat us, can affect how motivated and satisfied we feel. This is determined by the fulfillment of our basic psychological needs for autonomy, competence, and relatedness. When these needs are met, we are likely to feel more engaged and motivated at work, which facilitates enhanced performance. Interestingly, when organizations and managers promote autonomy, the fulfillment of the other two psychological needs – competence and relatedness – is also addressed. When managers and the organization support employees' independence, it usually means they also care about meeting other needs employees have, like feeling competent and connected. When employees have freedom in their work, they tend to figure out ways to meet these needs on their own. So, when employees feel supported in their independence, they also tend to feel more connected to the organization and more confident in their abilities. This could explain why employees often dislike workplace mandates, such as mandatory training or strict directives regarding office/home working arrangements. Responses to mandates at work can infringe on our autonomy needs because they often dictate how things should be done, leaving little room for individual choice or self-direction. When employees feel that their autonomy is restricted, they may perceive their actions as controlled by external forces rather than being driven by their own volition. This can lead to feelings of frustration, disengagement, reduced motivation, and a tendency to feel less invested in the tasks they are required to complete. I always feel a sense of disappointment when I invite participants attending my leadership workshops to share their motivation for joining, to be told, "Because it's mandatory." That tells me they probably don't want to be there, and their organization is not sending out the right message about the value of the training. It is important employees feel empowered, not coerced – nobody likes "being done to."

Across a range of professions, studies examining how workplaces influence motivation have looked at how employees view their managers' support for their autonomy needs. This includes behaviors like listening to employees, giving them choices, providing helpful feedback, encouraging them to take the lead, giving them challenging tasks, and explaining why certain tasks are important. Studies across different cultures and industries affirm the utility of SDT in understanding employee motivation at work. The satisfaction of autonomy has been related to greater personal well-being, even in cultures for which collectivism is a core value.[5]

Autonomous Motivation versus Controlled Motivation

Central to SDT is the distinction between autonomous and controlled motivation. The autonomous motivation continuum is a useful way to understand how people are motivated to do things at work.[6]

- **Intrinsic Motivation:** At one end of the continuum, we have intrinsic motivation, this is when employees are motivated to work because they genuinely enjoy their tasks. They find their work interesting, challenging, and personally fulfilling. For example, someone who loves problem-solving might feel intrinsically motivated in a role that requires a lot of analytical thinking.

- **Autonomous Motivation:** Moving along the continuum, we have autonomous motivation. In this middle ground, employees are motivated by factors that are important to them, even if they don't necessarily find the work inherently enjoyable. They might see their work as aligned with their personal values or long-term goals. For instance, someone might work diligently on a project because they believe it contributes to the greater good of their team or organization, even if the specific tasks aren't so engaging.

- **Controlled Motivation:** At the other end of the continuum, we have controlled motivation. Here, employees feel pressured or obligated to work due to external factors such as rewards, punishments, or fear of negative consequences. For example, an employee might work overtime because they fear being reprimanded by their boss if they don't meet deadlines.

In summary, the autonomous motivation continuum in the workplace spans from intrinsic motivation, where employees work because they love what they do, to *autonomous motivation*, where their work aligns with their values and goals, to *controlled motivation*, where they work because of external pressures or incentives. Understanding where employees fall on this continuum can help employers create environments that cultivate more intrinsic and autonomous motivation, leading to higher job satisfaction and performance.

Locus of Control

One final concept relevant to this topic relates to locus of control. While autonomy is about experiencing a sense of control; *locus of control* refers to an individual's belief regarding the extent to which they can control events affecting them. There is a clear link between locus of control and autonomy. Individuals with an internal locus of control tend to believe that they have control over their own lives and outcomes. Consequently, they are more likely to exhibit autonomous behavior, taking initiative and making decisions based on their own beliefs and values. They may feel empowered to shape their destiny and are less dependent on external influences. Conversely, individuals with an external locus of control believe that their lives are largely influenced by external factors such as luck, fate, or powerful others. This belief can undermine their sense of autonomy, as they may feel less capable of controlling their circumstances. They may rely more on external cues or directions, feeling less empowered to make independent decisions. Interestingly, job autonomy has been found to promote the development of an employee's internal locus of control.[7]

Proactivity and Autonomy

It is thought that perceptions of high job autonomy can also give employees time, energy, and freedom to engage in future-orientated behaviors, thereby providing the conditions for proactivity to flourish. Of the international research that demonstrates how vital autonomy is in powering proactivity, here are the studies I have found most insightful, along with some practical considerations.

Proactive Personality

It's been suggested that proactive individuals value challenging tasks and autonomy more than those less inclined to be proactive.[8] There also appears to be a virtuous circle involving job autonomy and complexity. When individuals experience high levels of job autonomy and complexity, they have a greater sense of control, and they strive to achieve even higher autonomy and complexity by showing initiative. This, in turn, leads to even greater job control and job complexity in the longer term.[9] While there is mixed evidence on the relationship between proactive personality and locus of control, there is some certainty around the tendency for proactive individuals to perceive higher levels of psychological empowerment, autonomy, and job control.[10] With this knowledge, managers design roles and allocate tasks that challenge proactive employees, allowing them the freedom to solve problems creatively, take initiative, and contribute new ideas. By doing so, managers not only boost engagement but also tap into the full potential of their team.

Job Crafting

The importance of job autonomy in activating positive experiences of career proactivity, such as job crafting, is well documented. When job autonomy is high, employees may feel more empowered to modify their jobs without the need for encouragement from their leader.[11] Arnold Bakker, a prominent organizational psychologist renowned for his research on stress and burnout, illustrated the link between job crafting and work engagement. He showed that individuals experience heightened levels of energy and enthusiasm when they can tailor their jobs to align with their interests and skills.[12] Continuing in the vein of positive feelings and mood, proactivity at work has been linked to the satisfaction of basic psychological needs: competence, autonomy, and relatedness, thereby inducing feelings of vitality and enthusiasm. I'm not going to pretend job crafting is always easy to facilitate and accommodate, and there is plenty of evidence to suggest the potentially negative consequences associated with job crafting if not done well. Recent studies highlight the risk of tensions arising when co-workers observe job crafting in others, and this may contribute to perceptions of unfairness, which we know from Chapter 6 can be highly problematic. It's important to remember the power of job crafting lies in promoting a sense of autonomy and tailoring to an individual's needs. However, its success depends on a positive team dynamic.

Proactive Innovative Behavior

The importance of autonomy is underscored in driving innovative behavior, from studies in government institutions to agricultural settings. A group of researchers from Japan conducted a study among over 600 employees of a forging factory, to investigate the relationship between autonomy and proactive innovative behavior. This study is interesting because it reinforces the importance of autonomy regardless of the type of industry. I also found it interesting because the researchers examined autonomy with some granularity. They assessed whether different facets of work autonomy have a stronger effect on innovative behavior for those with high proactive personality than for those with low proactive personality. Rather than treating autonomy in its broadest sense, they broke it down to:

i **Methods:** the discretion employees possess regarding their work procedures.
ii **Scheduling:** the extent to which employees have control in timetabling their work.
iii **Criteria:** the ability of employees to determine the measures used for evaluating their performance.

They found that work method and work schedule autonomy resulted in innovative behavior among all participants. Interestingly, the effects of work criteria autonomy differed depending on whether individuals identified as having a proactive personality or not and were more susceptible to variability. This suggests that strengthening autonomy within work criteria could effectively encourage innovative contributions, especially from employees who may not be naturally proactive.[13]

Speaking Up and Taking Charge

It's generally accepted that because speaking up comes with interpersonal risk, employees will need more autonomous motivation to offer improvement ideas. Researchers from China found that job autonomy strengthened the relationship between empowering leadership and speaking up via so-called *harmonious passion,* which is a form of deep intrinsic motivation. Findings demonstrated that empowering leaders stimulated *harmonious passion,* which in turn fuelled employees to speak up. This was premised on the idea that when employees enjoy their jobs and their need for autonomy is satisfied, they will feel more motivated to speak up to offer improvement ideas because they feel vested in the organization.[14] So, when leaders empower their team members, it not only makes them like their work more but also helps them understand its meaning. As a result, employees become more passionately engaged in their work, seeing it as part of who they are, which can lead them to take interpersonal risks, like speaking up to make their work better. Further research from China, but this time among almost 200 front-line workers in 5-star hotels, also found that autonomy strengthened "pro-social" personality traits. So, when employees perceived high levels of job autonomy, it gave them greater freedom to consider how to improve outcomes for their co-workers and the organization, thereby fuelling a desire to engage in more proactive taking charge behavior.[15] These examples highlight the value of autonomy-supportive work environments in creating a committed and concerned workforce. Conversely, when less autonomy is given, these opportunities for improvement and a sense of seeking responsibility will only decrease.

We've explored the evidence that shows the positive relationship between autonomy and proactivity, let's now take a deep dive into the consequences at work when proactive individuals find themselves in environments depicted by low autonomy.

The Harmful Effects of Low Autonomy + High Proactivity

My colleagues and I conducted a systematic literature review of 37 different studies to identify when proactivity at work had harmful consequences.[16] A key finding was the interplay between proactive behavior at work and stress-related outcomes in environments characterized by low levels of autonomy. A study carried out in Germany showed that when the motivation for proactivity was driven by external motives, e.g., reward/avoidance of chastisement, there was a higher propensity for irritability and rumination, leading to higher levels of disengagement.[17] Similarly, research carried out across various sectors in Australia found that when proactive employees took charge at work but experienced low levels of autonomous motivation, they were more likely to encounter difficulties in switching off, which exacerbated energy depletion and resulted in job strain.[18] We'll go further into how proactivity can fuel and deplete our energy in Chapter 12, in the meantime, there is little doubt that engaging in proactive behavior when we feel autonomously motivated to do so is better for our health and well-being.

Promoting Autonomy – Cultivating Empowering Leaders

Empowering leadership behaviors that focus on sharing power with team members to enhance their motivation is most effective in promoting autonomy at work. This involves leaders providing opportunities to make work more meaningful, encouraging greater participation in decision-making, and encouraging self-directedness. Autonomy-support and independence sets empowering leadership apart from other leadership styles. For this reason, this type of leadership has been linked to boosting proactive behavior, which makes sense given proactive actions are usually self-started. Empowering leadership behaviors provides the fuel to activate our *Can-do*, *Reason-to*, and *Energized-to* motivational states, as defined in Chapter 2. To drive greater levels of proactive innovative behavior, leaders must provide autonomy, appropriate levels of support, and the resources required for their employees to explore new ideas. In doing so, they can evoke positive emotions among team members, generating heightened creativity levels.[19]

Training managers and leaders to be more autonomy-supportive is possible. Such training has been reported to increase job satisfaction and trust in organizations,[20] resulting in greater levels of engagement and yielding a return on investment of more than 3 to 1.[21] Training interventions of this kind typically encourage managers to develop interpersonal skills to:

i Take the employees' perspective and encourage the expression of emotions.
ii Encourage greater levels of group participation to encourage team members to take more personal initiative.
iii Provide motivating, constructive feedback.

Trusting relationships are at the heart of empowering leadership behaviors. Conventional work practices that closely monitor employees do not boost autonomy. Conversations between supervisors and their direct reports should be modeled on adult-to-adult interactions, not those of parent-child. Instead of constantly assigning tasks and monitoring their actions, managers could utilize more empowering techniques to boost constructive suggestions from employees.

Practical Considerations

In this section, I want to situate autonomy within two current challenges facing many organizations that also relate to proactivity at work: organizational change and hybrid/remote working. In addition, there's also practical value in considering the role of autonomy in goal setting to drive individuals' contribution and commitment.

Autonomy and Change

When implementing organizational changes, one of the early stages of a change project is to assess "organizational readiness." This is often associated with identifying any "resistance" that may be counter-productive to the change effort.[22] I have always found the word resistance deeply uncomfortable, as, in many contexts, resistance is simply a response to attempts to impose authority without considering the perspectives or autonomy of those involved. If we interpret resistance through the eyes of those impacted, it is more helpful to acknowledge resistance as a response to a perceived threat, for example, a fear of the unknown, which can be extremely disconcerting. By taking a more humanist approach, mobilizing energy for change can be achieved by engaging the groups who will be impacted by the change, first and foremost, as a more positive way to address readiness and acceptance. The power of participation cannot be underestimated, not only for the benefits it has in determining and shaping the change effort but also as an empowering process that can help facilitate a smoother transition process. During a significant period of change at a Canadian telecommunications company, researchers looked at how supportive managers were towards employees' autonomy at two different times: when the change started and 13 months later. Autonomy support was measured by how much employees felt their managers listened to their perspectives, gave them choices, and explained why certain tasks were important. At the same time, these employees shared their attitudes toward the changes happening in the company. The results showed that the more supportive managers were perceived by employees at the start of the change, the more accepting those employees became of the changes over the 13 months.[23] Allowing people as much autonomy as possible during change initiatives to find their way of doing things is recommended. While targets are vital, handing over responsibility for how things are achieved can be empowering and highly effective. That said, I also appreciate that there will be times when employees will have fewer opportunities to influence or effect an organizational change. I would suggest in these cases, open and honest conversations are had at the onset regarding what is within one's scope of control to influence and what is not. Most employees will recognize that there will be decisions that go beyond their ability to control or influence, and being transparent with this will help manage expectations and prevent the risk of seeking perspectives only for them to be undermined.

Autonomy and Hybrid/Remote Work

Since the pandemic, there has been a significant rise in more flexible working arrangements, with knowledge workers choosing to balance time spent in the office with time working from home. Decades of research give us a good understanding of how working from home affects both employees and organizations. On the one hand, it can boost proactivity, improve work-life balance, and support well-being. On the other hand, it brings challenges like managing workplace relationships, health and safety concerns over the workspace, and the risk of intensification of work from blurring work/home boundaries.[24] The debate seems to have become somewhat divisive. According to a Microsoft survey of over 20,000 knowledge workers across 11 countries, 85% of leaders express challenges in confidently assessing employee productivity.[25] Consequently, leaders may experience "productivity paranoia," with some organizations resorting to tracking activity rather than assessing impact and mandating office days.

This acts to undermine trust and autonomy among employees, which, as highlighted, can have serious consequences for engagement, motivation, and proactivity. In Chapter 5, I introduced you to the *stimulation* aspect of the SMART teamwork model developed by Sharon Parker. The same framework emphasizes the value of promoting "agency" or autonomy (terms used interchangeably).[26] They provide the following tips for increasing autonomy for leading virtual teams, which I believe is invaluable for reaping the benefits associated with hybrid/remote work:

i **Avoid micromanagement,** instead, provide enough decision-making discretion which will ultimately drive autonomous teams and facilitate self-management. This means setting clear goals and providing the necessary tools so that team members can complete tasks in a self-managed way.
ii **Remove boundaries,** whether that be technological or organizational that hinder progress. This means ensuring teams have access rights and permissions to read and edit virtual folders.
iii **Grant autonomy** to teams to guide when and how activities are carried out.

With high levels of autonomy, teams can make decisions and plan work activities at their discretion. Teams that have a lot of freedom to make their own decisions are often called "self-managing teams" or "autonomous teams." These teams can handle their duties independently, like deciding what tasks are most important, assigning tasks to team members, and keeping track of how well the team is doing. Self-management works well for teams that work remotely because they might not get feedback from the organization, praise from a boss, or pressure from colleagues – the things that usually motivate teams. The importance of creating an autonomy-supportive environment that has been designed to balance both individual and organizational needs is critical. One-size-fits-all solutions simply won't work.

Autonomy and Goal Setting

Another notable shift I've recently observed among large organizations is conversations around contribution versus traditional performance management approaches. In other words, encouraging manager-employee conversations that promote discussion around how an individual's contribution influences the collective achievement of the organization while driving a greater sense of purpose and collective success. At the heart of these approaches is ensuring there's a clear line of sight between an individual's goals and that of the overall organization. Yet, in creating that alignment, there is a risk that goals are cascaded without considering the importance of "making them your own." Given the insights shared in this chapter, the imperative of co-creating, not "setting" others' goals, should not be understated. When individuals have the autonomy to craft their own goals, they are more likely to feel a sense of ownership and commitment to those goals.[27] There is also merit in ensuring employees are coached to determine how to pursue their goals, to enable some alignment between their actions with their values and preferences, again, this contributes to greater goal commitment. When individuals are more committed to their goals, they are more likely to persist and persevere even when the going gets tough. This approach speaks to the difference between leading for compliance and control vs. cultivating commitment and shared purpose, outlined by Brené Brown in her illuminating book Dare to Lead.[28]

This chapter concludes with a case study from Timpson, showcasing their upside management approach, which is rooted in driving autonomous motivation.

Box 7.1 Case Study

Empowering Excellence – How Timpson's Radical Culture of Autonomy Drives Success

Established in 1865, Timpson is the UK's leading retail service provider employing just short of 5,000 colleagues. The family-owned business is a trailblazer in the retail sector, renowned for its innovative management approach. The company has consistently demonstrated an ability to innovate and grow organically and through strategic acquisitions. Over the years, Timpson has developed a reputation for exceptional customer service and a people-first culture. An upside-down management philosophy introduced 25 years ago is central to its success, which has transformed how the company operates and interacts with its stakeholders.

Upside Down Management

Upside-down management at Timpson inverts the traditional corporate hierarchy, placing decision-making power in the hands of colleagues rather than senior executives. This innovative management style was first introduced by Sir John Timpson, now Chair, in response to a belief that "the only way to provide truly great customer service is to trust our customer-facing colleagues with the freedom to serve customers the way they know best." Initially, this transformation led to some churn, as it did not suit those who preferred a more traditional, hierarchical approach to management. However, those who embraced the new model discovered a workplace that valued autonomy, trust, and personal initiative, and it has continued to go from strength to strength.

There is an entrenched belief at Timpson that great people will take ownership when given autonomy. The company focuses on recruiting individuals who are driven, passionate, and capable of thinking independently. Trust is the cornerstone of Timpson's culture, with an emphasis on mutual respect and care for colleagues. The company's mantra, "affecting someone's day in a positive way," encourages colleagues to engage in acts of kindness and community support daily. Senior leadership at Timpson views their roles as servants to their employees, focusing on removing obstacles and providing the necessary tools and resources for colleagues to thrive. This leadership model reinforces the company's strong customer service ethos and commitment to excellence.

Impact and Results

The impact of Timpson's upside-down management approach has been profound. The company has experienced consistent double-digit growth in profits in recent years, a testament to the effectiveness of its unique culture. Colleague tenure is exceptionally high compared to industry averages, with many colleagues staying for over 20 years. Notably, one colleague is celebrating 50 years of service this year, highlighting the deep sense of loyalty and satisfaction among the workforce.

The company's growth strategy includes acquiring new companies, which are expected to embrace the Timpson way and its core values. The onboarding and probationary periods are critical in ensuring that new colleagues are a good fit for the culture, and that goes both ways. Those who align with the company's values of trust, autonomy, and exceptional customer service thrive, while those who do not often self-select out during the early stages.

Area managers are "home-grown," having risen through the ranks by gaining firsthand experience in various roles within the company. This internal promotion strategy ensures that managers understand the challenges and nuances of the business, further reinforcing the company's commitment to excellent customer service. Colleagues are empowered to take initiative without seeking permission, provided their actions align with the company's values. Examples of this include a colleague growing tomato plants at a branch and giving them away to customers, and many others initiating fundraisers for local causes. These acts of kindness and community support exemplify the company's mantra and demonstrate how autonomy within a clear framework can drive positive outcomes.

Testimonial and Advice

Janet Leighton, Director of Happiness, is responsible for ensuring that colleagues have access to support and resources when needed. She emphasizes the importance of maintaining a people-focused culture through the positive emotional energy that becomes contagious within the organization. According to Janet, the key to sustaining such a culture is the commitment from senior leadership to serve their colleagues, remain dynamic and visible, and connect with colleagues at all levels.

In offering advice to other organizations looking to create a more autonomous, people-focused culture, Janet highlights several critical factors:

1 *Commitment from the Top*: Leadership must walk the talk and embody the values they wish to instill in the company.
2 *Trust:* Trust is paramount. Leaders must be open to giving up control and have faith that their colleagues will do the right thing. This trust fosters a culture of mutual respect and encourages employees to take ownership and initiative.
3 *Clear Framework*: While autonomy is essential, it must exist within a clear framework of expectations. Colleagues should know what is expected of them, including delivering excellent results, being trustworthy, providing exceptional customer service, and positively impacting others.
4 *Positive Emotional Energy*: Leveraging positive emotional energy can be a powerful tool in maintaining a vibrant and engaged workforce. Acts of kindness, community support, and recognition of achievements contribute to a positive work environment.

The Timpson journey with upside-down management demonstrates that with the right values, trust, and commitment, a company can create a thriving, autonomous, and people-focused culture. This approach not only drives business success but also fosters a deeply loyal and engaged workforce.

Key Takeaways

- In workplaces where supervisors are willing to empower and encourage their team members to be self-directed and take charge, employees' basic need for autonomy is met, and they will feel motivated to do their best.
- When supervisors are more autonomy-supportive, benefits include higher job satisfaction for employees, greater trust in senior leaders in the organization, and a higher propensity for proactive behaviors to be enacted.
- A lack of perceived autonomy can have significant depletive effects on proactive individuals, which can have major consequences at every level of the organization.

Reflective Questions

- How is autonomy being supported in your organization?
- What's your biggest takeaway from reading this chapter?
- What three things would you like to see more of in your organization?

My Implementation Intentions

Jot down in this space any actions you will take in response to the reflective questions.

References

1. Maier, S. F., & Seligman, M. E. (1976). Learned helplessness: Theory and evidence. *Journal of Experimental Psychology: General, 105*(1), 3.
2. Health & Safety Executive. (2017). *Management Standards Framework.* Health & Safety Executive.
3. PwC. (2019). Secure your future: People experience. PwC. Retrieved from www.pwc.com/gx/en/people-organisation/pdf/secure-your-future-people-exp erience-pwc.pdf
4. Deci, E. L., & Ryan, R. M. (2000). The "what" and "why" of goal pursuits: Human needs and the self-determination of behavior. *Psychological Inquiry, 11*(4), 227–268.
5. Chirkov, V., Ryan, R. M., Kim, Y., & Kaplan, U. (2003). Differentiating autonomy from individualism and independence: A self-determination theory perspective on internalization of cultural orientations and well-being. *Journal of Personality and Social Psychology, 84*(1), 97–110.
6. Deci, E. L., Olafsen, A. H., & Ryan, R. M. (2017). Self-determination theory in work organizations: The state of a science. *Annual Review of Organizational Psychology and Organizational Behavior, 4,* 19–43.
7. Wu, C. H., Griffin, M. A., & Parker, S. K. (2015). Developing agency through good work: Longitudinal effects of job autonomy and skill utilization on locus of control. *Journal of Vocational Behavior, 89,* 102–108.
8. Ohly, S., Friebel, G., Heinz, M., Kulisa, J., & Plückthun, L. (2013). *What do proactive students of economic and business studies value about their future job? In Paper presented at the 17th European Congress of Work & Organizational Psychology, Münster.*
9. Li, W. D., Fay, D., Frese, M., Harms, P. D., & Gao, X. Y. (2014). Reciprocal relationship between proactive personality and work characteristics: A latent change score approach. *Journal of Applied Psychology, 99*(5), 948.
10. Crant, J. M., Hu, J., & Jiang, K. (2016). Proactive personality: A twenty-year review. *Proactivity at Work,* 193–225.
11. Den Hartog, D. N., & Belschak, F. D. (2012). When does transformational leadership enhance employee proactive behavior? The role of autonomy and role breadth self-efficacy. *Journal of Applied Psychology, 97*(1), 194.
12. Bakker, A. B. (2010). Engagement and "job crafting": *Engaged employees create their own great place to work. In Handbook of employee engagement.* Edward Elgar Publishing.
13. Takaishi, K., Sekiguchi, K., Kono, H., & Suzuki, S. (2019). Interactive effects of work autonomy and proactive personality on innovative behavior. *Asian Business Research, 4*(1), 6.
14. Gao, A., & Jiang, J. (2019). Perceived empowering leadership, harmonious passion, and employee voice: The moderating role of job autonomy. *Frontiers in Psychology, 10,* 456028.
15. Cai, Z., Huo, Y., Lan, J., Chen, Z., & Lam, W. (2019). When do frontline hospitality employees take charge? Prosocial motivation, taking charge, and

job performance: The moderating role of job autonomy. *Cornell Hospitality Quarterly*, 60(3), 237–248.

16. Gray, J., Dhensa-Kahlon, R., Lewis, R., & McDowall, A. (2024). Unintended consequences: Why proactive behaviour at work can be harmful to individuals, teams, and organizations. A systematic review *(manuscript submitted for publication)*.

17. Pingel, R., Fay, D., & Urbach, T. (2019). A resources perspective on when and how proactive work behaviour leads to employee withdrawal. *Journal of Occupational and Organizational Psychology*, 92(2), 410–435.

18. Cangiano, F., Parker, S. K., & Yeo, G. B. (2019). Does daily proactivity affect well-being? The moderating role of punitive supervision. *Journal of Organizational Behavior*, 40(1), 59–72.

19. Mehraein, V., Visintin, F., & Pittino, D. (2023). The dark side of leadership: A systematic review of creativity and innovation. *International Journal of Management Reviews*, 25(4), 740–767.

20. Deci, E. L., Connell, J. P., & Ryan, R. M. (1989). Self-determination in a work organization. *Journal of Applied Psychology*, 74(4), 580.

21. Hardré, P. L., & Reeve, J. (2009). Training corporate managers to adopt a more autonomy-supportive motivating style toward employees: An intervention study. *International Journal of Training and Development*, 13(3), 165–184.

22. Sullivan, K., Kashiwagi, D., & Lines, B. (2011, *September). Organizational change models: A critical review of change management processes*. In RICS construction and property conference (p. 302).

23. Gagne, M., Koestner, R., & Zuckerman, M. (2000). Facilitating acceptance of organizational change: The importance of self-determination 1. *Journal of Applied Social Psychology*, 30(9), 1843–1852.

24. Wheatley, D., Broome, M. R., Dobbins, T., Hopkins, B., & Powell, O. (2024). Navigating choppy water: Flexibility ripple effects in the COVID-19 pandemic and the future of remote and hybrid working. *Work, Employment and Society*, 38(5), 1379–1402.

25. Microsoft. (2022). Work Trend Index 2022. Retrieved from www.microsoft.com/en-us/worklab/work-trend-index

26. Parker, S. K., & Knight, C. (2024). The SMART model of work design: A higher order structure to help see the wood from the trees. *Human Resource Management*, 63(2), 265–291.

27. Locke, E. A., & Latham, G. P. (Eds.). (2013). *New developments in goal setting and task performance* (Vol. 24, p. 664). Routledge.

28. Brown, B. (2018). *Dare to lead: Brave work. Tough conversations. Whole hearts*. Random House.

Chapter 8

Communication

In this chapter, I reveal the complexities around communication and the challenges of decoding and interpreting proactive individuals' behavior. I suggest creating a culture of supportive communication, whereby negative narratives around individuals' intentions and actions are avoided in favor of extending the most generous interpretations of others' behavior. This perspective challenges the over-simplified, traditional binary classification of proactive action being motivated by either self-interest or pro-social tendencies, appreciating that proactivity can simultaneously serve both organizational and individual needs. I go on to provide insights on how to set employees up for success by aligning the different forms of proactivity to the organization's overall goals. Tips and techniques are also offered to boost communication skills to create an inclusive, supportive work environment.

The Crucial Role of Communication

Organizational excellence is frequently associated with effective communication. It is the glue that holds the organization together, just as glue binds separate pieces together, communication facilitates connections between individuals, departments, and levels within an organization, ensuring that information flows smoothly, goals are understood, and teamwork is facilitated. So, when communication is poor or breaks down, the cohesiveness and effectiveness of the organization will suffer. Communication involves the exchange of information between individuals or groups through a shared system of symbols, such as language, gestures, or visual cues. Encoding and decoding are two fundamental processes that occur during communication; the former involves creating a message for communication, while decoding involves interpreting and understanding the received message. These are essential for effective communication to occur, enabling individuals to exchange information, share ideas, and connect with

DOI: 10.4324/9781003480693-11

others. Undoubtedly, proactivity is a social endeavor that relies on great communication, but often, the intentions of proactive individuals get misinterpreted, which causes problems with interpersonal relationships. So, in this chapter, we'll discover how some psychological processes interfere with decoding processes and can hinder our efforts to be proactive at work. To counter this, I provide some tools and techniques for building communication competence and strengthening communication within teams to create an environment where proactivity can flourish. In Chapter 10, we'll explore encoding effective communication utilizing influencing skills to maximize success in implementing proactive endeavors.

Challenging Conventional Wisdom: Self-Interest Reconsidered

Before getting into the intricacies of communication and its connection to proactive behavior, let's reflect on some of our human tendencies that can influence how we perceive the behaviors and actions of others. *Self-interest* theory suggests that individuals primarily act to maximize their own gain and has roots in various philosophical, economic, and sociological theories. This doctrine that humans are innately selfish dates to the Ancient Greeks and has been perpetuated over the centuries, from the works of philosopher Thomas Hobbes in the 1600s, *The Wealth of Nations* by Adam Smith in the 1700s, to Taylor's scientific management of work in the early 1900s. While self-interest may seem more overt in contexts where individualism is emphasized, such as in Western cultures, it is considered a fundamental aspect of human nature that can manifest in various contexts. Richard Dawkins' pioneering research and influential book *The Selfish Gene*,[1] published in the late 1970s, introduced the idea that genes are "selfish," meaning they act in ways that help them survive and replicate, sometimes at a cost to the individual. While Dawkins was talking about biology, this idea has influenced the way some people think in the realm of business, fuelling a perception that everyone is out for themselves and assuming the worst of others. Such beliefs have informed surveillance, monitoring, and tracking practices at work, such as time and attendance systems, access control systems, performance metrics, and computer monitoring software. Interestingly, Dawkins himself later clarified that the term "selfish" had been used metaphorically, highlighting that his findings represent simplifications and idealizations of real-world behavior. And that, in reality, human motivation and decision-making are influenced by a complex interplay of factors beyond self-interest alone. In his book *Humankind*, Rutger Bregman suggests that the "carrot (reward) and stick (punishment)" approach to motivating workers stems from this perception of human nature as inherently selfish. While he acknowledges that business practices have indeed moved on in recent decades, he suggests this view of humanity is as pervasive as ever and plays into how we make sense of other's behavior.[2] Keep this in mind, as we explore how we might interpret the actions and behaviors of proactive individuals at work.

Understanding and Reacting to Social Cues

The social cognition approach to communication explores how individuals perceive and interpret social cues in different situations. It emphasizes how cognitive processes, such as attributions and judgments, influence communication behavior, including how individuals regulate their own and others' actions during interactions.

When it comes to interpreting the proactive behaviors of others, *attribution theory* provides a useful lens. *Attribution theory* occupies a central position within social psychology, being the study of how people make sense of their behavior and that of others.[3] Central to the theory is that humans perceive behavior as being caused by something, someone, or for some reason. In this regard, an intention to act is viewed as a conscious choice that flows from a reasoning process. The problem lies in the fact that reasoning is subjective, so in our attempts to make sense of the behavior of others, we are trying to reconstruct the considerations that person went through, but with missing or inadequate information, which means it is prone to error. I find this fascinating and mind-blowing in equal measure. *Misattribution of intention* at work refers to the process of incorrectly interpreting the motives or intentions of a colleague's actions or behaviors. This can lead to misunderstandings, miscommunication, and interpersonal conflict in the workplace. Common forms of misattribution that relate to interpreting proactivity in others are:

- **Assuming Negative Intent:** This is when one assumes negative intentions behind a colleague's proactive actions, even when they may be neutral or positive. For instance, if a co-worker proactively offers feedback on a project, it might be misattributed as an attempt to undermine one's work rather than genuinely help improve it. Or, if a co-worker speaks up on a safety issue, it might be misattributed as being destructive and harmful to the organization rather than helping to safeguard it.

- **Attributing Personal Motives:** Another form of misattribution involves attributing personal motives or agendas to a colleague's behavior. For example, suppose a proactive co-worker receives praise from a supervisor for taking initiative. In that case, others might misattribute their success to "playing politics" or seeking personal gain, rather than recognizing their hard work and competence.

In addition to misattribution, the concept of *hostile attribution bias* is often studied in the context of social interactions, particularly in situations where conflict may arise. *Hostile attribution bias* is a cognitive tendency where individuals interpret social cues as intentionally hostile.[4] In other words, they perceive others' actions or intentions as threatening, even when there may not be any hostile intent present. For example, in a scenario where someone is proactively taking charge at work, hostile attribution bias could lead to misunderstandings or conflict if colleagues interpret the individual's assertive behavior as aggressive or domineering, leading them to react defensively or confrontationally. Several factors may contribute to the development of hostile attribution bias, including past experiences of conflict or victimization, socialization processes, and individual differences in temperament and personality traits. We'll return to hostile attribution in Chapter 15 as it is something that can be more pronounced among neurodivergent individuals. In the meantime, it's clear that when it comes to interpreting the proactive behavior of others, both misattribution and a hostile attribution bias can have significant implications for interpersonal relationships at work, contributing to misunderstandings, escalation of conflicts, and putting a strain on relationships. Managers and leaders must be attuned to the potential for misattribution to occur and its associated risks to working relationships and team dynamics. From my experience, managers often find it difficult to lean into conflict resolution and trust repair in their teams because it is "difficult," particularly if they've had no training. My advice is simple: managers must recognize that conflict is an inherent part of organizational life, and rather than avoid it, they should proactively manage and resolve it. Left unchecked, unresolved conflict will only escalate, adversely impacting a team's ability to function well.

Another social cognitive consideration in communication and interpretation processes relates to *impression management*, which I introduced in Chapter 5 concerning psychological safety. Impression management refers to the strategies individuals use to shape others' perceptions of themselves in communication interactions. It involves self-presentation tactics aimed at conveying desired impressions and influencing others' evaluations. Impression management can be conscious or unconscious and may involve verbal, nonverbal, or online communication behaviors. Given the risks associated with misattribution or hostile attribution bias, proactive individuals may be reluctant to take charge for fear of negative judgment from others. This aligns with findings from my research, in which several participants suggested they'd had experiences at work where they felt compelled to hold back on proactive efforts for fear of "rocking the boat" and being judged negatively by bosses or co-workers. To stimulate proactivity in those who may be more hesitant, leaders must clarify which types of proactive behaviors are valued and set expectations for how employees should best demonstrate them.

Proactive Motivation: Self-interest or Pro-social

Returning to the notion of self-interest and how we perceive and judge proactivity in others, we also have a human tendency to evaluate and categorize such behavior as either for the good of "oneself" or "others," in other words, self-interested versus pro-social. A review of 95 published articles found that leaders and co-workers are more likely to judge acts of proactivity by others in a positive light if they perceive their motives to be pro-social and in the interests of others.[5] This has genuine consequences for proactive individuals. In two separate studies, one with 103 managers and their direct supervisors and the other with 55 firefighters and their supervisors, the role of proactive voice, issue-selling (that is, explicitly raising issues to senior management), taking charge, and anticipatory helping was explored in relation to performance evaluations. Findings from both studies suggested that when supervisors perceive acts of proactive behavior to be self-interested and not in the interests of the group, being proactive will not translate into higher performance ratings.[6] In another study exploring the consequences of different forms of speaking up, researchers concluded that when employees raise issues in a way that is perceived as being negative or defensive, it is seen as an indication they don't care about the organization and, therefore, not pro-social, which makes others think poorly of them.[7] So, when proactive individuals speak up on issues that are perceived by others to be challenging, confrontational, and potentially damaging to the organization, it carries some risk. These studies underscore a tendency for managers to reward proactive employees with higher performance evaluations only when they perceive the employee is motivated by pro-social intentions and a concern for the organization. While on the surface, this may seem intuitive and inconsequential, I'd argue it oversimplifies human behavior at work by assuming managers are skilled in accurately predicting the intentions of their team members, which, as I highlighted earlier, is highly questionable.

My research added some nuance to the self-interest vs. pro-social dichotomy. While study participants were all considered to be in the mid to late stages of their careers and therefore influenced by maturity and experience, most participants described their proactive endeavors as simultaneously being personally driven (self-interest) while also being in the interests of their organization (pro-social). For example, an executive who was a keen environmentalist proactively took charge of driving the organization's strategy toward a pathway to net zero carbon. This was intrinsically motivating to them while serving the sustainability goals for the organization and the wider world. In another example, an HR business partner who had a keen interest in legal and regulatory issues proactively took charge to build organizational readiness for a significant change in UK tax laws that would impact a sizeable proportion of their workforce. So, when it comes to our "reason to be" proactive, perhaps it's not a case of either self-interested or pro-social, it's more nuanced. This reinforces the value of not assuming our proactive co-workers are simply out for themselves, inviting us to avoid creating negative narratives around the intentions of others.

Communicating Valued Proactive Behaviors

As I already alluded to, there is significant value in leaders being more explicit in communicating the forms of proactivity that are valued in the organization. My research highlighted that all too often, job descriptions and role profiles highlight proactivity as a desirable behavior, yet when proactive employees attempt to speak up, propose new ideas, and take charge, they are stifled by others, which leads to frustration, disengagement, and withdrawal. Table 8.1 considers different organizational strategies and provides some examples of the forms of proactive behavior that may be appropriate to the organizational context.

Once you have identified the valued forms of proactive behaviors for your organization and/or team, they can be communicated to employees. One word of caution, we should not forget that proactivity is a self-directed, autonomous behavior; there is a fine line between clearly

Table 8.1 Aligning Organizational Strategy to Valued Proactive Behaviors

Organizational Strategy	Valued Forms of Proactivity
Innovation & change	Problem solving Innovative behavior Taking charge
Operational efficiency	Personal initiative Taking charge
Risk management	Safety proactivity Problem prevention Speaking up
Talent management	Career-initiative Job crafting Feedback-seeking
Corporate social responsibility	Speaking up Strategic scanning Issue-selling

communicating which forms of proactivity the organization values and conveying an expectation for these to be enacted by everyone. When employees feel pressured or coerced into being proactive, it can lead to negative consequences, including work-related stress[8] and work-family conflict.[9] The aim, therefore, is to become more granular in highlighting which forms of proactive behavior will drive organizational goals, rather than assuming all proactive endeavors are either a help or hindrance.

Sensitivity in Communication

One of the ways to address some of the challenges associated with mis-attributing proactive behavior is to build communication competence within teams. Communication competence is at the heart of problem-solving, effective decision-making, conflict resolution, organizational change, creativity, and innovation. Effective communication continues to be a primary concern for contemporary organizations that want individuals to exhibit strong interpersonal skills. Globalization and technological advancements have heavily influenced how we communicate and our ability to communicate competently, introducing further layers of complexity when considering intercultural communication.

Drawing from these insights and my experience in developing and coaching leaders, prioritizing the enhancement of sensitivity skills to bolster communication competence within teams and organizations is essential. Sensitivity in communication involves awareness and responsiveness to the needs, feelings, and perspectives of others. It encompasses empathy, emotional intelligence, and cultural competence. Sensitivity enables individuals to recognize and respect diverse viewpoints, communicate with tact and diplomacy, and adapt their communication style to accommodate different audiences and situations. It nurtures positive interpersonal relationships, reduces misunderstandings and/or misattribution, and promotes inclusivity and mutual respect. In her illuminating book *Dare to Lead*, psychologist Brené Brown breaks down the concept of trust, to show how we can trust others and be trusted by others. A key component of her model is the importance of *Generosity*, encouraging the most generous interpretation of the intentions, words, and actions of others.[10] This emphasis on assuming the best in others could be the antidote to misattribution, which as highlighted hinders our endeavours to be proactive at work.

A synthesis of studies exploring communication competence underscores the importance of:

i **Listening:** actively paying attention to the speaker, seeking to understand, and providing appropriate responses.

ii **Adaptive Style:** the ability to adjust one's communication style, tone, and approach based on the needs of the audience and/or situation.

iii **Expressing Emotion:** acknowledging and validating your own feelings, articulating them clearly and appropriately, actively attuned to the emotions in others, and responding sensitively.

iv **Empathy:** the ability to understand and share the feelings, perspectives, and experiences of others during interactions.

v **Knowledge-sharing:** seeking information and answering questions, in other words, two-way dialog.

Practical Resources

If we assume that more open, honest, and trusting conversations (e.g. sensitive communication) lead to better outcomes associated with being proactive at work, the key is to develop the skills for such quality conversations to happen. So, in this section, I'm sharing a collection of activities and resources that I have used in workshops and in my coaching practice to help clients develop some of the core communication competencies outlined in this chapter (Boxes 8.1–8.5).

Box 8.1   The Art of Listening

Solo or Small Group Exercise

In this reflective activity or group exercise, you will consider what active listening looks and feels like and uncover what gets in the way of having more empathetic conversations. If doing this activity alone, it may be helpful to write down or capture your reflections on a voice note, so you can return to them at any point.

Step 1: Think about a conversation you've had in recent days or weeks where you were truly listened to, how did that make you feel?

Step 2: What did the person listening do to make you feel listened to?

Step 3: What gets in the way of having these kinds of active listening conversations more often?

Step 4: Following your reflection or group discussion, capture the key insights you will take away and consider what might you do differently going forward?

Box 8.2   Active Empathic Listening

Solo Activity – Micro-Actions

Active empathic listening is the practice of being attentive and responsive to others' input during a conversation. This form of deep listening is almost impossible when we are operating in "busy" mode, we can only truly listen when we switch off our internal and external distractions. The following tips highlight how we might be able to improve our active empathic listening skills:

- **Non-verbal Involvement** – show attention and engagement by nodding and using facial expressions (e.g., smiling, which is associated with likeability, trust, warmth, and kindness).
- **Attention on the Speaker, Not Your Own Thoughts** – it's important to see the world as the person talking sees it, that means being present in the moment, observing your thoughts but resisting the temptation of engaging in them.
- **Avoid Judgment** – A skillful active listener can simply receive the message without the need to judge or respond with their own bias (I'm not going to pretend this is easy – it takes a lot of practice).
- **The Power of the Pause** –resist the urge to fill the gaps, even if it does feel a little uncomfortable initially. One way to do this is to highlight to the person you are listening to that you will deliberately embrace silence to allow you both to process the conversation in the moment.
- **Repeat Back** – mirroring or repeating back what you believe the other person said can create a greater sense of closeness and ensure you are aligned on what is being said and what is being heard.
- **Delve Deeper** – resist the impulse to tell your story on the topic (I find this tricky, particularly if the topic is something I am passionate about – it takes some discipline to keep your attention focused on the person you are listening to). Instead, ask follow-up questions to get more insight and show attentiveness using phrases such as "I can imagine you..."

Box 8.3   Connecting with Emotions

Solo or Small Group Activity

In this exercise, you will reflect on or share with the group a recent experience at work that triggered an emotional response for you. You will then take some time to understand and label these emotions. If doing this as a group exercise, it would be important to agree on some ground rules and/or allow participants to opt out, given the potential for sensitive information or feelings to be shared. High levels of psychological safety are a pre-requisite for this activity.

Step 1: Reflect on a moment in the last week where you are aware that you experienced an emotion that left you feeling a level of comfort or discomfort, jot down the experience.

Step 2: Based on this experience, establish what top-level emotion was being evoked (e.g., love, joy, surprise, anger, sadness, fear, disgust). Would you describe the energy that came with this emotion as positive or negative? Would you describe your mood as being pleasant or unpleasant?

Step 3: Use the following questions to understand your emotional response:

- How were you feeling leading up to this experience?
- What triggered this experience?
- What might be the underlying reason for feeling like this?
- How might you respond to this emotion in a way that serves yourself and others in the best way?

Step 4: What key insights have you taken from this exercise?

Box 8.4   Minimizing Attribution Bias

Solo Activity – Micro-Actions

De-biasing strategies are designed to force us out of unconscious pattern recognition and to move us into a more objective mode of thinking. Strategies to overcome attribution biases include

- The Power of Hindsight: reflect on past attributions you have made about someone at work and the outcomes, e.g., you assumed a co-worker who was missing deadlines and seemed less engaged in meetings was lazy or disorganized. Yet, in reality, the employee was experiencing burnout from personal stressors outside of work. Use the benefit of hindsight to consider whether you are falling into the misattribution trap. It's particularly important to consider the individuals who you value highly or who you consider underperformers, as we're most likely to fall into the *halo and horn effect* bias in these instances (that is, where one positive/negative trait leads us to view someone entirely favorably/unfavorably).[11]

- **Encourage Explicit Conversations:** rather than second-guessing the intentions of others, which we've already established is prone to error, just ask! You could demonstrate curiosity by simply asking, "Can you tell me what your motivation is...?"
- **Challenging Your Own Viewpoints:** try to identify weaknesses in your own thinking and assumptions. We tend to look for evidence to support our existing views (it's called *confirmation bias*), whereas we should be looking for counter-evidence to ensure we are seeing the full picture.
- **Critically Evaluate:** assess all the information available to you and ask yourself "What information am I missing?" or "Whose perspective haven't I heard?"

Box 8.5 Perspective Taking and Knowledge Sharing

Job Shadowing

This activity provides employees with a practical opportunity to gain first-hand insight into the perspectives and responsibilities of their colleagues to boost empathy, understanding, collaboration, and knowledge-sharing in the workplace. This is an effective way to break down silos in organizations and increase *role breadth confidence* which is essential for stimulating proactivity (discussed in Chapter 5).

- **Partner Up:** Pair employees, whether that be from within the team or different departments or roles within the organization.

- **Schedule a Shadowing Half-day or Day:** Set aside a day for each pair to shadow each other in their respective roles. Each participant spends time observing and participating in the daily tasks and responsibilities of their partner.
- **Reflective Discussion:** At the end of the shadowing day, participants meet to discuss their experiences. They share insights gained from experiencing a different role first-hand, including challenges, priorities, and perspectives.
- **Key Learnings:** Encourage participants to identify key takeaways from the experience, such as areas of overlap, differences in priorities, and opportunities for collaboration.
- **Action Planning:** Based on their reflections, participants develop action plans for how they can better support and collaborate with colleagues from different roles or departments in the future.

Key Takeaways

- Human behavior is complex and multifaceted. We must be careful in making assumptions about the proactive intentions of others, which is both common and prone to misattribution.
- In workplaces, exchanging suspicion and negative judgment of an individual's intention to be proactive for a more positive view, can lead to an upward spiral of recognition and trust that can be contagious and enable proactive behaviors to flourish.
- Being more explicit in communicating the forms of proactive behavior that are valued and aligned with organizational goals provides employees with parameters in which to enact their proactive endeavors.
- Nurturing an environment of supportive communication will fuel greater levels of engagement, commitment, and proactivity.

Reflective Questions

- What are some of the communication pitfalls in your organization?
- What's your biggest takeaway from reading this chapter?
- Which of the practical resources might you be able to utilize?

My Implementation Intentions

Jot down in this space any actions you will take in response to the reflective questions.

References

1. Dawkins, R. (1976). *The selfish gene*. Oxford University Press.
2. Bregman, R. (2020). *Humankind: A hopeful history*. Bloomsbury Publishing.
3. Malle, B. F. (2022). Attribution theories: How people make sense of behavior. In *Theories in social psychology (2nd ed.*, pp. 93–120).
4. Smeijers, D., Bulten, E. B., & Brazil, I. A. (2019). The computations of hostile biases (CHB) model: Grounding hostility biases in a unified cognitive framework. *Clinical Psychology Review, 73*, 101775.
5. Parker, S. K., Wang, Y., & Liao, J. (2019). When is proactivity wise? A review of factors that influence the individual outcomes of proactive behavior. *Annual Review of Organizational Psychology and Organizational Behavior, 6*, 221–248.
6. Grant, A. M., Parker, S., & Collins, C. (2009). Getting credit for proactive behavior: Supervisor reactions depend on what you value and how you feel. *Personnel Psychology, 62*(1), 31–55.
7. Maynes, T. D., & Podsakoff, P. M. (2014). Speaking more broadly: An examination of the nature, antecedents, and consequences of an expanded set of employee voice behaviors. *Journal of Applied Psychology, 99*(1), 87.
8. Pingel, R., Fay, D., & Urbach, T. (2019). A resources perspective on when and how proactive work behaviour leads to employee withdrawal. *Journal of Occupational and Organizational Psychology, 92*(2), 410–435.
9. Chen, P., Xu, Y., Sparrow, P., & Cooper, C. (2023). Compulsory citizenship behaviour and work-family conflict: a moderated mediation model. *Current Psychology, 42*(8), 6641–6652.
10. Brown, B. (2018). *Dare to lead: Brave work*. Tough conversations. Whole hearts. Random House.
11. Kahneman, D. (2011). *Thinking, fast and slow*. Farrar, Straus and Giroux.

Chapter 9

Time

The Dreaded "T" Word

When I ask workshop participants what gets in the way of being pro-active at work, I am repeatedly met with the same response: "Time." We have a strange relationship with this finite resource, we claim never to have enough of it, yet if we're honest we often don't always make the best use of it. It also provides us with the perfect excuse for not doing certain things. Our obsession with time, or a lack of it seems ubiquitous. Understandably, for many employees, work has intensified so the demands feel more demanding than ever. This time pressure has no doubt been fuelled by technological advances giving rise to a 24/7 "always on" culture[1] and economic factors driving a need for workers to deliver more but with fewer resources. However, a "busy" work culture that glorifies constant activity at the expense of thoughtful reflection, creativity, and balanced relationships leads to missed opportunities for genuine growth and innovation. So, in this chapter, I'll highlight the importance of giving time and space for proactivity at work and offer some practical tips to prioritize future-focused activities. In reinforcing the importance of setting aside time for proactive efforts, I explore the essential steps in setting and achieving proactive goals, providing insights into the actions and activities deserving of dedicated time allocation. I then spotlight proactive innovative behavior and introduce the *CLEAR IDEAS* model, which helps with developing new ideas and encourages time spent on both creating and implementing these ideas to boost innovation at work.

Taking Back Control of Time

In his game-changing book *Busy – How to Thrive in a World of Too Much*,[2] Organizational Psychologist Tony Crabbe suggests that when we decide to stay busy, we miss out on opportunities and end up choosing more chaos instead of less. To bring his ideas to life, he introduces the

DOI: 10.4324/9781003480693-12

Siamese fighting fish, a species of fish that will eat itself to death – not because there is too much food, but because this fish keeps on choosing to eat. Crabbe suggests that in our world of too much, we need to be bolder in making choices and taking back control of time. He emphasizes the opportunity cost of being busy; in choosing "busy-ness" we neglect creative thinking time, which has already been highlighted as critical to proactivity. Taking back control of time requires focusing on making an impact and making more deliberate decisions on how we manage our time and attention. In my research examining participants' positive and negative experiences of being proactive at work, there was a recurring theme that spoke to the importance of taking one's time to do the "groundwork" to ensure the success of the proactive endeavor. However, doing so can be challenging for various reasons, I call these *Time Traps*, which I'll outline along with some mitigating strategies.

Common Time Traps

Firefighting

Firefighting in organizations refers to a reactive approach where immediate, short-term urgencies take precedence over long-term, strategic planning, and proactive actions. This mode of operation prioritizes addressing crises and urgent tasks, often at the expense of future-focused initiatives and sustainable growth. I've observed a rise in this approach in recent years, which is concerning as it poses risks to employees, such as stress and low morale. Additionally, it jeopardizes the quality of work, as our best thinking seldom happens when we feel rushed and under pressure. To redress the balance from reactivity toward proactivity, a cultural shift may be required. This might involve reinforcing organizational values that speak to the importance of future-focused work, whether that be by emphasizing a desire to drive innovation, sustainability, and/or strategic competitive advantage. In turn, there needs to be a leadership commitment to establishing clear priorities and modeling behavior that focuses on long-term goals. This also requires having clearly defined processes and approaches for effective time management. This chapter is not intended as time-management self-help, a simple search online will provide an abundance of tools and techniques for helping with prioritization. That said, I find the Urgent-Important matrix a helpful and intuitive way to keep focused on important work. As demonstrated in Figure 9.1, it helps with determining priorities by arranging tasks by urgency and importance in a 2 × 2 matrix. The aim is to spend more time working on important activities in the top half of the grid by being more disciplined on the less important tasks that sit in the bottom half, which often eat up our time. However,

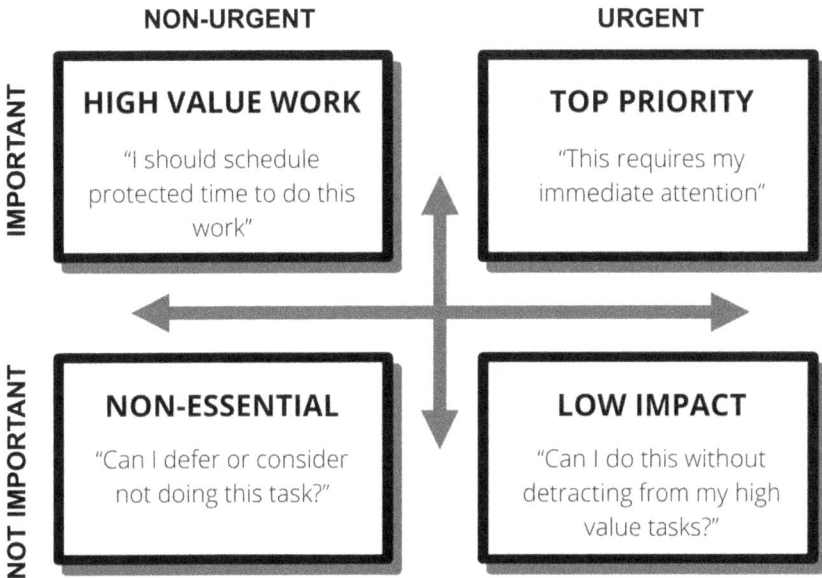

Figure 9.1 Urgent-Important Matrix.
Source: Created by the author.

adhering to these principles requires us to tame our tendencies to favor instant reward, which leads me to cognitive biases.

Cognitive Biases

Temporal discounting is a cognitive bias that describes the tendency to devalue rewards or outcomes that are set to occur in the future compared to those available immediately. You may be familiar with the famous marshmallow test,[3] a psychological experiment linked to temporal discounting that tests self-control and delayed gratification in children by seeing if they choose to eat the marshmallow immediately or wait for a second one (though the test's validity is widely debated!) Temporal discounting at work refers to the tendency of employees to favor immediate tasks that give us instant gratification over those that offer greater benefits in the future. This can lead to procrastination on long-term, high-value projects by prioritizing short-term tasks that may not be as important. This behavior often results in reduced contribution, impact, and ultimately missed opportunities. Building self-awareness of this tendency can be helpful for managers and leaders in coaching their team members to recognize the pitfalls of this unconscious bias. In goal-setting conversations, it can be helpful to encourage long-term proactive projects to be broken into bite-sized chunks to create short-term tasks. Encouraging individuals to allocate time to focus on these smaller important, but not necessarily urgent tasks is also key, emphasizing the importance of avoiding the temptation to de-prioritize these tasks in favor of short-term wins. Advocating that individuals calendarize "focus time" or "protected time" in their diaries to tackle high-value work tasks is also helpful for maintaining discipline in attending to proactive work.

Distractions

While technology has been an enabler of progress at work, it has also emerged as a significant source of distraction. Take social media apps for example, these have been carefully designed to capture and command our attention, which in turn distract us from spending uninterrupted time on important tasks. I recently heard a joke about how the only firms that describe their customers as users are tech firms and drug dealers! Jokes aside, the levels of distraction employees are experiencing are a cause for concern. With remote work becoming more common and meetings transitioning to virtual platforms, staying focused has become increasingly challenging, with constant distractions from emails and instant messages. This in turn forces us to do more *mental switching*, also known as task switching, whereby we shift our attention and focus from one task to another. One study suggests that people compensate for interruptions by working faster, but this comes at a price: employees end up experiencing more stress, higher frustration, time pressure, and exerting more effort, all of which are exhausting and depletive.[4] Strategies for turning off distractions will vary by individual, what works for one person may not work for another. I find the *Pomodoro Technique* helpful; it's a time management technique (named after the tomato-shaped kitchen timer) that improves focus by encouraging uninterrupted periods of work. This technique is particularly interesting because it encourages us to break work down into shorter intervals and separate them by short breaks, which reinforces the importance of pausing, reflecting, and recuperating. For example, by working in bursts of 25 minutes and then having a full 5-minute break before starting on the next 25 minutes. By gaining more control over tasks and enabling more focused time, we also have a higher propensity to experience the *flow state*, whereby we feel fully immersed in an activity that induces feelings of engagement and enjoyment.[5]

People-pleasing

I am not a huge fan of this phrase because I'd argue the concept is more complex in reality, but it is a term many of us are familiar with and understand. *People-pleasing* at work often results in prioritizing tasks that are neither urgent nor important, simply to satisfy others. This behavior can lead to a focus on low-impact reactive activities, diverting time and energy away from more critical, future-focused projects. Like temporal discounting, it can hamper proactivity, as important goals and deadlines may be neglected in favor of less important tasks. As someone who has people-pleasing tendencies, I'm aware of the detrimental effects this can have in terms of overcommitting and feeling time-pressured. While being considerate and helpful are positive traits and critical for successful team-related proactive endeavors, there is value in creating more boundaries at work to minimize the risks of taking on too much and protecting time to be change-focused and future-orientated. Some useful approaches to managing boundaries include setting and communicating clear parameters, whether that be around your availability, deadlines, or preferred ways of working. For me personally, saying, "Can I get back to you?" to enable me to consider a request before committing to it has been revolutionary in preventing impulsive responses that may lead to over-committing myself. Also, saying, "I can help you, but not yet" can be a good strategy for expressing a willingness to assist while also setting boundaries and managing expectations. These microactions can be particularly useful in taking back control of time to focus on the tasks and activities that will make a difference. In organizations, leaders and managers can be great role models of this boundary-setting behavior. They can also coach their team members to be more explicit in setting, communicating, and managing boundaries. Boundaries should not be perceived as barriers or someone being difficult; rather, it's about creating a healthy balance that enhances proactivity, productivity, and well-being. Let's now move on to consider what activities merit time allocation when generating and striving toward proactive goals.

Allocating Time to Proactive Work

In Chapter 2, I introduced you to the four stages of the proactivity process.[6] In this section, I'll outline activities and tasks to optimize the potential for positive outcomes linked to proactive behaviors. I'll focus on allocating time to tasks related to innovative behavior, taking charge, and proactive safety measures. These are summarized in Table 9.1.

i Envisioning
  As a reminder, the proactivity process starts with perceiving a problem or opportunity and imagining a solution, this is called the *envisioning* phase. At this stage, time is best allocated to analyzing the status quo and determining the need for change. Mapping out the "what" (issue

Table 9.1 Allocating Time to Proactive Phases

	Envisioning	Planning	Acting	Reflecting
Important Activities to Give Time To	'What & Why' => Compelling Vision	Stakeholder Engagement	Project Management Processes	Power of Hindsight Thinking
	Situational & Social Factors Assessment	Objections, Risks & Mitigators	Communication Plan	

and opportunity) and the "why" (rationale and benefit) is a helpful starting point. In addition, it is worth giving time to reflect on situational factors, by asking, "Is what I am proposing appropriate to the situation and current context?" For instance, if the organization or team has recently experienced a significant structural change and is still in the recovery phase, and your proposal has the potential to cause additional disruption, it may be prudent to delay until stability is restored. There is also an important *Can-do* and *Reason-to* question to reflect on at this point, which is "Am I the right person to be proactive in this instance, and am I doing it for the right reasons?" Finally, consideration should be given to the social context and those who are likely to be affected by asking, "What is the impact on others?" Assuming the answers to these questions lead you to conclude that the proactive endeavor is worth pursuing, then spending some time developing and articulating a vision is also an essential part of the early "groundwork." There is merit in not rushing this part of the process, and there is value and power in "percolation time." Allowing ideas time to percolate can lead to more refined and innovative solutions. The very act of going back to an idea and revisiting it after a day or so can be helpful. From a leader and manager perspective, there is scope to coach team members to proactively carve out time to attend to these reflective questions and tasks associated with envisioning proactive activities. By doing so, you will be setting your proactive employees up for success.

ii Planning

The next phase of the proactivity process is *planning*, that is, deciding on appropriate actions. Again, emphasis should be given to allocating time to consider the situational and social factors that need to be addressed. Stakeholder mapping and engagement are critical activities at this phase. Stakeholders can be thought of as those who are affected by and/or can impact the achievement of one's proactive objectives. To maximize the success of proactive change-orientated endeavors, participation is key. This involves gathering insights to enhance readiness and acceptance of the proposed change. One way to do this is by identifying common aspirations and shared visions to promote higher levels of engagement, this again highlights the importance of employee participation, while also touching on the idea of vision setting which is predominant in several change models.[7] Finally, carving out time to map out potential objections, risks, and mitigators is vital to stakeholder buy-in, and safeguards against potential setbacks. It's worth noting that for proactive individuals who are naturally optimistic,[8] it can be more challenging to engage in thorough risk assessment and planning.[9] Optimistic people tend to focus on positive outcomes and possibilities, which may lead them to overlook potential risks or downplay their significance. This can result in incomplete planning and inadequate preparation for contingencies. Again, coaching to raise self-awareness and guide a more deliberate effort to balance optimism with realistic assessment, can enhance one's ability to anticipate and address risks effectively.

iii Acting

The third phase of the proactivity process is *acting*, so engaging in the proactive goal, implementing the plan to bring about that different future, and making the change happen. At this stage, identifying and engaging a core team to bring about the change is advisable, which speaks to the importance of interdependency between individuals and teams which I have reinforced throughout this book. A project team and ongoing project management are critical in creating shared responsibility for the outcome and maximizing the chances for success. It's not within the scope of this book to outline the various project management tools available, but if I were to offer any advice it would be to build some confidence using the Critical Path Method (CPM). This is a simple, yet powerful technique used to determine the longest sequence of dependent tasks and activities required to complete a project. It identifies the critical path, which is the series of tasks that must be completed on time for the project to finish as scheduled. By analyzing the critical path, project managers can identify tasks that cannot be delayed without delaying the entire project, allowing them to allocate resources and manage the project timeline effectively.[10] Once the critical path is determined, providing that visually to stakeholders in the form of a calendarized time plan is useful in gaining commitment to deadlines and allocating the appropriate time to tasks.

It would be remiss of me not to reinforce the importance of communication as a central facet of the *acting phase*, which requires time and attention. Poor communication can lead to confusion, conflict, derailment, and delays. Therefore, it is important to engage key stakeholders with the "right" communication at the "right" frequency, using the "right" medium. I am deliberately not spelling out what I mean by "right" because it will be dependent on the organization, its established norms, and what has been agreed upon. From my experience, assigning time to formal gate meetings is beneficial in keeping communication flowing. Gate meetings, also known as stage-gate meetings or phase-gate reviews, are formal checkpoints or decision points in a project's lifecycle where key stakeholders assess the project's progress and determine whether to proceed to the next phase or stage. These meetings typically occur at the end of each project phase or stage and involve evaluating deliverables, milestones, risks, and overall project performance against predefined criteria or benchmarks. Gate meetings help ensure alignment with project objectives, manage risks, allocate resources effectively, and make informed decisions about the project's future direction. Instituting robust processes within an organization helps to stimulate a culture where proactivity flourishes. It provides a structured framework for proactive individuals to anticipate challenges, identify opportunities, and take initiative toward achieving goals that are aligned with those of the organization.

iv Reflecting

Finally, the *reflecting* stage aims to evaluate outcomes to inform future proactive endeavors. In my conversations with various organizations, this seems to be the phase that often gets forgotten or side-lined in favor of moving on to the next big thing. I am a strong advocate of taking time to engage in reflective practice to aid continuous improvement and ultimately lead to more successful outcomes of proactivity at work. A useful technique to guide self-reflection and/or group discussions is the *keep doing, stop doing, do differently* approach. First, consider and capture what went well and is important to continue to do in future endeavors. Second, consider and capture what did not work well and what you'd want to avoid doing in the future. Third, with the power of hindsight, consider what you would do differently if given this opportunity again. If conducted as a group exercise, to generate meaningful insights, there needs to be high levels of psychological safety (as detailed in Chapter 4). Otherwise, there is a risk the reflections will be marred by impression management and lack substance. This final stage does not need to be a burden on time – by using a simple template, inviting team members to come prepared, and keeping it focused on future improvements rather than onerous post-mortems of what went wrong. When organizations value a mindset of continuous improvement, and leaders and managers emphasize the importance of giving time to learn lessons to inform future projects, a learning culture ensues. A learning culture has been proven to be good for business, with higher levels of job satisfaction, commitment, and employee retention.[11]

Proactive Innovative Behavior – CLEAR IDEAS

To conclude this Chapter, I'd like to introduce an evidence-based approach to idea generation and implementation developed by Kamal Birdi, an Occupational Psychologist and Professor at Sheffield University. I was fortunate to attend a CLEAR IDEAS workshop delivered by Kamal and instantly connected the dots between this model and some of the elements of my PROACTIVE work design framework, specifically when considering proactive innovative behavior. Several of my research participants shared stories of their proactive efforts at work having negative consequences due to rushing and missing key steps necessary for success. So, I chose to include the CLEAR IDEAS model in this chapter because I think seeing the different steps involved further reminds us of the importance of making time to take a more intentional approach to our proactive goals at work. Furthermore, if organizations are looking for greater levels of proactive innovative behavior, developing the knowledge and skills needed to both generate ideas and effectively implement them as innovations is critical. Fortunately, these skills can be learned and developed; the CLEAR IDEAS creativity training model was created for this very purpose. Figure 9.2 provides a visual representation of the model. The first five steps of the model are concentrated on IDEAS generation:

i   *Illuminate*
    First off, we need to illuminate an area where innovation is required; this may be a product, process, or strategic goal. This step involves posing a "How do we…" question to a current problem. For example, one organization that tried this approach was looking for ways to improve the efficiency of fitting smoke alarms, which was a key function of their business. Other organizations have used it to create new business opportunities, to reduce costs, or to create social impact.

ii *Diagnose*
    Diagnosis involves identifying the different causes of the problem. When working in groups this stage is best carried out by asking individuals to capture their initial thoughts individually, before sharing them with the wider group. Each person shares one reason with the group in a round-robin style, once all the reasons have been shared, they can be clustered into themes and then ranked to determine what creative ideas can be generated to tackle the priority causes.

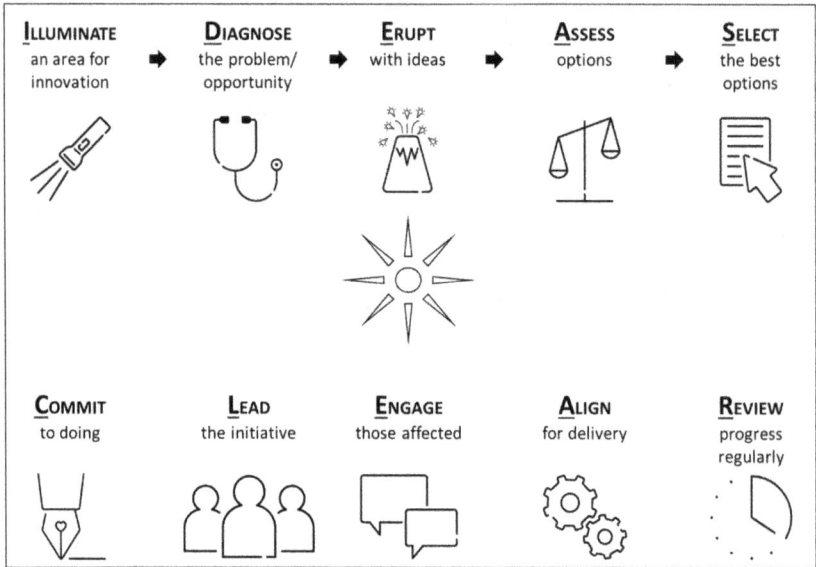

Figure 9.2 The CLEAR IDEAS Model of Innovation Development.
Source: Created by Professor Kamal Birdi.

iii   *Erupt*

As the name suggests, this step involves coming up with as many ideas as possible for dealing with the priority cause. Again, initially, this is done individually, and everyone is encouraged to be as wild and original as they want to be – no idea is considered a bad idea. Creative thinking triggers can be used to stimulate ideas, for example, by asking individuals to take their real-world problem to a fantasy land and consider how it might be resolved in this context or thinking about how your favorite historical figure might tackle the problem. This sounds a bit off the wall, but believe me, it works!

iv   *Assess*

Ideas are then shared, developed, and then assessed against criteria for selection. It is useful to determine the assessment criteria in advance to maintain objectivity and assign ratings of 1–5 to each criterion to calibrate scores from each assessor. Objective criteria may include projected sales volumes, projected savings, ease versus complexity, environmental impact, and so on.

v   *Select*

Select is the step for taking the best options forward for implementation. Based on the outputs of the previous step, ideas can be ranked and voted upon, with the idea receiving the most votes going forward.

Good ideas don't work out in practice for many reasons, whether that be a lack of skills to make it work, a lack of motivation, poor project leadership, little input from others, unclear roles and responsibilities, a lack of monitoring, and/or poor communication. So, the next five steps of the model are concentrated on implementation and reinforce some of the insights outlined in the previous section around the *Planning* and *Acting* stages of the proactive process. I will outline each of these briefly.

v   *Commit*
This step involves developing strategies to engage and persuade different stakeholders to buy-in to the solution. This draws on the importance of stakeholder mapping and engagement already discussed. Further insights into influence and persuasion are covered in Chapter 10, which can be drawn on at this stage.

vi   *Lead*
This step involves considering some of the important characteristics required to lead the innovation project, including good interpersonal skills, utilizing networks, and being able to adapt one's style at different stages of the innovation process.

vii *Engage*
Engage is about identifying methods for engaging with users of the proposed innovation to get their early views, this has some parallels with the points around participation introduced in the earlier *Planning* phase section.

viii *Align*
This involves strategically defining the target audience for the innovation and determining the resources needed to deliver it. For example, new innovative work processes often rely on employee training, or the introduction of new software may involve piloting with a smaller group before the full-scale rollout.

ix   *Review*
A lack of assessment and review has been identified as a barrier to successful innovation implementation, so this step reinforces the need to develop an action plan. This chimes with the project management processes outlined in the *Acting* phase discussed in the earlier section.

It is possible for The CLEAR IDEAS (CI) creativity training to be delivered by an experienced in-house L&D facilitator. But if choosing this option, I recommend further immersion into the model, either by reading Kamal's article featured in the Journal of Work and Organizational Psychology[12] or watching a public engagement seminar on CI that is available on YouTube.

Alternatively, engaging with the team at Sheffield University or bringing in an Independent Practitioner Organizational Psychologist with expertise in change management would be advantageous for effectively delivering this training in your organization.

Key Takeaways

- To move beyond reactivity, organizations must establish a culture and environment that prioritizes future-focused work. This can be done by reinforcing organizational values such as innovation, continuous improvement, and sustainability.
- At an individual level, employees must take charge and allocate their time effectively, resisting the temptation of chasing short-term wins.
- Successful proactive endeavors rely on time being allocated to doing the "groundwork," this involves thinking, planning, and acting under the contextual constraints of the organization.
- Instituting processes and utilizing models and frameworks to guide these different stages will maximize the chance of success.

Reflective Questions

- Which of the *Time Traps* (firefighting, cognitive biases, distractions, people pleasing) do you observe most often in your organization?
- What could you do to mitigate against these *Time Traps*?
- What processes and approaches can you introduce to help individuals and teams successfully implement their proactive goals?

My Implementation Intentions

Jot down in this space any actions you will take in response to the reflective questions.

References

1. McDowall, A., & Kinman, G. (2017). The new nowhere land? A research and practice agenda for the "always on" culture. *Journal of Organizational Effectiveness: People and Performance*, 4(3), 256–266.
2. Crabbe, T. (2014). *Busy: How to thrive in a world of too much*. Hachette UK.
3. Mischel, W. (2014). *The marshmallow test: Understanding self-control and how to master it*. Random House.
4. Mark, G., Gudith, D., & Klocke, U. (2008, April). *The cost of interrupted work: More speed and stress*. In Proceedings of the SIGCHI conference on human factors in computing systems (pp. 107–110).
5. Csikszentmihalyi, M., & Csikzentmihaly, M. (1990). *Flow: The psychology of optimal experience* (Vol. 1990, p. 1). Harper & Row.
6. Bindl, U. K., & Parker, S. K. (2009). *Investigating self-regulatory elements of proactivity at work*. In Working paper. Institute of Work Psychology, University of Sheffield.
7. Boyd, N.M., & Bright, D. S. (2007). Appreciative inquiry as a mode of action research for community psychology. *Journal of Community Psychology*, 35(8), 1019–1036.
8. Wang, S., Tu, Y., Zhao, T., & Yang, Y. (2022). Focusing on the past, present, or future? Why proactive personality increases weekly subjective well-being. *Journal of Happiness Studies*, 23, 1543–1560.
9. Son, J., & Rojas, E. M. (2011). Impact of optimism bias regarding organizational dynamics on project planning and control. *Journal of Construction Engineering and Management*, 137(2), 147–157.
10. Rudder, A., Bottrff, C., & Watts, R. (2024). *Critical Path Method (CPM): The Ultimate Guide*. www.forbes.com/advisor/business/critical-path-method/
11. CIPD. (2020). *Creating learning cultures: Assessing the evidence*. Chartered Institute of Personnel and Development.
12. Birdi, K. (2021). Insights on impact from the development, delivery and evaluation of the CLEAR IDEAS innovation training model. *European Journal of Work and Organizational Psychology*, 30(3), 400–414.

Chapter 10

Influence

The Important Role of Influence

Social structures inherently involve power dynamics. The animal kingdom provides many examples of this, whether it's matriarchal elephants guiding critical survival decisions, or the hierarchical structures of bee colonies that ensure efficiency and order. Organizations are no different. Workplaces often mirror these dynamics, with unevenly dispersed power, and certain individuals possessing more authority and influence than others. While "playing politics" at work has negative connotations, it's important to distinguish between ethical and toxic politics, the former is not about harming others or deliberately misleading others for one's gain, it's about using relationships and influence to good effect. Navigating complex power structures can be challenging, particularly when being proactive at work. Proactivity in the workplace frequently requires influencing others to gain their support, whether it's for a new product, a new process, or a different way of doing things, yet this is not always straightforward. In Chapter 8, we revealed how issues arise at work when others misinterpret the intentions behind our proactivity. In this chapter, we'll explore how leaders and managers can help support their team members to build interpersonal influencing skills, to maximize the success of proactive endeavors. After a brief introduction to the psychology of influence, consideration is given to how proactive individuals can best engage their colleagues to support new initiatives. The concepts of political skill and situational judgment effectiveness are outlined, with ideas provided for enhancing these important skills. Considerations and tactics for proactive issue-selling and upward influence are also presented, reinforcing the importance of planning, framing, and effective communication.

The Psychology of Influence

Like other concepts introduced in this book, ideas relating to influence date back to Ancient Greek philosophers and then, as now, the question

DOI: 10.4324/9781003480693-13

of ethics regarding persuasion prevailed. Aristotle's rhetorical triangle underscores the importance of influencers demonstrating *ethos* (e.g., being credible, a trustworthy expert), connecting with *pathos* (e.g., appealing to emotions), and utilizing *logos* (e.g., sound logic, being rational).[1] Take a moment to reflect on a person you consider as influential at work, what is it you observe in them that tells you they are effective influencers? I imagine they are adept at connecting with others through heart and mind, have strong interpersonal skills, and make convincing and compelling arguments. We must differentiate influence from manipulation, the former is about guiding or persuading someone through open, honest communication; whereas the latter usually involves deceptive or underhand tactics to control or coerce someone for personal gain. When it comes to influencing tactics, they are typically regarded as *hard* (e.g., coercive, applying pressure), *rational* (e.g., using logic/data), and *soft* (e.g., using interpersonal skills). The most effective influencing tactics are *rational* or *soft*, perhaps unsurprisingly, after all, who likes to feel coerced, pressured, or bullied? An analysis of 39 studies, surveying over 9,000 participants, concluded the six most effective influencing tactics at work are[2]:

i **Rational:** the ability to form logical arguments and convince others by making claims based on reliable data.

ii **Inspirational Appeal:** appealing to the values and ideals of others to gain their commitment to an idea.

iii **Apprising:** the practice of explaining how the fulfillment of a request will benefit the person being influenced e.g., outlining "what's in it for you."

iv **Collaboration:** providing the resources and assistance to help the person accomplish what the influencer is asking them to do.

v **Ingratiation:** the custom of making the person being influenced feel good about themselves by authentically using flattery or giving praise.

vi **Consultation:** involves co-creation and participation, focused on enabling the person being influenced to play an active role in shaping the final approach.

Other less effective tactics, described in the same analysis, were those utilizing the authority of others, so using someone else's hierarchical position to convince others. In these cases, this was often perceived as calculative and impersonal. Coalition techniques that involve seeking the help of others to influence can also potentially backfire, particularly if the person you are attempting to influence perceives this as being "ganged up" on.

That said, when it comes to upward issue-selling, there is some evidence that coalition forming can be effective, and we will discuss that further in this chapter. From my research, a cluster of participants claimed to dislike engaging in office politics and found navigating power dynamics tedious and frustrating. These individuals had the most negative experiences of being proactive at work, usually because they were unable to influence and convince others to support their endeavors, leaving them feeling stifled and despondent. On the other hand, participants who were adept at navigating power dynamics and who simultaneously drew on several of the effective influencing tactics shared more positive stories of proactive successes at work.

Peer Reactions to Proactive Actions

It was evident from my research that proactive team members often need their peers to help them implement their proactive ideas, and the way peers respond can ultimately impact the outcome. Few studies have investigated peer reactions to proactivity, but an interesting study carried out amongst IT professionals within the energy sector in the Netherlands revealed some illuminating findings.[3] The study explored proactive episodes within teams relating to problem prevention, taking charge, and innovative behavior. It showed that proactive individuals are likely to trigger negative reactions from their peers when their suggestions are perceived as threatening in some way. Whether it's a perception that the proactive idea is disruptive to regular work and will require additional time or effort, or it is conveyed in a way that is felt to be overly dominant or condemns the team in any way. Disgruntled responses from peers also transpire if the distribution of work seems unfair, particularly if proactive individuals delegate responsibilities, to avoid doing the work themselves. Negative reactions from peers were either targeted directly at the proactive person, in the form of belittling comments; or targeted at the initiative, viewing it as a waste of time and resulting in a lack of commitment, or even deliberately sabotaging or slowing down the process. Interestingly, peers who defined their role more narrowly were more likely to respond negatively to proactive ideas, typically with a "this is not part of my job" response, touching on the insights shared in Chapter 5 around role and remit. Either way, negative reactions from peers fuelled team conflict, and broke team cohesion, with the potential to negatively impact productivity.

On the flip side, the same study also demonstrated that when proactive individuals shared their initiative with a visionary tone, reinforced the benefits for all, and emphasized a favorable effort-to-reward ratio, peers responded more positively. Touching on the *consultation* influencing tactic mentioned earlier, this study also reinforced the value of proactive individuals allowing some flexibility, negotiation, and tweaking of their ideas to drive motivation and commitment in their peers. Ideas that were not deemed to "feel like hard work" were welcomed by peers, particularly when the proactive person initiating them was also seen to be "rolling their sleeves up" and "going the extra mile" to drive the initiative forward. In these cases, positive proactive experiences became contagious, fuelling more proactivity and creating a sense of team cohesion and effectiveness. The findings of this study remind us of the importance of "how" proactivity is communicated and influenced, knowledge of influence tactics is not enough, and that is where political skill and situational judgment effectiveness come in.

Political Skill

Political skill is defined as "the ability to effectively understand others at work, and to use such knowledge to influence others to act in ways that enhance one's personal and/or organizational objectives."[4] As such, political skill is premised on the idea that individuals who can accurately gauge the needs of others and calibrate their behavior to match the social situation are more likely to receive positive evaluations from others. In fact, a study of 225 employees and their supervisors from 12 companies across different industries in Indonesia showed that proactive employees low in political skills are more likely to receive negative performance evaluations from their supervisors.[5] There are four dimensions of political skill, as follows:

i **Self and Social Astuteness:** this refers to having self-awareness and being aware of the behaviors of others, to adapt to the needs of the social situation.

ii **Interpersonal Influence:** this is a personal style associated with the ability to exert influence on others, by drawing on appropriate influencing tactics for the given situation.

iii **Network Building:** those high in political skill tend to forge diverse networks of people, build strong alliances, openly ask for support from others, and are willing to reciprocate.

iv **Sincerity:** politically skilled individuals display high levels of integrity and authenticity, they are open, honest, and trusted by others.

While possession of political skill is partly down to personality, it can be shaped and developed. Coaching is particularly well suited to enhancing political skill, as a development technique. One-to-one coaching sessions can help individuals recognize political situations and give them time and space to explore how to respond appropriately. Table 10.1

Table 10.1 Interventions to Develop Political Skill

Dimension of Political Skill	Development Opportunities
Self and social astuteness	• One-to-one coaching sessions to reflect on previous handling of social situations and explore alternative approaches. • Buddying with a peer and using time together to share real-life scenarios, and acting as an objective sounding board, mentor or coach. • Group simulations using scenarios of interpersonal dilemmas found on the job and discussing optimal approaches.
Interpersonal influence	• Coaching to build "confidence to convince," utilizing "what have I got to lose/gain?" and "what's the worst/best that can happen?" questions. • Mentoring – assigning individuals skilled mentors or experienced members of the team to help them develop influencing skills. • Group simulations using work-related influence situations, discussing which combination of influencing tactics would be most effective.
Network building	• Providing opportunities for cross-functional teamwork or training courses that bring diverse groups together. • Encourage setting up and/or participation in employee network groups. • Mentoring programs that encompass both traditional mentoring and *reverse mentoring*, whereby younger individuals mentor an older colleague, typically in areas where the mentor has more up-to-date knowledge or skills. • Encourage volunteering opportunities to provide experiences in helping others and building reliability and trust with new groups. • In hybrid teams create virtual social spaces to encourage spontaneous connections with others, e.g., virtual coffee calls. • Consider creating a profile and building connections to groups using sites such as LinkedIn.
Sincerity	• Communication skills training that emphasizes the use of verbal and non-verbal cues to ensure messages are conveyed honestly and clearly. • Share personal stories and experiences as a communication technique to foster authenticity, connection and relatability. • Empathy training or Emotion Coaching training to help develop the ability to actively listen and understand and share the feelings of others

summarizes some of the other development techniques used to develop each of the dimensions of political skill at work. Some of these interventions can be facilitated in-house, while others may benefit from external expertise.

Situational Judgment Effectiveness

Proactive individuals often tenaciously seek to alter situations they perceive to be problematic by championing change and making things happen. But as highlighted, this involves navigating complex social processes, that's why *situational judgment effectiveness* is important in enabling effective enactments of proactive behavior. Situational judgment effectiveness, or practical intelligence is a measure of how adept individuals are at making effective judgments and/or responses in each situation, it is rooted in social expectations and norms. A study of 139 employees at a rehabilitation agency in Singapore found that proactive individuals who are low in situational judgment effectiveness are more likely to encounter lower job satisfaction, lower organizational commitment, and relational problems with their colleagues.[6] In part, this can be explained by an inability to assess the situation, leading to perceptions of unfairness, which can result in the proactive person demonstrating behaviors such as frustration, cynicism, and complaining, which ultimately impacts relationships at work. In other words, the success of proactivity at work is contingent upon an individual's ability to effectively "read the situation." Several factors contribute to ineffectively judging the situations we find ourselves in at work, these include a lack of knowledge of the organization; unconscious biases (resulting from "too much" or "not enough" information); emotions being triggered and overriding logical decision-making; and stress leading to selective attention that reduces our capacity to consider other perspectives. Table 10.2 summarizes interventions that can be used to develop situational judgment effectiveness.

To summarize, proactivity at work is a complex social process that relies on possessing political skills and situational judgment effectiveness. To maximize successful outcomes, proactive individuals need to acknowledge and adapt to the needs of others, and this can be developed and sharpened. Another form of proactive behavior at work that generates a lot of interest is proactive issue-selling, requiring upward influence. From my research and in discussions with middle-level managers, this can be one of the trickiest forms of proactive behavior, so I will conclude this chapter by providing some guidance on how to maximize outcomes related to this form of proactivity.

Table 10.2 Interventions to Develop Situational Judgment Effectiveness

Intervention	*Aim*	*Practical Considerations*
Developing procedural knowledge	To help individuals know their job well and understand the implications of their actions in the organization.	Importance of robust on-boarding for new starters and the socialization of organizational norms, to develop a depth of knowledge about the job and the organization.
Slow down and step back	To help individuals step back and view situations from a wider lens, to help them move from automatic to deliberate thinking, to combat unconscious bias and minimise *selective attention*.	Provide opportunities for pause and reflect moments. Provide opportunities to engage in mindfulness activities and those that slow down our thinking. Provide coaching and mentoring to explore alternative perspectives.
Group simulations	To develop strategy-based problem solving and help with understanding the perspectives of others.	Provide opportunities for groups to discuss real-life, job-related scenarios and consider the implications of different decisions and actions.

Upward Influence and Proactive Issue-Selling

While speaking up is similar to issue-selling, the latter specifically relates to explicit attempts to influence top-level management to attend to broader issues that relate to strategic or organizational goals, and sometimes societal issues. Selling issues are particularly challenging, whether that be due to the difficulty in gaining access to senior decision-makers, reputational risks if attempts fail, or the interpersonal risks that might ensue. For example, in a previous company, I attempted to advocate for improvements in the maternity policy, which was only offering the bare minimum and was not competitive with similar companies. Unfortunately, I was unsuccessful because the ultimate decision-makers believed I was pushing for these changes solely because I was a woman of reproductive age, potentially seeking to benefit from the policy personally. This outcome certainly didn't leave me feeling motivated and committed to the organization – if you read Chapter 8 – this is a real scenario of misattribution in action. Recently, I was discussing hybrid working policies with a group of leaders, who were feeling disgruntled and demotivated by their companies' office working mandate. The anger and fury felt by many of these leaders was evident, yet not one of them felt able to raise this important issue with their senior leaders, for fear of repercussions. Similarly, issues with selling strategic ideas emerged in my research involving participants aged between 50 and 60 years old. These experienced professionals, despite their efforts to promote strategic initiatives, found the lack of receptiveness from senior decision-makers deeply demoralizing. To optimize the effectiveness of upward issue-selling, proactive individuals can be coached in the following ways:

- **Window of Opportunity** – knowing when to raise an issue and when to hold off is critical, this requires being aware of what else is going on in the organization and asking, "Is the time right?" Windows of opportunity tend to be "closed" in periods of downsizing and uncertainty.[7]

- **Preparation** – doing research, gathering data (from reputable sources), and building a business case is paramount. It is also important to know what key stakeholders value and are interested in, to tailor your communication accordingly. Research findings on issue-selling episodes indicated that conducting thorough research and presenting a robust business case increased the likelihood of success threefold.[8] Drawing on the experience of mentors who have familiarity with selling issues in the organization can be beneficial.

- **Issue-Packaging** – this is about how we present the issue. Framing issues positively as "opportunities" tend to be less threatening to senior leaders. While opportunities evoke excitement, issues may lead to a perception that the organization lacks control. Choice of language is also critical, using business-friendly terminology (e.g., efficiency, risk management) and minimizing technical jargon is advisable. Similarly, using economic arguments (market share, profit, sales) is more likely to influence decision-makers over personal appeals. When the issue is explicitly tied to the mission and vision of the organization, there is also likely to be greater resonance with senior leaders.

- **Influencing Tactics** – Getting the balance between rational/factual and emotive is important: express emotions in a regulated manner to show you care but focus on demonstrating knowledge and expertise. Coalition building might be appropriate where the issue requires higher levels of convincing and recognizes that some individuals or groups have higher levels of social capital in some organizations than others. It is regrettable that some voices get listened to, while others simply do not (we will explore this further in Chapter 15). For example, when it comes to raising gender issues in the workplace, it is advisable not to just leave it to the women, deploying male allies to speak up is likely to add weight to the overall argument.

There will no doubt be some cross-cultural differences, shaped by cultural values that will influence some of the factors above, so it is again important to understand the situation and context within which you are operating. However, increased awareness of these considerations could potentially influence the outcome of one's issue-selling efforts, for the better.

This chapter concludes with a case study from Avon, which showcases their approach to coaching and mentoring to build social capital and influence.

Box 10.1   Case Study

Empowering Confidence – How Avon Uses Coaching and Mentoring to Drive Proactivity

Avon was founded in 1886, with a radical business model rooted in the power of community and driven by a desire to give women economic freedom. Today, Avon is part of Natura &Co, a global purpose-driven group uniting Natura and Avon Brands. With over 5,000 associates and millions of independent Representatives in over 35 countries, Avon continues to be driven by a desire to create a better world for women, to do business responsibly, and to be inclusive. It is a transformational time for Avon as it continues to evolve into an omnichannel business. Their "open and grow" strategy recognizes the importance of proactive behaviors such as taking risks and providing constructive challenge, which have been enabled and strengthened through developing self-confidence across the workforce. This, in part, has been achieved through a commitment to providing access to coaching and mentoring.

Coaching and Mentoring Initiatives at Avon

At Avon, relationships are at the heart of the company's culture. But, with teams spread across various geographies and many associates working in hybrid or remote setups, building personal connections can be challenging. To address this, Avon considers coaching and mentoring as cost-effective and powerful tools for employee development, allowing meaningful relationships to flourish despite physical distance. Avon offers a comprehensive suite of coaching and mentoring interventions designed to support employees at different stages of their careers. Their coaching program is divided into two primary offerings: one for the executive team and another for emerging leaders or individuals transitioning into new roles. Executive coaching begins with a thorough assessment to identify strengths and areas for growth, which guides the coaching process. The emerging leaders' program, meanwhile, targets aspiring individuals nominated by their business leaders and utilizes a digital platform, Coach Hub. This provides a structured yet flexible environment for coaching. The platform facilitates the initial assessment, tracks progress, and allows unlimited coaching sessions over four months, offering participants the opportunity to focus on the areas that matter most to them.

In addition to individual coaching, Avon integrates coaching into its leadership development programs. For example, the "Leading with Heart" program includes a dedicated module on coaching skills, serving as an introduction to the "manager as coach" ethos. Similarly, the "Leading with Purpose" and "Embrace Your Power" programs incorporate team coaching elements, underscoring the company's commitment to embedding a coaching culture across the organization.

Avon's mentoring program launched a few years ago and has also played a pivotal role in employee development. Housed on the company's Workday platform, the mentoring program is flexible and self-nominating, allowing employees to easily opt-in as mentors or mentees. The program's launch was supported by a "Just Click" campaign, highlighting its ease of access. Mentors are equipped with e-learning resources to clarify the principles of mentoring and manage expectations regarding time commitments. To date, over 150 mentors have signed up, eager to support their fellow Avon associates. A recent enhancement to the mentoring program is the introduction of the *Career Hub*, an AI-powered feature that matches mentors and mentees based on their skills and experiences. This technological integration is a key factor in the success of Avon's mentoring initiative, making it more accessible and easier for associates to engage with.

Impact and Results

The impact of Avon's coaching and mentoring programs has been significant, particularly in nurturing a "Can-Do" attitude among employees. By building confidence, enhancing knowledge, and supporting the development of strengths, these programs have empowered individuals to take risks and challenge the status quo, knowing they have the support of their peers, mentors, and coaches. One of the most significant outcomes has been the increase in internal succession, notably senior roles being filled by homegrown talent. The focus on coaching and mentoring has also boosted motivation and engagement across the organization. Mentees regularly provide feedback on the transformative nature of the mentoring program, with one associate expressing gratitude for their experience, which had been a "huge learning curve that enabled a mindset shift." They were left feeling like they'd been "imparted a gift." For mentors, the program offers a sense of giving back and contributes to their personal growth and confidence. These programs have helped Avon maintain a culture of supportive relationships, enabling employees to navigate changes confidently and constructively.

Advice to Other Organizations

For other organizations looking to implement or enhance their coaching and mentoring programs, Avon's experience offers several valuable lessons. First and foremost, these initiatives require ongoing focus and attention to keep momentum. While the programs are designed to encourage self-sufficiency and empowerment, some individuals may need encouragement to engage in personal development, which requires an ongoing emphasis from the organization on the value it places on learning and personal growth. Avon's People Team also notes that preferences can vary across different markets. Some teams may prefer more structure and guidance, while others thrive in a more informal and fluid environment. Striking a balance between providing direction and fostering empowerment is key to the success of these initiatives.

Another challenge the People Team faced when proposing these interventions was demonstrating these development programs' value and return on investment. While there is abundant anecdotal evidence to support coaching and mentoring initiatives, providing concrete evidence was more difficult. Digital platforms like *Coach Hub* and *Career Hub* have helped address this by providing metrics and analytics to showcase the programs' effectiveness, which has helped support the business case.

Finally, Avon's People Team offers the following top tips for kickstarting coaching and mentoring initiatives:

- Recognize the importance of executive sponsorship in driving a coaching culture.

- Don't wait for perfection in program design, instead launch a "good enough" version and refine it based on user feedback.
- Take a flexible approach, for example, while Avon's mentoring approach is based on self-nomination, there have been cases where individuals have been recommended for mentoring based on their specific needs or the needs of the business.
- Don't let budget concerns limit your imagination. For example, Avon has creatively leveraged its internal coaches across the organization to minimize costs while maximizing impact and engagement.

As Avon continues to evolve, the emphasis on coaching and mentoring will continue to be a crucial feature in its approach to talent development.

Key Takeaways

- The ability to effectively influence is at the heart of successful proactive initiatives, understanding and navigating power and relationships is fundamental. Naively assuming politics don't exist and/or actively not engaging in politics can adversely affect outcomes associated with proactivity.
- Knowledge of influencing tactics is not enough, understanding "how" to influence is critical. From a training perspective, developing proactive individuals' political skills and situational judgment effectiveness can be an effective way to minimize the potential for conflict amongst co-workers and misattribution by line managers.
- Upward influence and proactive issue-selling can be challenging. However, these tasks can become more effective by applying situational judgment and adhering to guiding principles of planning, framing, and effective communication.

Reflective Questions

- Which of the four aspects of political skill are less prevalent in your organization and would benefit from being emphasized?
- Who in your team would benefit from enhancing their influencing skills, and which development techniques do you believe would be most appropriate?
- What's your biggest takeaway from reading this chapter?

My Implementation Intentions

Jot down in this space any actions you will take in response to the reflective questions.

References

1. Demirdöğen, Ü. D. (2010). The roots of research in (political) persuasion: Ethos, pathos, logos and the Yale studies of persuasive communications. *International Journal of Social Inquiry*, 3(1), 189–201.
2. Lee, S., Han, S., Cheong, M., Kim, S. L., & Yun, S. (2017). How do I get my way? A meta-analytic review of research on influence tactics. *The Leadership Quarterly*, 28(1), 210–228.
3. Twemlow, M., Tims, M., & Khapova, S. N. (2023). A process model of peer reactions to team member proactivity. *Human Relations,* 76(9), 1317–1351.
4. Ferris, G. R., Treadway, D. C., Kolodinsky, R. W., Hochwarter, W. A., Kacmar, C. J., Douglas, C., & Frink, D. D. (2005). Development and validation of the political skill inventory. *Journal of Management,* 31(1), 126–152.
5. Sun, S., & van Emmerik, H. I. (2015). Are proactive personalities always beneficial? Political skill as a moderator. *Journal of Applied Psychology,* 100(3), 966.
6. Chan, D. (2006). Interactive effects of situational judgment effectiveness and proactive personality on work perceptions and work outcomes. *Journal of Applied Psychology,* 91(2), 475.
7. Ong, C. M., & Ashford, S. J. (2016). Issue-selling: Proactive efforts toward organizational. *In Proactivity at work* (pp. 156–186). Routledge.
8. Bishop, K., Webber, S. S., & O'Neill, R. (2011). Preparation and prior experience in issue-selling success. *Journal of Managerial Issues,* 23(3), 323–340.

Chapter 11

Values and Motivation

The Value in Understanding Values and Motivational Drivers

Understanding the values and motives driving proactive behaviors at work is crucial in creating the conditions for such behavior to flourish. When employees' proactive goals are intrinsically motivated, they are likely to experience feelings of pride and satisfaction when successfully taking charge and bringing about change. In addition, recognizing and respecting individual values promotes a positive work environment that nurtures inclusivity and cooperation among team members. After distinguishing between values and motives, I bring your attention to the different types of work-related values and introduce the concept of values alignment, outlining the benefits to individuals and the organization. With a greater appreciation of individuals' values and motivational drivers, leaders can tailor their management styles and strategies to better support their teams, facilitating both personal and professional growth for employees. To enable such tailored approaches, I will highlight how certain circumstances at work can influence how proactivity is expressed, depending on one's values. Four personas identified in my research will exemplify this, exploring the implications for supporting proactivity within each group. Values exercises and activities are offered as practical resources, along with a case study from Virgin Money which highlights the importance of leaders' investing time in getting to know their colleagues' motivational drivers.

Distinguishing Values and Motives

Values – Our Compass

Our values serve as a compass, guiding, and directing our behavior. They are fundamental beliefs that drive our attitudes, decision-making, and

DOI: 10.4324/9781003480693-14

actions. Values tend to be determined by a combination of personal experiences, social interactions, cultural influences, and education. It is generally accepted that values remain fairly stable over time. Social Psychologist Shalom H. Schwartz's seminal work on the theory of *Basic Human Values* identified ten distinct values: achievement, power, hedonism, benevolence, universalism, security, tradition, conformity, self-direction, and stimulation. Extensive studies from across the world have provided cross-cultural support for his model.[1] Value orientations affect how people behave at work, and a psychometric assessment has been developed to capture the work-related values, drawing on Schwartz's *Basic Human Values*. The ten distinct values correspond to four higher-order values: *Self-Transcendence, Openness to Change, Self-Enhancement,* and *Conservation*.[2] Table 11.1 provides definitions of each of the work values, along with an example of the value in action. *Openness to Change* values relates to independence of thought and is associated with being proactive. *Openness to Change* is also associated with being anxiety-free, which increases resources for proactive goal striving, whereas individuals high in *Conservation* values report lower levels of personal initiative, in favor of certainty and structure.[3]

Motivation – Our Fuel

The word "motivation" is derived from the Latin word "movere," which means "to move." Motivation refers to the process that initiates, guides, and sustains goal-oriented behavior. While our values serve as our compass, our motivation is the fuel that energizes action. Motivation theory is complex; there are several different theories used to explain motivation at work, some are based on satisfying our needs (e.g., achievement, status), while others are based on the thought processes we engage in (e.g., equity and fairness). Motivators tend to be categorized as either intrinsic or extrinsic, with the former being driven from within (e.g., aligns with one's interests) and the latter being influenced by external rewards (e.g., status, salary, recognition). I introduced the *self-determination theory* of motivation in Chapter 7, highlighting that intrinsic motivation is linked with satisfying our basic human need for autonomy, a sense of belonging, and competence (often referred to as the A, B, and C of motivation).[4]

You'll notice some overlap between values and motivation, for example, achievement. If achievement is a core value for someone, they are likely to be motivated by goals that allow them to succeed and accomplish tasks. The achievement value drives behaviors aimed at gaining competence and recognition. It has been suggested that an individual's work values are fundamental for managing their motivation and commitment, influencing how they relate to their organization. Job satisfaction is, in part, determined by the degree of alignment between the organizational environment and an individual's values.

Table 11.1 Definitions of Work Values

Value	Work Value Definition	Example
Higher order value: self-enhancement		
Achievement	Work success defined by recognition of one's abilities	Someone who sets themselves challenging goals and is resourceful in striving to deliver them
Power	Social status and prestige expressed through leadership and influence	Someone who enjoys guiding and/or directing other people's actions, and puts themselves forward to speak up for the group
Higher order value: self-transcendence		
Benevolence	Devoting oneself to the needs of others at work, creating harmonious and supportive relationships	Someone who proactively demonstrates care for their colleagues by providing support, empathy and nurtures collaboration
Universalism	Advocating fairness, respect, and protection against discrimination for everyone	Someone who proactively acts as an ally to under-represented groups and/or encourages socially responsible policies
Hedonism	Pleasure in doing work, while achieving work/life balance	Someone who puts the fun into work, by engaging in work they enjoy and being a contagion for positivity
Higher order value: openness to change		
Self-direction	Independent thought and decision-making, creating and exploring ideas	Someone who enjoys the freedom to choose how to perform their job and initiates new projects
Stimulation	Enjoyment from variety, novelty and problem-solving	Someone who has access to a wide variety of different tasks within their job, so no one day is the same
Higher order value: conservation		
Security	Avoids risks, promotes safety and stability	Someone who enjoys identifying and mitigating risks that could threaten the company's operations
Tradition	Respects and accepts organizational traditions, culture and customs	Someone who is unlikely to speak up or challenge the norms that exist within the organization
Conformity	Complies to management expectations, sacrifices personal desires to preserve organizational order	Someone who takes pride in carrying out one's assigned role and doing what the position requires

Values Alignment and Proactivity

Research suggests that where there is alignment of values between employees and their organization, it leads to positive outcomes, such as improved retention. It is premised on the idea that shared values are likely to reduce conflict as a result of their association with shared goals and shared priorities regarding what is important.[5] Values alignment is also associated with trust, which, as highlighted in Chapter 5, is essential in building psychological safety, which helps stimulate proactive behavior at work. Interestingly, a company's values can help or hinder employees' proactive efforts. Individuals who identify with the organization or leader are more likely to demonstrate a promotive proactive voice (e.g., suggesting improvement ideas) because they can connect with and relate to the vision and feel invested in sustaining the organization in the future.[6] Furthermore, employees are more likely to share ideas if they have a good relationship with their manager. When managers create an atmosphere where people feel comfortable speaking up, it encourages more open communication. A study of nearly 500 people from various industries in the United States found that when managers' and employees' values are aligned, employees are more likely to speak up. This, in turn, boosts their commitment to the company, encourages them to help others, and improves their overall well-being.[7] Equally, employees are more likely to engage in safety proactivity in collectivist organizational cultures, where managers demonstrate a commitment to safety, are involved in promoting safety at work, and explicitly communicate its importance.[8] In the context of successful proactive issue-selling, when there is a perceived fit between organizational values and the issue being proactively raised, there is a higher chance of senior stakeholders being receptive to it.[9] This reminds us of the importance of creating a connection between an individual's personal values, leaders' values, and those of the organization, which will require thoughtful consideration in a diverse workforce. Fostering alignment relies on actively engaging employees and creating opportunities for dialogue to identify common ground and to build upon shared values to align personal beliefs with overarching organizational values.

Providing opportunities for employees to express themselves in ways that feel authentic to their values is crucial. Psychologists refer to this as identity-based motivation, and this type of motivation emphasizes how one's sense of identity can drive behaviors and goals.[10] As an example, a teacher who values self-direction and is committed to nurturing creativity in their students is likely to be motivated to design engaging lessons, look for innovative ways to enable young people to learn, and advocate for curriculum changes that support creative thinking. Similarly, for individuals with a proactive personality, the very act of being proactive serves the purpose of expressing oneself, which can become self-fulfilling. For instance, if a person sees themselves as a "fixer" or problem-solver, they are more likely to engage in proactive problem-solving and innovative behavior when they see an issue at work that needs resolving. Group identity follows a similar trajectory; when individuals identify with a group, they are more likely to engage in proactive behavior that is aimed at shaping the future of the group. Values alignment is a vital ingredient for driving collaboration and reducing conflict in teams, creating common values helps to build a cohesive culture and a sense of community. Identity-based motivation is a powerful force that can drive individuals to pursue goals that are aligned with their values. By understanding their team members' values, leaders and managers can leverage identity-based motivation to drive greater levels of engagement and commitment.

Throughout this book, I've reiterated the importance of creating the right environment for proactivity to flourish, so now let's consider some of the contextual and situational factors that might affect values and proactivity.

Contextual and Situational Factors

Employees are more inclined to behave in ways consistent with their identity when the opportunities within their work environment align with their self-perception, and this helps explain why different employees engage in different forms of proactivity. To illustrate, a study conducted in the United States and China found that individuals who value self-determination and independence in their jobs – and who were granted higher levels of autonomy – were more likely to demonstrate proactive behavior oriented towards their careers and to exhibit career commitment. Whereas employees in highly interdependent teams who value benevolence and prefer collaborative work exhibited higher levels of team-oriented proactive behavior.[11] Another study explored ambiguity as a condition under which employees express their values and proactivity differently. Traditionally, ambiguity was thought to stimulate proactive behavior at work on the basis that uncertainty prompted proactive individuals to attempt to improve the status quo. However, it would appear that ambiguity also has the propensity to inhibit proactivity in some people. Adam Grant and Nancy Rothbard's research conducted in a water treatment plant in the United States found that employees high in security values were more likely to perceive ambiguity as a threat. The reaction to the threat heightened the perceived dangers of being proactive, causing employees to adopt a more inflexible approach and reducing their likelihood of engaging in proactive behavior. By contrast, employees who held strong pro-social values (benevolence and universalism) perceived the ambiguity as an opportunity to change the situation for the benefit of the wider organization and, therefore, were more proactive in confronting the challenging circumstances to make a meaningful change.[12] This provides a useful explanation of why employees engage in different forms of proactivity and under what circumstances. In turn, managers can promote specific forms of proactivity where there is a values match and/or provide opportunities that enable values alignment. From a practical perspective, rather than alter the situation across the board, it may be prudent to adapt to individual needs. Using the ambiguity example, it may be more fruitful to actively clarify the forms of proactive actions beneficial for individuals with high-security values while also offering extra support to help ease their fears and anxiety. Let me demonstrate this further by introducing you to different proactive personas I identified in my research.

Proactive Personas

In my qualitative study, I investigated individuals' motivations for engaging in proactive behaviors at work, exploring their varied experiences – both positive and negative, and the resulting outcomes. My findings suggest proactivity is commonly associated with a desire to achieve (achievement motive), though in a nuanced way. The achievement motive was associated with either wanting to prove oneself, to accomplish goals, a drive to be competitive, or a striving towards collective success. Participants rarely pinpointed one *reason-to* be proactive, instead conveying a combination of personally driven and socially driven motives. Alongside the desire to achieve were values-driven motives, which were clustered based on participants' experiences. While my research participants were late-careerists aged 50–60 years old, it was interesting to note that the values driving their proactive motivation were evenly split among the four higher-order value categories (outlined in Table 11.1). I heard some participants refer to *self-enhancement* values, such as a need for social recognition and ambition, or *openness to change* values, such as a need for creativity and stimulation. Others spoke of *conservation* values associated with conforming to expectations or values associated with *self-transcendence*, such as social justice and environmental protection. As participants described their proactive experiences at work, the metaphors they chose to use were striking, especially those related to combat, such as "getting shot down" or "having their head blown off," and those linked to gameplay, such as "playing the waiting game" and "dealing with a bunch of poker players." As such, I developed four different proactive personas named after gameplay techniques: *Strategists, Sandboxers, Tacticians,* and *Co-operators*.[13] Let me explain these different personas in more depth to provide insight into their values, associated behaviors, and implications for managers:

i **Strategist – Self-Enhancement Values**
  Strategy games, such as Monopoly, usually involve having a plan, and outcomes are dependent on both the actions of the player and others in the game. In this instance, the *Strategist* metaphor is used to reinforce the groundwork, influencing skills, and risk-taking involved in being pro-active. The *Strategist* is ambitious and influential; they also like to feel in control and be empowered to make autonomous decisions. Their pro-active endeavors are motivated by achievement, a desire to do a good job, and recognition, and they enjoy a challenge, often describing themselves as competitive. *Strategists* often recounted stories about taking charge and issue-selling as their favored proactive behaviors, frequently initiating large-scale change projects that would substantially impact their business.

  Implications for Managers => *Strategists* are likely to be engaging in proactive efforts that require persistence, overcoming obstacles, and dealing with challenges from others, which can be effortful and exhausting. Managers should be mindful of this and help coach their proactive *Strategists* to ensure they are adequately recuperating and switching off from work outside of work hours. (Energy depletion and restoration are covered more fully in Chapter 12).

ii **Co-operator – Self-Transcendence Values**
  Co-operative games involve players working with one another to achieve a common objective, for example, deck-building games. The *Co-operator* metaphor is used to reinforce the value of universalism and the need for affiliation, linked to the self-transcendence higher-order value. The *Co-operator* values equality, inclusion, and a sense of fairness at work and would proactively advocate for equity and/or engage in allyship. They are motivated by a love of learning, working collaboratively, and doing work that is aligned with their interests, as such, there is a strong drive towards intrinsically motivating work. *Co-operators* with strong benevolence values may also prefer to engage in proactive activities as part of a team, they are more likely to want to operate with dispersed power and take a "divide and conquer" approach.

  Implications for Managers => Fairness and harmony are important for *Co-operators*, therefore, all of the components of fairness outlined in Chapter 6 will be important to consider for this group. Organizational approaches such as implementing DEI (diversity, equity, and inclusion) initiatives and holding regular listening groups to ensure employees feel that their voices are valued and heard will be beneficial. *Co-operators* may also value being given opportunities to provide support in the form of mentoring or coaching to others within the organization. Encouraging team-focused proactive activities may also be beneficial to achieve value alignment.

iii **Sandboxer – Openness to Change Values**
Sandbox games include computer games like Minecraft, which often provide the game player with autonomy, control, and creative license. In this instance, the *Sandboxer* metaphor is used to reinforce the preference toward independence, freedom, and creativity, in the higher-order value of openness to change. *Sandboxers* value opportunities that allow them to take charge and create change. They describe themselves as being different and having different perspectives from other people and take pride in having innovative ideas or ways of working. *Sandboxers* frequently shared stories about coming up with new ideas or suggesting more innovative ways of working as their preferred proactive behaviors. They also frequently recounted stories of the challenges associated with convincing others to support their proactive endeavors.

Implications for Managers => *Sandboxers* typically struggle with *political skill* and influencing others and may become frustrated, demotivated, and withdrawn when they perceive their proactivity to be stifled by others. *Sandboxers* may benefit from working with a mentor or coach to help them enhance their influencing skills and provide an alternative perspective to aid sense-making. (Further strategies for developing influencing skills are discussed in Chapter 10.)

iv **Tactician – Conservation Values**
Tactical games, such as Connect Four, tend to involve everyday moves one takes to remain in the game. In this context, the *Tactician* metaphor is used to reinforce the more opportunistic approach taken to proactive behavior. The *Tactician* values tradition, conformity, and security associated with the higher-order value of conservation, so they are more likely to follow customs within the organization and tend to operate within the boundaries of their role. Their desire to be proactive is associated with achievement motive, along with wanting to do the "right thing" for the organization and meeting their supervisor's expectations. The *Tacticians'* preferred proactive behaviors often revolved around process improvements, or responding to changes being triggered by external factors, such as regulatory requirements.

Implications for Managers => Proactivity for *Tacticians* is likely to be a learned behavior rather than a personality trait. *Tacticians* who hold strong security values are less likely to exercise personal initiative and may be more avoidant of innovative or change-related activities for fear of social judgment. As highlighted earlier in this Chapter, coaching for confidence and helping individuals overcome their fears may be useful to enhance their engagement in proactivity. *Tacticians* may also benefit from interventions aimed at developing *role breadth confidence*, to broaden their perspectives around the work-related tasks they should engage in, as outlined in Chapter 5.

I developed different proactive personas to enable leaders and managers to take more tailored approaches to support their team members. While my research used a small sample, and generalizations about the four distinct proactive personas cannot be made at this stage, I believe future research will validate my findings. However, there may be more than four distinct proactive personas, and it is highly plausible that individuals may adapt from one persona to another depending on the context they find themselves in – though, of course, that would potentially mean them not being true to their values, which might have some consequences. That said, the four personas map to the higher-order values in the validated Work Values Questionnaire,[14] which provides some reassurance. Therefore, use the personas as a guide rather than a definitive reference; they are intended to help with tailored conversations, not to put people in boxes!

Practical Resources

Throughout this chapter, I have encouraged you to invest time in getting to know your work-related values and those of your team, to create a greater sense of values alignment. Here are some activities that I have carried out with teams looking to understand their values more fully (Boxes 11.1–11.3). I also use the first activity when starting with new coaching clients, as it provides me with a greater sense of their needs and what is important to them.

Box 11.1   Connecting with Your Values

Solo Exercise

What is important to you, what upsets you, and what underlies your decisions, are all connected to your personal values. They are a shorthand way of describing your motivations; together with your beliefs, values are the causal factors that drive your decision-making.

Whether personal, professional, social, or life-oriented, values make room for knowledge, wisdom, and heightened self-awareness. Unsurprisingly, given we are all unique, we all choose different combinations of values in life, and these choices shape our actions and decisions.

Assessing and clarifying our values is a great way to prioritize our life goals and understand what we truly desire to become.

Step 1: Review the Values List in Table 11.2 and check all the values that resonate with you most. Don't overthink it, just pick the words that pop out at you.

Step 2: Of the values you picked out, select those that are most important to you to refine your list down to about ten different values.

Table 11.2 Our Basic Values List[15]

Value Categories	Values List				
Power	Social power	Authority	Wealth	Public image	Social recognition
Achievement	Successful Self-respect	Capable	Ambitious	Influential	Intelligent
Stimulation	Daring	A varied life	Exciting life		
Self-direction	Creativity	Curious	Freedom	Choosing own goals	Independent
Hedonism	Pleasure	Enjoying life			
Universalism	Environment Harmony	Nature Wisdom	Broad-minded World peace	Social justice	
Benevolence (kindness)	Helpful Friendship	Honesty Spiritual	Forgiving Mature love	Loyalty Meaningful life	Responsible
Tradition	Committed to a cause Doing the right thing	Accepting your lot in life	Humble	Moderate	Respect for tradition
Conformity	Politeness	Honoring of parents/ elders	Obedient	Self-discipline	
Security	Good health Belonging	National security	Social order	Family Security	Reciprocation of favors

Step 3: Based on the refined list, select the ones you believe you couldn't live without:

i   ... ...
ii   ... ...
iii ... ...
iv   ... ...
v   ... ...

Step 4: Based on Step 3, can you see any themes relating to the Value Types, which categories do your values fall into? Is there a dominant Value Type category?

Step 5: Reflect on the following question alone or as part of a team discussion: Do you believe you are currently living your values at work? If not, what would help you to become more aligned with your values?

Box 11.2   Living Your Values

Solo or Small Group Exercise

Creating a values tree is a creative and reflective activity that helps you identify and visualize your core values. You will first need to have completed the *Connecting with Your Values* activity. For this activity, you will need your list of top values, paper or canvas, and pens, pencils, or paints. Follow these steps to create your own values tree:

Step 1: Begin by drawing the trunk of your tree in the center of your paper or canvas. Make it sturdy and strong, symbolizing the foundation of your values. Add branches extending from the trunk. These branches will hold the leaves where you will write your values.

Step 2: Draw leaves on the branches. You can choose to make them simple ovals or more detailed leaf shapes. Make sure you have enough leaves to represent all the values you want to include. You can add more branches and leaves as needed.

Step 3: Using the list of your values, you can start labeling your leaves. Write one value on each leaf. Add color to your tree. Feel free to add additional details such as flowers, fruits, or roots to further personalize your values tree – I added a sketch of my cat on mine!

Step 4: Spend some time looking at your completed values tree. Reflect on why each value is important to you and how it influences your life.

Step 5: Place your values tree somewhere you can see it regularly, such as on a wall in your room or in a workspace. Let it serve as a reminder of your core values and guide your actions and decisions.

Tips:

- Don't worry about artistic perfection. The goal is to create a personal and meaningful representation of your values.
- If the words on the values list aren't quite right for you, feel free to come up with your own.
- Revisit and update your values tree periodically as your values may evolve.

Box 11.3   Aligning Our Values

Team Exercise

This exercise is aimed at helping team members identify personal and shared values, which can help strengthen an understanding of one another and build team cohesion. It's a great activity to include in a team meeting or team building day and can be done in 45–60 minutes. For this activity, you will need sticky notes, marker pens, and a whiteboard or large sheet of paper, and you may want to refer to the values list in Table 11.1 to guide the discussion.

Step 1: Begin by asking each team member to reflect on the following question and to capture their responses on sticky notes: What personal values guide your decisions and behavior at work?

Step 2: Ask team members to verbally share their core values and provide an example of when they've demonstrated one of these values at work. Once everyone has contributed, ask the group to discuss any recurring themes and insights.

Step 3: Now, ask each team member to reflect on what they've heard and invite them to consider which three values they believe are essential for the team's success – start by doing this individually and capturing the values on a sticky note, then opening it up for discussion.

Step 5: The aim is to cluster and align values, so start by asking the team to work together to group the values they believe are most important for the team's success on the board. Agree on up to five core values that best represent the team's shared identity.

Step 6: To drive alignment and accountability, you may want to take the team's core values and create a Team Charter, which would encompass the team's purpose, goals, values, expectations, and success measures. Display this in a prominent place and revisit it periodically to ensure it remains relevant.

This chapter concludes with a case study from Virgin Money, which emphasizes the importance of leaders' investing time in getting to know their colleagues' motivational drivers.

Box 11.4   Case Study

Leaders' Understanding of Motivational Drivers at Virgin Money

Virgin Money is a banking and financial services brand operating in the United Kingdom, with over 7,000 colleagues. The organization prides itself on doing banking differently, being innovative, and working collaboratively. **Living** *a life more Virgin* is premised on living well, purposeful working, inspiring change, and building a community, and is at the center of their people practices. Following a merger with Clydesdale Bank plc in 2018, Virgin Money recognized the need to establish a consistent approach to leadership. Central to their strategy was the development of "Great Leadership," underpinned by Suzanne Jacob's research on drivers of intrinsic motivation.[16] By leveraging these insights, Virgin Money refined its leadership behaviors framework and implemented a series of initiatives to empower leaders and enhance colleague engagement.

Initiatives for Great Leadership

Virgin Money identified six key behaviors of great leaders, and these behaviors formed the foundation of their leadership development approach. In the first instance, leaders were invited to participate in a series of "Sprint" workshops focused on bite-sized learning to develop skills and knowledge supporting team engagement and motivation. These workshops were supplemented by a digital learning platform, enabling leaders to put their learning into action. The "Sprint" workshops were designed to be interactive and engaging, with a mix of theoretical concepts, case studies, and practical exercises. Leaders learned how to recognize and leverage the intrinsic motivations of their team members, fostering a culture of empowerment and autonomy.

As part of its commitment to developing effective leadership and nurturing a culture aligned with its values, Virgin Money also introduced the "Accelerate" program. Designed to socialize new leaders into the organization and reinforce leadership behavioral expectations, "Accelerate" is a comprehensive onboarding initiative that equips leaders with the skills, knowledge, and mindset needed to succeed in their roles. New leaders participate in a series of workshops and training sessions focused on developing essential leadership competencies. These sessions cover topics such as communication, goal setting, and performance management. A central component of the "Accelerate" program is the motivation and values module. With a focus on practical application, leaders are encouraged to discuss how they keep motivational drivers switched on. For example, to reinforce a sense of inclusion and belonging, one participant shared how they facilitate a daily team call to encourage open dialogue and knowledge-sharing, providing a sense of support. In addition to the workshop, participants are equipped with resources, including a template to capture individual team members' drivers, a conversation starter with recommended questions to prompt and guide discussions regarding motivation and aspirations, and practical tips to help managers ensure their team members' motivational drivers are being met.

Impact and Results

Program evaluations revealed participants' praising the practicality and relevance of the "Sprint" workshops, noting that they provided actionable strategies for enhancing team motivation and performance. The combination of theory and real-world examples resonated well with leaders at all levels of the organization. One-third of leaders who had previously not engaged in personal development attended "Sprint" workshops, indicating an increased interest and participation in leadership development initiatives. As for the "Accelerate" program, despite initial perceptions about the utility of the motivation module, it received the best evaluation scores among participants. In fact, many found it to be the most useful session, highlighting its value in understanding colleague motivations.

Virgin Money went on to implement a leadership index to measure colleagues' views of their people leaders. Following the "Sprint" and "Accelerate" initiatives, the quality of people leadership experienced by colleagues increased by eight percentage points, with improved consistency across leaders. The positive impact of the leadership development initiatives was also evident in colleague engagement surveys, with colleagues reporting higher levels of satisfaction and motivation. Leaders were better equipped to address colleagues' needs and concerns, resulting in improved morale and productivity. Perhaps unsurprisingly, colleagues who reported to leaders who participated in development sessions scored more favorably across all six leadership behaviors compared to those whose leaders did not participate.

Testimonial and Advice

A new leader at Virgin Money shared their experience of applying learnings from the "Accelerate" program, particularly regarding motivations and values. They found that understanding team members' motivational drivers led to more productive feedback and personal development conversations and accelerated interpersonal relationship building.

In providing advice to other organizations, the team responsible for designing these initiatives emphasized the importance of alignment across functions and stakeholder engagement. They highlighted the importance of having a comprehensive launch plan and sustained efforts to ensure the longevity and effectiveness of values and motivations training.

Virgin Money's commitment to understanding motivational drivers and values has transformed its leadership approach and significantly enhanced colleague engagement. By empowering leaders with the skills and insights to motivate their teams effectively, Virgin Money has created a culture of high performance and alignment with its organizational goals.

Key Takeaways

- While everyone's work-related values are unique and shaped by individual experiences, they tend to fall into one of four higher-order categories: self-enhancement, self-transcendence, openness to change, and conservation.
- By understanding the values that drive proactive behavior, leaders and managers can create a more supportive, motivating, and effective working environment.
- Understanding one another's values within a team can help create a collaborative culture that supports inclusivity and individual differences.
- Where there is alignment of values between employees and their organization, it leads to positive outcomes.

Reflective Questions

- What is your biggest insight from this Chapter?
- How can you apply any of these insights within your organization?

My Implementation Intentions

Jot down in this space any actions you will take in response to the reflective questions.

References

1. Schwartz, S. H. (2007). *Basic human values: Theory, methods, and application*. Risorsa Uomo.
2. Consiglio, C., Cenciotti, R., Borgogni, L., Alessandri, G., & Schwartz, S. H. (2017). The WVal: A new measure of work values. *Journal of Career Assessment*, 25(3), 405–422.
3. Fay, D., & Frese, M. (2000). Conservatives' approach to work: Less prepared for future work demands? *Journal of Applied Social Psychology*, 30, 171–195.
4. Deci, E. L., & Ryan, R. M. (2000). The "what" and "why" of goal pursuits: Human needs and the self-determination of behavior. *Psychological Inquiry*, 11(4), 227–268.
5. Presbitero, A., Roxas, B., & Chadee, D. (2016). Looking beyond HRM practices in enhancing employee retention in BPOs: Focus on employee–organisation value fit. The International Journal of Human Resource Management, 27(6), 635–652.
6. Den Hartog, D. N., & Belschak, F. D. (2016). Leadership and employee proactivity. *In Proactivity at work* (pp. 429–451). Routledge.
7. Weber, T. J., & Avey, J. B. (2019). Speaking up when values are aligned: Manager value congruence and the mediating role of employee voice. *Baltic Journal of Management*, 14(4), 578–596.
8. Curcuruto, M., & Griffin, M. A. (2016). Safety proactivity in the workplace: The initiative to improve individual, team, and organizational safety. *In Proactivity at work* (pp. 123–155). Routledge.
9. Ong, C. M., & Ashford, S. J. (2016). Issue-selling: Proactive efforts toward organizational. *In Proactivity at work* (pp. 156–186). Routledge.
10. Oyserman, D. (2015). Pathways to success through identity-based motivation. Oxford University Press.
11. Wu, C. H., Parker, S. K., Wu, L. Z., & Lee, C. (2018). When and why people engage in different forms of proactive behavior: Interactive effects of self-construals and work characteristics. *Academy of Management Journal*, 61(1), 293–323.
12. Grant, A. M., & Rothbard, N. P. (2013). When in doubt, seize the day? Security values, prosocial values, and proactivity under ambiguity. *Journal of Applied Psychology*, 98(5), 810.
13. Gray, J., & Dhensa-Kahlon, R. (2024). Proactive motivation through the lens of older workers. *Occupational Psychology Outlook*, 3(2), 6–13.
14. Schwartz, S. H. (2012). An overview of the Schwartz theory of basic values. *Online Readings in Psychology and Culture*, 2(1), 11.
15. Consiglio, C., Cenciotti, R., Borgogni, L., Alessandri, G., & Schwartz, S. H. (2017). The WVal: A new measure of work values. *Journal of Career Assessment*, 25(3), 405–422.
16. Jacobs, S. (2017). *DRIVERS: Creating trust and motivation at work*. Panoma Press.

Chapter 12

Energy

Proactivity as Vitalising and Depletive

Proactivity at work is double-edged in that it can be vitalizing and depleting. The pride and satisfaction we experience from using our initiative and making things happen can be a source of energy. On the other hand, if our efforts are being stifled or undervalued, it can leave us feeling frustrated and emotionally exhausted. In this chapter, I consider some of the risks to our well-being by engaging in proactive behavior at work, with suggestions for mitigating such negative consequences. Taking a resource-building approach, considerations and prompts are provided for individuals, managers, and at the organizational level to create a healthy environment for proactive behavior to flourish. Additionally, tools and techniques are shared to help build and restore our energy to keep us feeling actively engaged at work.

Before exploring the energy drains of proactivity, it is helpful to understand some of the factors contributing to exhaustion and stress at work through the lens of the demands-resources model.[1] Imagine a set of weighing scales, with job demands on one side and job resources on the other. To minimize stress at work, we need "our scales" to be balanced or in equilibrium. Demands and resources are typically associated with workload, perceived control, support, social relationships, role clarity, and change-related initiatives at work.[2] For example, if a team is under-resourced, workloads may be too high, and if support structures are not in place, it's likely the scales will be tipping toward demands outweighing available resources, increasing the risk of stress. Some behaviors associated with being proactive can use up valuable resources, leaving us feeling depleted, and this can be exacerbated when job resources are in short supply, which we'll now go on to explore.

DOI: 10.4324/9781003480693-15

Understanding the Energy Drains of Proactivity

Proactive Personality

Having a proactive personality goes hand in hand with striving – the act of making a sustained effort to achieve a goal or overcome challenges. Striving for career opportunities and enhanced performance at the expense of personal well-being is not uncommon among proactive people. I experienced this firsthand – in my early career, I pushed myself so hard that I collapsed on a flight during a business trip. Despite that wake-up call, I didn't learn my lesson and ended up experiencing something similar years later in a different job when I agreed to take on an expanded role that was beyond the scope of one person. In this instance, I developed a persistent eye twitch that lasted for six months, and when I finally went to the doctor, I discovered I was suffering from exhaustion. These examples are a stark reminder that a relentless, proactive drive can come at a real cost to one's health. Striving to bring about change through taking charge was a prominent feature of the conversations I had with participants in my research, who I refer to as *Strategists*.[3] I recall a participant expressing something along the lines of, "If the front door is closed, you need to find another way in, even if it means going through the back." However, persistence and tenacity have the potential for resource depletion because they heavily rely on an individual's self-control strategies. When our change endeavors at work are stifled by others, we are expected to manage our emotions and behave in a socially acceptable way, and that can be exhausting. Unsurprisingly, emotionally exhausted employees are more likely to suffer from poorer performance, and exhausted proactive individuals are more likely to leave an organization as a result.[4]

Job Crafting

Job crafting has been hailed as an effective way to boost engagement and job satisfaction by allowing employees to shape and align their job roles to their personal preferences and interests. Proactive job crafting provides a better sense of "fit" and allows us to use our strengths more effectively. When we spend more time working on the things we are good at and enjoy, we are more likely to experience a positive state of flow and enhanced well-being. However, recent studies suggest there may be some unintended consequences of job crafting, which can be energy-depleting. When we experience the flow state,[5] we can become so absorbed that we lose track of time, giving rise to overworking. This may be exacerbated when we are motivated to engage in more complex and/or challenging work, which requires more time, energy, and effort. Interestingly, job crafting has also been associated with presenteeism, the practice of attending work while ill. While presenteeism is often attributed to job insecurity, there is the potential, particularly in job roles associated with service and duty, that individuals can craft their jobs in such a way that they permit themselves to work when they should be recuperating. In a study of hospital physicians in Norway, doctors described being concerned about colleagues having to cover their tasks if they were unwell, so they made sense of their decision to go to work ill by cognitively crafting their job to prioritize meaningful work and good colleague relations over their health.[6] Anecdotally, I have several friends working in client-facing positions in creative and professional services, where there is a heavy emphasis on both sales and fulfilling clients' needs at all costs. Just like the doctors, I often hear them justifying their decision to work beyond their contracted hours (often until late in the evening and over the weekend) as an important part of the job, where being responsive is valued and expected. Yet, we know that overworking is bad for our health, contributing to stress and burnout.[7] Work-related stress is on the rise, contributing to higher absenteeism and staff turnover. Staggeringly, on average, each case of stress-related health problems results in the loss of 30.9 working days per annum.[8] Organizations have a duty of care to their employees; therefore, managers and leaders must resist glorifying over-working and be aware of the unintended consequences that can culminate from certain job-crafting behaviors.

Though not all job crafting is motivated by wanting to do more, sometimes employees craft their roles to reduce their workload or deprioritize tasks they don't like doing, which may not have been agreed with one's manager. While this sounds like an intuitive way to achieve balance, it could backfire. When an individual is motivated to reduce the complexity of their role, it can lead to boredom and disengagement, which in itself can be energy depleting. There is a fine balance to maintain in ensuring work remains within manageable limits, avoiding extremes of boredom and overwhelm. Furthermore, there is also a risk to others within a team when co-workers engage in task-reduction job crafting in that others may inadvertently have to pick up the slack and take on more work. Not only can this contribute to risks associated with overworking but it can create conflict across the team when the distribution of work is perceived as unfair. It is important that managers emphasize interdependencies and encourage their team members to consider the wider impact of their job-crafting behaviors, recognizing the potential for a negative ripple effect.

Proactive Work Behavior – Speaking Up, Taking Charge, Innovative Ideas

Using personal initiative to speak up, take charge and drive change often involves negotiating and influencing others in the process, which can be effortful and anxiety-inducing. Worrying about how others will respond to our proactive endeavors is natural, particularly given the *initiative paradox*, whereby organizations encourage proactivity, yet frequently punish it if it is considered misguided.[9] Consistently questioning whether one has permission to be proactive and fearing being reprimanded for taking initiative is like being on an emotional rollercoaster and poses a genuine risk to physical and psychological health. Recent studies suggest that the fear of social judgment from one's supervisor for being proactive can make it difficult to disconnect from work. This can lead to exhaustion, leaving individuals too drained to engage in hobbies outside of work that typically help replenish their energy reserves.[10] In some cases, ruminating and worrying about the reactions of others can also lead to insomnia.[11] Insufficient recuperation sets off a vicious cycle, where the proactive person feels increasingly drained of energy, and begins to disengage and withdraw. This, in turn, reduces their motivation to continue their proactive efforts, ultimately impacting overall organizational performance.

Anxiety and fear of judgment for being proactive can extend beyond one's supervisor. Colleagues can be just as important in making, breaking, or even preventing someone's proactive endeavors. Workplace gossip has been identified as a major contributor to the anxiety employees feel. This is particularly evident in work environments where gossip becomes a way for people to exert social pressure without openly confronting issues, it's almost a form of passive aggression. In these contexts, employees may become hyper-aware of how their actions are perceived by their peers, leading to heightened anxiety. This, in turn, can prevent individuals from taking personal initiative or proposing new ideas. Instead of embracing proactive behavior, which requires stepping out of the norm, employees may opt for the safer option of keeping quiet to prevent becoming the subject of workplace gossip. This can create a self-perpetuating cycle whereby the more anxiety employees experience, the less likely they are to act proactively, which can lead to feelings of detachment and disengagement. While this effect will be more prominent in individuals who are more sensitive to social stressors, there is a risk that, over time, a lack of initiative can erode both individual and team performance, further reinforcing a negative atmosphere.[12] While gossip can subtly undermine proactive behavior by sowing doubt and discouraging personal initiative, a more direct form of opposition, such as explicit rejection of others' ideas, can significantly heighten stress levels for those who are eager to drive change and innovation. As described in Chapter 10, it's not uncommon for peers to react negatively to the suggestions of others, particularly if they feel threatened by what's being proposed. This can have some nasty consequences, including peers deliberately sabotaging initiatives, bullying, and ostracism. When we feel socially excluded, it is not so different from the pain of physical injury; rejection has serious implications for an individual's psychological state.[13] It is, therefore, crucial for leaders to be attuned to the social dynamics within their team; gossip should be curtailed and conflicts addressed promptly. As mentioned in an earlier chapter, conflicts rarely disappear without intervention, and ignoring issues can only act to escalate tensions and stress across the team.

Energy-Smart Proactivity: Reducing the Risk of Exhaustion

Having established the energy demands associated with proactivity, let's now turn to some ideas for mitigating the risks of exhaustion and depletion associated with being proactive at work. I'll start by reflecting on factors relating to workload, control, and social support before introducing the *Group-Wise Proactivity Framework*, designed to help minimize the unintended consequences of proactive behavior at work.

i **Tolerable workloads** mean having enough time to complete the required tasks within work hours. When it comes to getting work done, we often think things take less time than they do, this bias is known as the *planning fallacy*.[14] This can be problematic for proactive employees who regularly seek out new opportunities for doing things differently, particularly if they misjudge the impact on their workload. Managers and their direct reports should regularly discuss priorities, deadlines, and capacity concerns, ensuring work-life boundaries are well managed. When workloads are high, it's not uncommon to slip into unhealthy habits such as back-to-back meetings and skipping breaks, which, over time, will become depletive. The value of taking short, regular breaks throughout the day should also be encouraged to help maintain energy levels; these can be as brief as five to ten minutes. To enable this, meeting organizers should be encouraged to schedule 50-minute meetings rather than an hour to allow breakpoints between meetings.

ii **Job control** is a critical factor for maintaining the energy to be proactive, as feeling disempowered can be draining. Excessive bureaucracy and red tape can contribute to a sense of low job control and a feeling that permission needs to be granted to be proactive. So, finding opportunities to eliminate unnecessary rules and regulations to enable employees to make decisions can be beneficial. As a reminder, a range of tools and techniques to help create more autonomous working environments are detailed in Chapter 7. The key to enhancing perceptions of job control is to treat employees as adults, by providing them with clear expectations, and necessary resources, encouraging active participation, and providing latitude to make informed decisions.

iii **A supportive environment** is essential for workplace well-being. Support can come from colleagues and supervisors but also from a perception that the organization cares. Building and maintaining good relations at work requires ongoing effort and attention and is the responsibility of everyone. That said, managers should encourage their team members to invest time in getting to know one another and create opportunities to openly discuss issues regularly. Having shared objectives with other members of the organization can also be useful in helping to break down silos, thereby creating more collective responsibility. Employees who do not feel valued or supported by their organization are more likely to experience negative emotions and subsequent exhaustion when taking personal initiative. Organizations need to demonstrate that their employees are more than just numbers on the payroll, this relies on a strong culture built on recognition and appreciation of individual and team contributions.

In uncovering the potential costs to our health associated with proactivity, my colleagues and I developed a framework to maximize motivation and alignment, and to reduce well-being risks, such as work overload and burnout. Our framework, which addresses considerations and actions at the individual, managerial, and organizational levels, is called *Group-Wise* Proactivity.[15] By considering actions at these distinct levels, it ensures a comprehensive and holistic approach, accounting for each group's role in contributing to overall outcomes. We provide prompts for employees, managers, and those responsible for setting organizational strategy to consider at the ideation stage (e.g. when proactivity is being envisioned), and the implementation stage (e.g. when proactivity is being enacted). Figure 12.1 provides an overview of the *Group-Wise Proactivity* framework, designed to encourage thoughtful reflection, and help everyone to pause, assess, and create a healthy environment for proactivity.

INDIVIDUAL-LEVEL

IDEATION STAGE

What is my 'reason to be' proactive?

Do I have the energy to be proactive in this instance?

Is proactivity needed in this instance? If so, in what form?

Does my proactivity consider others' interests? What is the impact on others?

IMPLEMENTATION STAGE

What is within my control and influence? What am I prepared to let go of?

What are my energizers and depleters? What will I do to regularly recharge?

How do I frame the change? How do I adapt as the situation changes?

How do I pursue proactivity with compassion and consider the impact on others?

MANAGER LEVEL

IDEATION STAGE

Are there high levels of psychological safety in the team?

What is the current capacity within the team? Is work fairly distributed

Are team-members clear on strategic priorities?

How does one team-members proactivity impact other team members?

IMPLEMENTATION STAGE

Have clear expectation been communicated, with support and regular feedforward?

Are team-members appropriately 'switching off' outside of work?

Are team members spending an appropriate amount time on what's important?

Is conflict management adequately addressed– are interpersonal issues resolved before they escalate?

ORGANIZATIONAL LEVEL

IDEATION STAGE

Do we have a culture that values experimentation and adaptation?

Is there a shared approach to leadership? Does everyone feel appropriately empowered?

Which forms of proactivity are valued by the organization? How is this communicated?

Does our culture convey high levels of perceived organizational support?

IMPLEMENTATION STAGE

How are we harnessing diversity & creativity? What platforms do we have to recognise & celebrate successes?

How is the importance of work life balance communicated?

Is there scope in the system to leverage proactivity e.g. innovative ideas

Do we provide adequate training for employees to develop interpersonal skills?

Figure 12.1 The Group-Wise Proactivity Framework.

Source: Created by the author.

Powering-Up: Practical Ideas for Sustaining Vitality

In addition to the strategies that serve to mitigate risks of exhaustion associated with proactivity, there is value in considering techniques we can use to keep our batteries charged. A good starting point is to understand what depletes your energy; for some individuals, that may be spending the day firefighting issues and responding to short-term demands or pro-longed hours on video calls, while for others, it may be working on tasks that are not tapping into their key strengths, which requires them to have to try a bit harder and that can be draining. Remember, what drains your batteries might not be the same for everyone else; one person's stressor can be another person's impetus. Drawing on the large body of work and well-being research, I share some insights that I often refer to when supporting my coaching clients navigating well-being concerns; I also draw on these personally to sustain my resilience and energy levels. Let's walk through some key considerations and reflect on actions that could be taken.

i Experiencing the feel-good factor
   As human beings, we need to be able to feel good, hopeful, and inspired by the things we do and the life we live. When we truly experience, we allow our positive emotions to take the lead in our lives. Positive feelings help us in many ways, including being better able to tackle negative emotions or experiences when they arise. To feel good, we first need to ensure that our basic hygiene needs are met, for example, sleeping well, moving regularly, and having a nutritious diet. When these needs are met, we can then open ourselves up to exploring what can further fuel our positive emotions, such as intellectual and creative pursuits, relationships, and fulfilling work. One micro-action considered to boost feelings of optimism is gratitude journalling, which is the daily practice of writing down or saying three things you are grateful for. I often do this with my daughter at the end of the day and find it an enriching experience.

ii Finding your WHY?
   Building a sense of purpose in life and using that purpose to contribute to the community is one of the core ways to find meaning in life. Finding meaning and purpose isn't just about your actions; it's about your beliefs, self-perception, and how well your life aligns with those beliefs. Living in alignment with your values is essential for finding meaning and purpose in life. As a reminder, there are a range of

tools in Chapter 11 to help you do this. From my personal experience, knowing that equality is a fundamental value of mine has motivated me to actively seek out opportunities to make a positive impact in the Diversity, Equality, and Inclusion space in my work. Contributing to causes you believe in can make your work more fulfilling, so look for opportunities that allow you to do this. Even if you haven't fully discovered your life's purpose, the journey of seeking it can bring great happiness and fulfillment.

iii *Finding pleasure in our work*

When we find pleasure in our work, it fuels motivation and commitment to getting things done. We are more likely to feel engaged when our work aligns with our values and interests; we feel valued for what we do and feel like we are learning and growing. Not every working day will be filled with tasks that we'd consider engaging, as with all jobs, there will be some aspects we consider less enjoyable. Strive for a balance between enjoyable and essential work activities. Find ways to make the less pleasant tasks more fulfilling while still making time for the things that bring you joy. I often use the "eat the frog" principle, which prioritizes getting the task you least enjoy done first so that it is out of the way, and then you can focus on the more pleasurable tasks. What works for me in terms of prioritization might be different for someone else, as we all have different circadian rhythms that influence our performance throughout the day – it's important to find your own preferences.

iv *Challenging ourselves*

When we challenge ourselves, we can get a huge sense of satisfaction from achieving our goals. But it is not necessarily about winning or being competitive; it's about progress. Whether that's developing our strengths and skills further, both practically and emotionally. I strongly believe that the journey is the destination – it's the process of achieving a goal that is often more fulfilling than the goal itself. A wise friend once reminded me that as you climb the mountain of your goals, don't forget to look back and appreciate the view of where you've come from. It's easy to get caught up in striving toward the summit and miss the incredible journey you've taken. I found this advice invaluable during my studies, at each important milestone, I gave myself opportunities to celebrate successes and savor the moment, this often involved rewarding myself with cake! Finding achievement in these ways again helps to encourage further positive emotions and adds to our continued sense of well-being.

v   The power of social connection
As highlighted throughout this Chapter, feeling connected and a sense of belonging are a crucial part of our sense of well-being. The authenticity and depth of interactions with friends, family, loved ones, and our wider social circle have a significant impact on how we feel. Positive, useful, and inspiring connections lead to more positive emotions, enabling us to feel valued and supported. I truly believe in the value of building and nurturing a strong and diverse network, which requires ongoing attention. I'm aware some people find networking transactional, uncomfortable, and inauthentic, but it doesn't need to be. Instead, reframe networking as an opportunity to connect with interesting people, learn new things, and expand your perspective. The key to good relationships is reciprocation, maintaining a healthy balance of give and take. If you approach networking with a mindset of giving, asking for help later feels less awkward. Playing an active role within those relationships – by offering support, listening, and helping in return, without expectations – will also lead to greater positive emotions.

This chapter concludes with a case study from Harris Creative, which brings to life many of the ideas in this chapter.

Box 12.1   Case Study

Harris Creative – Cultivating a Collaborative and Supportive Culture

Harris Creative is a leading specialist construction marketing agency, based in the north of England. The independently owned, boutique agency offers a full suite of marketing solutions to clients across the £100bn UK construction sector. The agency was founded over 35 years ago, with current owners and joint managing directors, Neil Craven and Kirsty Scott, taking the helm in 2020. The business has grown organically in recent years, with almost 20 colleagues. As the name suggests, creativity is the driving force at the heart of the company. Harris Creative's culture is built on shared values of trust, integrity, and support, with a welcoming working environment and team spirit that resonates with both colleagues and clients.

Harris is a forward-thinking organization committed to creating a high-performance culture built on employee engagement and proactivity. Recognizing the pivotal role of collaboration in driving organizational success, Harris has developed a comprehensive strategy that not only promotes initiative and accountability but also nurtures a strong sense of camaraderie and support within the team. This approach ensures that while employees are encouraged to take the lead, they always feel backed by a supportive environment.

Supportive Initiatives

To cultivate a culture of proactivity, Harris Creative has implemented several key initiatives designed to develop and empower employees, encourage collaboration, and recognize achievements. The company has adopted a decentralized decision-making model, granting teams significant autonomy over their projects and processes. This approach fosters a sense of ownership and accountability, encouraging employees to take initiative and find creative solutions to challenges. But to ensure cohesion and connection, the company holds bi-weekly full-team production meetings. In these meetings, each team is allocated five minutes to provide project updates, share insights gained from training and projects, discuss client knowledge, and propose innovative ideas. This platform enables a culture of knowledge sharing, where teams openly discuss their work, celebrate achievements, and learn from each other's experiences. Importantly, the meetings serve as an arena for idea generation and dissemination, ensuring that valuable concepts are shared across the organization, promoting transparency and a collective approach to problem-solving. The ethos at Harris Creative is "give it a go, try it, and if it doesn't work out, then learn from it and move on." It is not uncommon for them to pilot new ideas and experiment with new initiatives, taking forward those that work for them.

One such idea proposed by a colleague is their rotational "buddy system," which has been piloted and subsequently rolled out to the entire organization. This initiative pairs employees from different departments to promote cross-functional collaboration and knowledge sharing. By connecting individuals with diverse perspectives and experiences, the buddy system breaks down silos, enhances communication, and creates a more connected workforce. Buddies serve as mentors, confidants, and resources for each other. They offer support, share insights, problem-solve collaboratively, and help one another find optimal ways of working. The program encourages open dialogue and knowledge exchange, allowing employees to learn from each other's strengths and expertise. True to Harris Creative's form, there is no agenda and no set way to conduct a buddy meeting, the only ask is that everyone prioritizes the initiative by allocating 30 minutes every 2–3 weeks. To maximize the impact of the buddy system, it was launched at a full team production meeting, setting out the expectations and benefits. Regular check-ins and feedback mechanisms are in place to ensure the ongoing success of the initiative.

Alongside this, they place a strong emphasis on personal development and continuous learning. The joint Managing Directors collaborate closely with people managers to implement a coaching-focused approach in Personal and Career Development meetings. Employees are actively encouraged to bring forward their ideas for training and development and work together to explore innovative solutions for meeting these needs within the training budget constraints. By integrating personal growth into their collaborative culture, they ensure that every team member has the resources and support to thrive both professionally and personally. Additionally, Kirsty reinforces the importance of taking the time out to celebrate everyone's successes. Team members are regularly acknowledged and celebrated for their contributions and for demonstrating creative, client-focused behaviors through various channels, including the full team production meeting and a weekly email from Kirsty and Neil. This approach creates a positive and motivating work environment where employees feel valued and appreciated for their efforts.

Impact and Results

The implementation of these supportive initiatives has generated significant results. There has been a notable increase in collaboration across projects, silos have been broken down and there is a greater understanding of each other's demands. Colleagues are more readily displaying empathy for one another and as a result, there is a heightened level of engagement and a stronger sense of belonging. The focus on autonomy and development has empowered the workforce, leading to improved problem-solving and innovation, all of which serve to benefit Harris Creative's clients. This is echoed by the Chief Marketing Officer at one of their leading clients, who suggested: "The team-based energy from Harris has grown materially, which is clearly underpinned by strong cultural integrity. This is super important for us in terms of fit, as it means there is trust between both parties which enables Harris to take pressure away from us and deliver what they're brilliant at in spades."

Advice to Other Organizations

Kirsty and Neil challenge the traditional emphasis on productivity, arguing that a relentless focus on "churning out work" can often overshadow the true measure of success: which is great creative work. They encourage other organizations to do the same. When launching the buddy system, they were faced with some initial concerns from colleagues, suggesting they didn't have time, and the initiative was perceived as a "nice to do" rather than a "need to do." Kirsty encouraged employees to shift their mindset, prioritizing quality conversations and collaboration over task lists. She emphasizes the importance of demonstrating the trust they have in colleagues to focus on delivering outstanding results for their clients, by working together to share knowledge and problem-solving.

Harris Creative is reaping the benefits of its people-centered culture, which promotes an experimental, creative mindset. By investing in its employees, empowering them, and creating a collaborative and supportive environment, Harris Creative has cultivated a high-performing organization where individuals thrive and contribute to the company's overall success.

Key Takeaways

- Proactivity at work is double-edged, it can be a source of energy but can also deplete our energy.
- Being proactive can come at a cost to our health, being aware of the unintended consequences is vital to ensure mitigators are in place to minimize stress and burnout.
- Everyone has a role to play in engaging in *Group-Wise Proactivity*, a healthy team-oriented approach to problem-solving and goal achievement, where everyone contributes to the overall success of the organization.

- Prioritizing self-care is essential for maintaining high energy levels. By building positive emotions, purpose, pleasure, challenge, and connections, you can build resilience and energy reserves.

Reflective Questions

- Did anything in this Chapter challenge your previous assumptions?
- Have you personally experienced or observed the signs of stress and burnout related to proactivity?
- How could you apply the *Group-Wise Proactivity Framework* within your organization?

My Implementation Intentions

Jot down in this space any actions you will take in response to the reflective questions.

References

1. Demerouti, E., Bakker, A. B., Nachreiner, F., & Schaufeli, W. B. (2001). The job demands-resources model of burnout. *Journal of Applied Psychology*, 86(3), 499.
2. Bakker, A. B., & Demerouti, E. (2017). Job demands-resources theory: Taking stock and looking forward. *Journal of Occupational Health Psychology*, 22(3), 273.
3. Gray, J., & Dhensa-Khalon, R. (2024). Proactive motivation through the lens of older workers. *Occupational Psychology Outlook*, 3(2): 6–13.

4. Nielsen, J., Firth, B., & Crawford, E. (2023). For better and worse: How proactive personality alters the strain responses to challenge and hindrance stressors. *Organization Science*, 34(2), 589–612.

5. Csikszentmihalyi, M. (2000). The contribution of flow to positive psychology. In J. E. Gillham (Ed.), The science of optimism and hope: Research essays in honor of Martin E. P. Seligman (pp. 387–395). Templeton Foundation Press.

6. Giæver, F., & Løvseth, L. T. (2020). Exploring presenteeism among hospital physicians through the perspective of job crafting. *Qualitative Research in Organizations and Management: An International Journal*, 15(3), 296–314.

7. Wong, K., Chan, A. H., & Ngan, S. C. (2019). The effect of long working hours and overtime on occupational health: A meta-analysis of evidence from 1998 to 2018. *International Journal of Environmental Research and Public Health*, 16(12), 2102.

8. European Commission. (2017). Healthy workplaces: A model for action. Examples of good practices. European Commission. Retrieved from https://health.ec.europa.eu/system/files/2017-06/2017_workplace_en_0.pdf

9. Campbell, D. J. (2000). The proactive employee: Managing workplace initiative. *Academy of Management Perspectives*, 14(3), 52–66.

10. Cangiano, F., Parker, S. K., & Ouyang, K. (2021). Too proactive to switch off: When taking charge drains resources and impairs detachment. *Journal of Occupational Health Psychology*, 26(2), 142.

11. Heydarifard, Z., & Krasikova, D. V. (2023). Losing sleep over speaking up at work: A daily study of voice and insomnia. *Journal of Applied Psychology*, 108(9), 1559.

12. Gao, C., Shaheen, S., & Bari, M. W. (2024). Workplace gossip erodes proactive work behavior: Anxiety and neuroticism as underlying mechanisms. *BMC Psychology*, 12(1), 464.

13. Sturgeon, J. A., & Zautra, A. J. (2016). Social pain and physical pain: Shared paths to resilience. *Pain Management*, 6(1), 63–74.

14. Kahneman, D., Sibony, O., & Sunstein, C. R. (2021). *Noise: A flaw in human judgment*. Hachette UK.

15. Gray, J., Dhensa-Kahlon, R., Lewis, R., & McDowall, A. (2024). Unintended consequences: Why proactive behaviour at work can be harmful to individuals, teams, and organizations. A systematic review *(manuscript submitted for publication)*.

Part III

Diversity in Focus

Introduction – Through Different Lenses

This final section of the book invites you to consider how some of the insights from the PROACTIVE work design framework might vary across individual experiences. I have chosen to focus on under-recognized groups, age, and neurodivergence as key areas of inclusive practices related to proactivity. These specific dimensions are often overlooked in discussions around workplace proactivity despite their profound impact on individual experiences and outcomes. Historically under-recognized groups, such as racial and ethnic minorities or marginalized gender identities, frequently encounter systemic biases that reinforce barriers to inclusion. Similarly, stereotypes around age and generational differences can shape expectations and stifle proactive behavior. Whereas neurodivergent workers may encounter unique challenges in enacting proactivity, such as difficulties associated with executive functioning or managing unpleasant feelings. Without inclusive support systems in place, these struggles can hinder their ability to fully engage in proactive behaviors, even though they may possess the motivation and creativity to do so. These challenges are further compounded by intersecting identities, where individuals belonging to multiple marginalized groups (e.g., neurodivergent and racially marginalized) face overlapping and intensified barriers to engaging in proactive behavior. By focusing on these areas, these chapters seek to illuminate how these barriers perpetuate exclusion and can impact proactive engagement. Addressing these specific challenges through inclusive practices is essential to creating an environment that supports proactive behaviors from everyone.

Sadly, there is limited research within the proactivity domain that directly addresses critical debates around diversity. So, I have drawn on the insights and expertise of researchers whose work focuses on under-representation and inclusion. By connecting their work to the proactivity literature, I aim to raise some important questions. There are three recurring

DOI: 10.4324/9781003480693-16

concepts across the following chapters: stereotyping, social norms, and ideal worker, for which I will provide a brief explanation to set the scene.

i *Stereotyping – mental shortcuts that can lead us astray*

Stereotypes, those mental shortcuts we often unconsciously take, are oversimplified beliefs or generalizations about a group of people. They can be based on many factors, such as race, gender, age, religion, or occupation. While they can sometimes help make quick judgments, they often lead to inaccurate and harmful assumptions. Stereotypes are often rooted in our experiences, upbringing, and the cultural and societal influences around us. Media, education, and personal interactions can all contribute to the formation of stereotypes. For instance, if we repeatedly see negative portrayals of a particular group in movies or news, we may come to associate those negative attributes with the entire group. One reason we over-rely on stereotypes is that they can simplify complex information and help us make decisions more quickly. When we encounter a new person, it can be easier to categorize them based on a stereotype rather than taking the time to get to know them as an individual. Additionally, stereotypes can provide a sense of comfort and familiarity. They can help us feel like we understand the world around us and our place in it. However, the problem with stereotypes is that they can be harmful and discriminatory and when we act on stereotypes, we can perpetuate biases and prejudices. Take a moment to reflect on some of the stereotypes you observe at work and how this might impact an individual's experience of being proactive at work.

ii *Social norms – unwritten rules that guide our behavior*

Social norms are the unspoken rules that govern our behavior in society. They are the expectations, beliefs, and values that are shared by members of a particular group or community. These norms can be formal or informal, and they can vary significantly across different cultures and contexts. While social norms may not be explicitly stated, they are powerful forces that shape our actions and interactions. They can influence everything from how we dress and speak to how we behave in public and at work. For instance, in many cultures, there are social norms at work about being punctual and not having emotional outbursts. These norms can be both beneficial and harmful. On the one hand, social norms can promote cooperation, harmony, and a sense of belonging. They can help us to navigate social situations smoothly and avoid conflict. On the other hand, social norms can also be oppressive and discriminatory. They can limit individual freedom and expression, and they can perpetuate harmful stereotypes and biases. Despite progress in gender equality, the social norm that the women "take care" and the men "take charge" continues to perpetuate. This feeds into stereotypes about how women should act at work, whereby women are labelled "bossy" or "difficult" for being assertive, while their male counterparts are praised for their "strong leadership" or "confidence."

iii Ideal worker norm – a deep-rooted threat to equality
The ideal worker concept was originally derived to emphasize different gendered experiences at work. The ideal worker was conceptualized as someone who had strict boundaries between work and personal domains, who was highly productive, and who prioritized work needs first and foremost. The concept has its roots in the breadwinner-homemaker model that dates back to the Industrial Revolution and endured until the 1960s. It has since been extended to other contexts (e.g., ethnicity, sexuality, disability) to acknowledge the privilege associated with being unencumbered, recognizing that in society, the ability to progress without anything holding you back is simply not readily available to all. This notion of the ideal worker is outmoded and unrealistic, yet it continues to linger beneath the surface of society, subtly perpetuating workplace norms and inequalities.

Given the complexity of these interrelated topics and variation across individual experiences, these chapters are purely intended as conversation starters. While I introduce these important areas, it is just the tip of the iceberg when it comes to understanding lived experiences across diverse groups. I will endeavor to dispel myths and shed light on some overlooked issues, but I encourage you to delve deeper into the rich body of knowledge available. Let's not forget that each person is unique, and tailoring support to what works for them is often the most effective approach. As such, I will signpost to relevant organizations and resources where possible to guide that exploration. I do hope this will spark some proactive thinking and action on your part to support a diverse workforce.

Chapter 13

The Under-Recognized Voice

The Roots of Workplace Inequality

We have been grappling with pervasive work-related inequalities for thousands of years. Dating back to when societies first transitioned to agriculture and the advent of the oxen plow, which drove competitive advantage and quickly created divisions between the haves and the have-nots.[1] Fast forward to the Industrial Revolution, whereby the distribution of wealth and the division of labor relied on such inequalities.[2] While the Industrial Revolution is often celebrated for its advancements in production and economic growth, this progress was built, in part, on the exploitation of slave and coerced labor, which entrenched deep inequalities and further marginalized vulnerable populations.[3] Around the same time, Enlightenment thinkers brought glimmers of hope to the historically oppressed by acknowledging that humans are indeed all born equal by nature.[4] However, the emphasis on equality raised ethical dilemmas and uncomfortable questions. In response, scientists of the time quickly got to work, conducting experiments to justify inequalities between sexes and races, characterized by what we now know to be some very bizarre claims (e.g., women's supposed inferiority was linked to brain size).[5] Advancing to the 20th century, the world of work began to transform significantly from the 1960s, driven by social movements advocating for civil rights, gender equality, and labor rights. Over the past several decades, equality laws have significantly shaped workplaces worldwide. Key legislative milestones in different regions have advanced equal rights in employment, ensuring protections based on characteristics like gender, race, disability, sexual orientation, age, and religion.

Why the brief history lesson? I wanted to show how inequality at work is so deeply rooted. Despite progress made in recent decades, stereotypes and pseudoscientific theories of old get lodged in public consciousness and become entrenched. It's disheartening to see comments on social media suggesting that gender equality has been achieved or calling for society to

DOI: 10.4324/9781003480693-17

be less "woke," often dismissing the ongoing challenges faced by historically under-recognized groups. These perspectives downplay the realities that many continue to face, reinforcing the need for ongoing efforts to create a truly fair and inclusive workplace.

I use the term historically under-recognized to describe groups of people who have been socially marginalized in the past due to their demographics, these include, but are not limited to race, ethnicity, gender, sexuality, and ability. There's limited academic research on proactive experiences among historically under-recognized groups. I aim to bridge this gap by drawing on existing research that highlights the barriers these groups often face and connect the dots to proactivity. I spotlight the research of academic peers who I have worked and studied with, and whose work I deeply respect. Rob Sayers-Brown's body of research examines the state of play for underrepresented groups in leadership and focuses on female and LGBTQ+ leaders.[6] While Zoe Nwosu's exploration of the career experiences of ethnically minoritized individuals, emphasizes how the *ideal worker* concept creates barriers. Their studies provide invaluable perspectives that shape the discussion that follows. I must highlight that this is merely a snapshot of a far more intricate and complex subject. While the scope of this book limits a deep examination, I aim to offer a glimpse into a much broader discussion, which I would encourage you to explore independently. This chapter focuses on a few key aspects of the PROACTIVE work design model, namely, Psychological Safety, Organizational Fairness, Influence, and Energy, and the implications for historically under-recognized groups.

Psychological Safety

The Importance of Inclusive Leadership

In Chapter 4, I explained how vital psychological safety is in stimulating proactivity at work. I highlighted that if there is a sense of low psychological safety, we are more likely to remain silent and be more accepting of the status quo for fear of repercussions. I introduced the concept of inclusive leadership and emphasized the importance of recognizing and valuing employees for bringing diverse perspectives and being treated fairly in diverse contexts. Herein lies the problem: inclusivity in organizations and teams is not always guaranteed. Zoe identified a sub-theme in her research she called "pushed against the career wall," which highlighted how ethnic minorities were stereotyped and subjected to various difficulties at work. Her participants shared experiences of receiving minimal leadership support and being denied opportunities for development and growth. Instead, they were stereotyped as incompetent, and treated as less capable than their peers, despite having to work extra hard to prove themselves, which negatively impacted their self-esteem. Self-efficacy and self-esteem are critical factors fuelling proactive motivation. So, it's clear how a vicious cycle of low recognition, limited support, perceived lack of psychological safety, and diminished self-esteem can take hold, ultimately stifling proactivity. In other words, self-directedness becomes less attainable where bias is a fundamental barrier.

Stigma and Its Impact on Psychological Safety

Coming from a different angle, Rob's research illuminates the barriers experienced by LGBTQ+ leaders, such as homophobia, transphobia, and heteronormative structures that make it difficult for them to reconcile their LGBTQ+ identity with their leadership role. With such low levels of psychological safety, they often navigate complex personal and professional dynamics, which means they may conceal parts of their identity to avoid judgment from others. This pressure to conceal one's true identity creates challenges around authenticity, leaving individuals feeling disconnected from their genuine selves. Authenticity has been identified as a core component driving confident performance at work.[7] In this case, I propose a different but equally damaging cycle that may ensue. Low psychological safety can lead to individuals feeling pressured to conceal their true identity, this lack of authenticity erodes self-confidence, which, in turn, weakens the proactive motivation process. I'm a firm believer in fixing the environment, not the person. However, I recognize changing the environment can take time. Targeted development programs that allow participants to reflect on gender-specific challenges and empower them to embrace their authenticity may be beneficial in building confidence and self-efficacy. But that does not negate the need to create a psychologically safe environment where people genuinely believe they can bring their whole selves to work. The practical resources for building psychological safety provided in Chapter 2 are a useful starting point, but a simple search online for inclusive leadership resources will provide a range of readily available reflective exercises and activities.

Organizational Fairness

Employees care about being treated fairly because it signals status within the group. When we feel like our views are deemed important, we are more likely to feel like valued members of the team. In Chapter 6, I discussed how perceptions of unfairness can negatively influence our desire to be proactive at work. In this section, I want to emphasize that while

workplaces can be unfair, they are more unfair to some than others, specifically historically under-recognized groups. I want to reveal some hard
truths and stress the critical importance of addressing bias in organizations
head-on, to create the conditions for everyone to engage in proactivity.

The Illusion of Fairness

Many organizations have made great strides in embracing Diversity, Equity,
and Inclusion (DEI), with an emphasis on belonging and fairness, which
is a positive step forward. However, actions speak louder than words, if
the actions taken within the organization don't align with DEI commitments, there's a risk of creating an *illusion of fairness*. This can happen
when organizations put diversity policies in place, in doing so they send
a message to senior stakeholders (who tend to be historically privileged)
that underrepresented groups are respected and valued. However, the *illusion of fairness* hypothesis suggests that even if these policies exist, senior
or high-status stakeholders may mistakenly believe the company is treating underrepresented groups fairly, even if, in reality, those groups are still
facing unfair treatment. This illusion can make it harder for organizations
to recognize discrimination. As a result, they may be more likely to dis-
miss discrimination claims made by underrepresented groups and may even
feel more negatively toward those who raise such issues. For organizations
to truly address injustice, leaders need to ensure that people can recognize
when unfairness, like discrimination, occurs. People must be empowered
to speak up about it when they see it happening.[8] This brings to mind a
thought-provoking study by Sonia Kang and colleagues, which explores
the practice of "résumé whitening," whereby attempts are made to avoid
anticipated discrimination by concealing or downplaying racial cues in job
applications.[9] One of the most interesting insights highlighted by this study
is that diversity statements do not necessarily result in less discrimination
against unwhitened resumes. Ironically, there is a suggestion that minority
ethnic groups might be more disadvantaged when applying to pro-diversity
organizations. This paradox is explained by the fact that the lengths one will
go to conceal one's ethnicity will be dependent on how the employer presents themselves from a Diversity & Inclusion perspective, with less résumé
whitening where organizations convey valuing diversity. So, if organizations
aren't walking the talk, discriminatory practices are plausible despite their
impressive DEI statements. This certainly acts as a good reminder that mer-
itocracy doesn't reign as much as we might like to think it does.

Implications for the "Unideal" Worker

In Chapter 6, I highlighted that leaders and managers are likely to be perceived as fair if they are seen to distribute resources equitably, whether

that be access to personal development, training, flexible working arrangements, or career progression. Yet, I also alluded to the fact managers tend to demonstrate greater fairness toward individuals they feel more positively about and that they trust.[10] Findings from Zoe's study, under the sub-theme "the preferred other versus the ethnic other," reinforced some of the consequences of not fitting in for ethnic minority workers. Individuals not complying with the expectations of the "ideal worker" can be considered the "unideal worker." They are judged as inferior, incompetent, and undeserving, regardless of their capability, and without giving them a chance to defend themselves. Zoe's research participants shared stories of facing discrimination and prejudice; they felt like they were seen as the "lesser" ethnicity due to their differences. The concept of the ideal worker often reinforces biases like similarity bias or in-group favoritism, where people tend to prefer those who are similar to them and treat others differently. This dynamic inevitably leads to inequality, whereby certain groups gain more access to power and resources while leaving others excluded or disadvantaged. Proactive behavior is resource-dependent, when resources aren't fairly distributed, it's understandable that some people will find it easier to take initiative than others. Without equitable access to resources, not everyone has the same opportunity to step up and succeed.

Influence

The Authority Gap

This leads us to consider challenges associated with power and influence amongst historically under-recognized groups. *Social capital* at work refers to the network of relationships, connections, and social interactions that individuals build, which provides access to valuable resources. Employees with strong social capital are often better positioned to navigate the organization, gain visibility, and access opportunities that others may not, such as advocacy from influential colleagues. *Social habitus* encompasses the patterns of behavior, speech, appearance, and thought that define a social group. At work, *social habitus* influences how individuals communicate and navigate social interactions. Those with habitus align with the dominant norms of the organization, and those whose habitus differs may face challenges and be excluded from informal networks.[11] Both of these dynamics impact an individual's ability to influence, which is vital for successful proactive endeavors at work. In *The Authority Gap*, Mary Ann Sieghart suggests that barriers to women succeeding at work consist of many small disadvantages that accumulate and are often rooted in social norms and stereotypes that undermine social capital and social habitus. For example, despite some progress in gender equality, women still face significant barriers in building professional networks. One factor is the deeply ingrained societal norm where men are expected to "take charge" and women to "take care."[12] Women disproportionately shoulder unpaid care work at home, which limits time and energy to invest in nurturing professional relationships, which is critical for various forms of proactivity, particularly career proactivity.

Besides the practical barriers to building social capital associated with "men as agentic and women as communal" stereotypes, challenges around social habitus can also arise from pervasive social norms. The *status incongruity hypothesis* suggests that agentic women are judged negatively for demonstrating powerful behavior that is typically not associated with their gender.[13] This provides a Catch-22 situation, particularly in male-dominant workplaces, whereby women who conform to the communal stereotype misalign with the dominant norms and face exclusion from informal networks. Or they act counter-stereotypically and face criticism and negative judgment, which also limits access to networks and impacts credibility. While I have spotlighted the barriers encountered by women in gaining access to influential networks, similar obstacles are faced by other historically under-recognized groups who are tethered to stereotypes, which can constrain and impact their ability to grow networks.

Systemic improvements

It's important not to put the onus solely on individuals to build *political skill* and develop diverse networks to fuel proactive behavior at work. When, in reality, barriers to influence are often the result of complex systemic issues. There is no magic bullet to solving these issues, but improving diversity in leadership roles will undoubtedly make a difference. As we observe more historically overlooked individuals in leadership roles, we send a strong message to young people who relate to them, showing that they too have the potential to become future leaders. Workplace *Employee Network Groups*, also known as *Employee Resource Groups* or *Affinity Groups,* can also be effective in bringing together individuals with shared experiences and backgrounds to form collaborative networks. They can play a crucial role in empowering employees to share their voices, drive cultural awareness, and enhance professional development. Finally, there are several microactions that leaders and managers can take to address some of the obstacles faced. Including, encouraging everyone to resist making assumptions that rely on stereotypes, and calling out harmful microaggressions when they occur.

Energy

In this final section, I want to emphasize the well-being consequences of navigating systemic issues that favor privileged groups over historically under-recognized individuals. The constant struggle against these inequities can lead to significant emotional and mental strain. Masking is a concept that describes how individuals may consciously or unconsciously suppress aspects of their authentic identity at work to conform to workplace norms or avoid discrimination. The cognitive load that comes with masking and muting one's identity is well documented in research on social inequalities and was also a central theme in both Rob and Zoe's research. The demands associated with being someone you are not or not being accepted for who you are can be exhausting.

Several LGBTQ+ leaders who participated in Rob's research shared experiences of feeling obligated to be "out and open," which felt pressuring, while others felt they had to suppress who they were to fit in. This is often related to perceptions of *stereotype threat*, which occurs when individuals fear reinforcing a negative stereotype or assumptions about their identity.[14] For example, in environments where being LGBTQ+ is stigmatized, someone might feel pressure to pass as straight or cisgender to avoid reinforcing stereotypes. The pressure to avoid reinforcing negative stereotypes can create an extra layer of stress, which has been associated with the *minority stress model*.[15] This has been used to explain how stress builds up for people facing stigma and prejudice. This includes dealing with unfair treatment and discrimination, constantly worrying about being judged or mistreated, concealing one's identity, and absorbing negative societal attitudes about who they are. Being *energized-to* be proactive may be extra challenging for individuals experiencing *minority stress*. That said, for some of Rob's participants, their experiences were conveyed as triumph-over-adversity stories in that their struggles made them stronger as a result. By acknowledging the pain and challenges involved while highlighting the inner strength, determination, and growth, these experiences can offer support to others. This reinforces the importance of providing opportunities for connection and mutual support through employee network groups.

The notion of "unideal workers" having to work harder to prove themselves was highlighted in Zoe's research and has been identified in previous studies. There is a sense that the bar is set very high for minoritized ethnic workers and almost an acceptance that they will have to work twice as hard to succeed. This, coupled with a sense of not being accepted as you are, and a pressure to conform and to "tone down" to fit in exacerbates exhaustion. This, of course, has implications for motivation and energy levels and will no doubt impact one's ability to be proactive. Again, despite the barriers, some of Zoe's research participants spoke to the idea of having to make yourself seen and rising above the challenges. It's always inspiring to hear stories of people rising above hardship, but we should be careful not to let these stories make us complacent about the inequalities that create such struggles in the first place.

Powering Proactivity – Where Do We Go from Here?

A powerful way to enable individuals to succeed in systems that were not inherently designed for them is by helping them to identify and leverage their unique strengths. Strengths-based approaches, rooted in positive psychology, can be beneficial in developing self-compassion, resilience, and confidence. Encouraging individuals to connect to their values to build an awareness of the things they can do, are proud to do, and love to do can fuel the proactive motivation process. The practical exercises in Chapter 11 provide valuable insights for developing a deeper awareness of one's values and motivational drivers. Similarly, the feedforward coaching approach that is outlined in Chapter 15 can provide a useful framework for identifying and amplifying strengths.

From an organizational standpoint, creating intersectional development programs that address the complexity of navigating multiple intersecting identities can help participants reflect on how their unique perspectives shape their contributions in the workplace. The implementation of inclusive mentoring and sponsorship programs can also play a significant role in the career proactivity and development of historically under-recognized groups, by providing access to networks and opportunities that these individuals might otherwise be excluded from. Finally, organizations should take responsibility for tracking and reporting leadership diversity across various identities. Clear data on the representation of diverse leaders can drive accountability and highlight areas where interventions are needed to promote systemic changes within the organization.

I hope that these insights encourage a shift toward action, motivating efforts to tackle some of the barriers that exist in organizations. As this chapter has highlighted, historically under-recognized groups often find themselves navigating an uphill struggle, we must find ways to create more equitable experiences at work.

References

1. University of Oxford. (2019, September 18). Roots of inequality traced back to Neolithic ox-drawn plows. www.ox.ac.uk/news/2019-09-18-roots-inequal ity-traced-back-neolithic-ox-drawn-plows
2. Madsen, J., & Strulik, H. (2024). Inequality and the industrial revolution. *European Economic Review*, 164, 104724.
3. Sherwood, M. (2021, July 15). *Slavery, coerced labour, and the development of industrial capitalism in Britain*. History Workshop. www.historyworkshop. org.uk/slavery/slavery-coerced-labour-and-the-development-of-industrial-cap italism-in-britain/

4. Facing History & Ourselves. (2017). *Who Is Human?* Facing History & Ourselves. Retrieved from www.facinghistory.org/resource-library/who-human

5. Rippon, G. (2019). *The gendered brain: The new neuroscience that shatters the myth of the female brain.* Random House.

6. Sayers-Brown, R. M. (2024). *Leadership identity: Insights from women-only leadership development programmes and LGBTQ+ leaders* (Doctoral dissertation, Birkbeck College, University of London).

7. Kane, A., Lewis, R., & Yarker, J. (2021). The development of the Embodied, Dynamic and Inclusive (EDI) model of self-confidence; a conceptual model for use in executive coaching. *International Coaching Psychology Review,* 16(1), 6–21.

8. Kaiser, C. R., Major, B., Jurcevic, I., Dover, T. L., Brady, L. M., & Shapiro, J. R. (2013). Presumed fair: Ironic effects of organizational diversity structures. *Journal of Personality and Social Psychology,* 104(3), 504.

9. Kang, S. K., DeCelles, K. A., Tilcsik, A., & Jun, S. (2016). Whitened résumés: Race and self-presentation in the labor market. *Administrative Science Quarterly,* 61(3), 469–502.

10. Seppälä, T., Lipponen, J., Pirttilä-Backman, A. M., & Lipsanen, J. (2012). A trust-focused model of leaders' fairness enactment. *Journal of Personnel Psychology,* 11(1), 20–30.

11. Mayrhofer, W., Meyer, M., & Steyrer, J. (2007). Contextual issues in the study of careers. In H. P. Gunz & M. Peiperl (Eds.), *Handbook of career studies* (pp. 215–240). Sage Publications.

12. Sieghart, M. A. (2022). *The authority gap: Why women are still taken less seriously than men, and what we can do about it.* WW Norton & Company.

13. Rudman, L. A., Moss-Racusin, C. A., Phelan, J. E., & Nauts, S. (2012). Status incongruity and backlash effects: Defending the gender hierarchy motivates prejudice against female leaders. *Journal of Experimental Social Psychology,* 48(1), 165–179.

14. Spencer, S. J., Logel, C., & Davies, P. G. (2016). Stereotype threat. *Annual Review of Psychology,* 67(1), 415–437.

15. Meyer, I. H. (2003). Prejudice, social stress, and mental health in lesbian, gay, and bisexual populations: Conceptual issues and research evidence. *Psychological Bulletin,* 129(5), 674.

Chapter 14

Implications of an Aging Workforce

Super Age, Ageism, and Generational Myths

The current global population of 1.9 billion adults aged 50 and over is expected to grow by 70% to 3.2 billion by 2050.[1] The Super Age, marked by increases in life expectancy and decreases in birth rates, inevitably leads to a new era, in which older populations will outnumber younger ones. This dramatic shift in demographics has huge and far-reaching implications. Our working lives are inevitably increasing, so the necessity to rethink workforce development and workplace design is critical, and motivating and retaining older workers becomes even more pertinent. Yet despite these significant demographic shifts, ageism continues to be one of the most permissible "isms" at work. An alarming report from Totaljobs suggests that 59% of recruiters make age-based assumptions. More concerning is that almost half of the recruiters surveyed considered candidates over the age of 57 "too old."[2] It never ceases to amaze me how openly ageist remarks go unchallenged, particularly those that suggest older workers are change-averse technophobes – this is simply not true. The over-reliance and misuse of generational stereotypes are part of the problem, in that discrimination based on generational cohorts appears to go unchecked.[3] Interestingly, the idea of generational archetypes has its roots in Sociology; it was intended to explain social change, not to define the attitudes and behaviors of swathes of people at work based on the year they were born. Applying generational theory in the workplace fails to acknowledge personality differences, it assumes we all make sense of historical events universally and is highly divisive. Organizational research does not support claims of generational differences when it comes to attitudes and behaviors at work; there is as much difference within generational cohorts as there is between them. That's not to say there are no differences between early, mid, and late-careerists, of course, there are – but it's better explained by age-related changes and maturity.[4]

DOI: 10.4324/9781003480693-18

This chapter aims to dispel myths and highlight opportunities to motivate an age-diverse workforce to engage in proactivity at work. I will focus on older workers, although it's important to acknowledge that ageism at work also includes prejudice toward younger people, it is not within the scope of this book to unpack that. Before discussing the implications around the PROACTIVE work design model, I will first share some insights on adult development, which contribute to some of the considerations within this chapter. I will then turn to the focal topics of Role and Remit, Autonomy, and Values and Motivation from the PROACTIVE work design model. To conclude, drawing on my research among the over 50s, I offer some practical recommendations for engaging an aging workforce in proactivity.

Understanding Age-related Changes – Lifespan Development

There is consensus among researchers that individuals' needs and motives evolve and are influenced by adult development and experiences throughout one's life. Lifespan development assumes that age-related changes can be multidirectional, including growth, maintenance, and decline.[5] From a growth perspective, as we age, we develop crystalized intelligence or wisdom, which is knowledge that has been built through education and experience. But we simultaneously experience loss, in the form of declines in fluid intelligence, which is associated with processing new information and the efficacy of working memory. Several interesting theories explain changes we may observe in ourselves and others as part of the aging process, which can be applied at work:

i   *Selection, optimization, and compensation (SOC) theory*[6]
    Suggests that older adults are more likely to engage in activities at work that allow them to minimize loss and maximize gains. This compensatory behavior could lead to older workers choosing proactive goals that do not require a lot of personal resources, usually linked with fluid intelligence. For example, working on activities that draw on existing experience and knowledge.

ii *Socioemotional selectivity (SES) theory*[7]
    Suggests that as we get older, we are more likely to seek out and maintain relationships that make us happy. Intrinsically motivating activities at work also become more important, as extrinsic motivators become less relevant. According to this theory, older adults are more likely to avoid activities associated with negative emotions, while actively seeking out those that stimulate positive feelings.

iii Generativity theory[8]

Aging can also be associated with a desire to leave a positive impact and is believed to affect our work motivation and how we interact with colleagues. Generativity involves nurturing and guiding the next generation; in the workplace, this can be observed in showing care and concern for co-workers and prioritizing cooperation and collaboration over personal gain and self-promotion.

iv Self-concept

As we age, our sense of identity and self-concept become more stable, resulting in fewer worries about social judgment. This may make us less likely to conform and more willing to speak up and stand out.[9] That said, older adults are also more likely to protect their self-concept and, as such, avoid situations that may expose any shortcomings, for example, in training and development settings.[10]

These lifespan development theories provide a helpful lens for understanding differences we may observe in older workers and can help tailor approaches to support mid-to-late careerists to engage in proactivity at work. My research aligned with many of these theories. I observed a preference among my participants toward more intrinsically motivated proactive goals, which for some was associated with a desire for a greater purpose and wanting to give back. The idea of setting themselves up for success was also observed, several participants drew on their work and life experiences to guide their proactive goals, drawing on what had worked in the past. While others spoke of focusing on proactive goals that had a higher propensity for success, these were often described using the "open door" metaphor. Furthermore, past experiences of engaging in proactivity had contributed to life lessons and wisdom, which boosted confidence and self-efficacy. Most participants in my research suggested that their drive to be proactive had increased with age, which was attributed to feeling more confident. These findings certainly refute the stereotype that older workers are less proactive, they are perhaps just more discerning when it comes to proactive goal-setting!

Role and Remit

Considerations for Life-long Learning

In Chapter 5, I highlighted the importance of training and development as a component for developing *role breadth confidence*, which is needed to stimulate proactivity at work. It is, therefore, important to spotlight some of the specific challenges that older workers may encounter relating to learning and development at work. Firstly, several challenges arise when it comes to accessing learning opportunities at work, which are often rooted in employer attitudes and biases. It is not uncommon for organizations to front-load formal training in favor of younger workers. This is often justified as a better return on investment because younger workers are expected to stay with the organization longer, allowing the cost of the training to be amortized more effectively. However, given younger workers tend to have shorter tenures in organizations, this logic simply doesn't ring true.[11] Another significant barrier is age stereotyping, where older workers are considered resistant to change, harder to train, less adaptable, and less receptive to feedback. These assumptions, while not based on evidence, lead employers to perceive older workers as having lower potential for development and a poorer return on investment when it comes to training. Overall, while the economic and stereotyping arguments against training older workers persist, they are largely unfounded. Both research and practical experience demonstrate that older workers can offer significant value, particularly when given equal opportunities for learning and development. In fact, there is some evidence to suggest that we can become more conscientious with age, so there is an argument older learners will be more committed and dedicated to engaging in personal development if given the opportunity.

However, barriers to training are not always one-sided. There may be a reluctance among some older workers to engage in learning opportunities for several reasons. One major obstacle is the fear of exposure, which touches on the points raised around self-concept. This fear of vulnerability can lead to hesitancy in participating in training, especially in environments where older learners might feel compared unfavorably to their younger co-workers. I have witnessed older workers being ridiculed when technology fails them during online learning sessions. It's ironic that when older workers face technical challenges, the blame often falls on them, yet when younger workers encounter the same difficulties, the technology itself is seen as the problem. In addition, for some older workers, negative school experiences may compound this issue, creating an aversion to "classroom" learning in adulthood. This reluctance can result in disengagement toward work-related training and development programs, even when they are crucial for career growth or job performance.

Together, these factors can create significant barriers for organizations striving to build and maintain a well-rounded, skilled workforce across all age groups. In overcoming these hurdles, an emphasis on life-long learning and creating psychologically safe learning environments will be critical for companies to fully develop their workforce and build *role breadth confidence*.

Considerations for Job Design

In Chapter 5, I introduced the SMART framework and job design practices to boost *role breadth remit, which is* also critical for driving proactivity.[12] *Stimulation, Mastery, and Autonomy* factors within the SMART framework that are particularly relevant to discussions relating to age-related changes at work. For this section, I will focus on *Stimulation* and *Mastery*, given *Autonomy* is a dimension of the PROACTIVE work design model, and will be discussed separately. When incorporating lifespan considerations into making work stimulating, it may be more beneficial for experienced workers to engage in problem-solving activities that allow the application of accumulated knowledge rather than activities that draw on working memory. Here's a scenario to bring this idea to life:

> An experienced manager in a large manufacturing company is tasked with resolving a long-standing conflict between two team members. The tension has been growing for months, impacting team morale and productivity. Instead of seeking a novel solution, the manager draws on their years of experience and knowledge of similar situations. They recall past conflict-resolution strategies that they learned on a training course and have put into practice previously, which involved the use of structured mediation. They used proven communication techniques to get to the root cause of the conflict and find common ground, which assisted in resolving the situation. This approach is not based on quick thinking, but on applying the accumulated knowledge and best practices developed over their career.

When considering the *Mastery* dimension, the significance of leveraging strengths becomes particularly crucial. Leading experts in the field of aging at work highlight the importance of helping older employees stay engaged and productive by drawing on their experience and knowledge. Studies show that this can be achieved when older workers take initiative, speak up, and share their ideas. Engaging in proactive behavior makes their work feel more meaningful, which in turn increases job satisfaction and engagement.[13] Too often, older workers' perspectives are dismissed as irrelevant, with the assumption that things have moved on or are so radically different from the past. We must emphasize experience as a resource for growth and not a barrier by enriching problem-solving processes with diverse perspectives, young and old.

Another form of proactive behavior that has been linked with engagement in older workers is job crafting. This means enabling older workers to adapt their jobs to their interests, skills, abilities, and needs in light of age-related demands. In considering skills and abilities, task crafting might involve focusing on the activities that leverage one's strengths while employing compensatory behaviors to more challenging activities. Let me bring this idea to life: my friend, an esteemed professor in his late 60s, continues to relish speaking at overseas conferences. However, he is aware of the increasing demands these events place on him; he has started to invite a colleague to co-host keynote sessions. This job crafting strategy has helped him maintain his role as a thought leader while adjusting to the physical and cognitive demands that come with age. Working flexible hours is another form of job crafting. Perhaps unsurprisingly, in the study commissioned by TotalJobs, flexibility at work was highly valued for job candidates over 55, with almost two-thirds (64%) prioritizing flexible hours compared to just half (49%) of those aged 18–34.[14] This may be reflective of a greater need for work-life balance, health considerations or caring responsibilities, which are ever more demanding. In fact, it's estimated that 23% of adults living in the United States contend with challenges associated with caring for both their children and their elderly parents, a term that's been called the *Sandwich Generation*.[15] Job crafting can take many forms, offering older workers the chance to tailor their roles in ways that allow them to give their best. However, this requires organizations to move away from a one-size-fits-all approach and embrace more flexibility in how roles are shaped.

Autonomy

In Chapter 7, I reinforced the importance of providing employees with a sense of autonomy over how they perform their work to power proactivity. When employees' need for autonomy is met, they respond with greater positivity, and those working in roles with high levels of autonomy tend to have higher levels of loyalty and commitment. The need for autonomy is generally accepted as universal, but it's particularly important for older adults in building self-efficacy and minimizing emotional exhaustion.[16] The relationship between autonomy and self-efficacy can be explained by *socio-emotional selectivity theory*. Autonomy allows older workers to carry out tasks using established methods without any interference or micro-management, leading to more positive experiences and reinforcing their sense of competence. The connection between autonomy and reduced emotional depletion can be seen in having control over one's work scheduling, which is particularly valuable to the *sandwich generation,* who are balancing significant work and home responsibilities. This is relevant to proactive motivation, given self-efficacy promotes our *Can-do* and feeling vitalized fuels our *Energized-to* motivational states. What's interesting is that younger workers seem to value autonomy, but for different reasons, which are associated with different outcomes. For example, autonomy in decision-making provides younger workers an opportunity to show-case initiative and demonstrate sound decision-making to their peers and supervisors, which can positively impact job satisfaction and engagement. Research is fairly conclusive in supporting the notion that increasing job autonomy benefits both employees and organizations, but it's not clear-cut; autonomy means different things to different people and may not be equally effective for individuals with varying needs and demographic backgrounds. Therefore, managers need to engage in conversations with their employees to determine the form of autonomy that best aligns with each individual's unique needs and circumstances.

Values and Motivation

Changing Motives Rather Than Declining

In Chapter 11, I described the role of values and motives in driving proactive behaviors at work. In earlier chapters, I referred to intrinsic motivation; this is when employees are motivated to work because they genuinely enjoy what they are doing. In other words, they find their work interesting, challenging, and personally fulfilling. Studies exploring the relationship between age and motivation at work suggest motives change rather than decline with age. With a tendency for older workers to be more motivated by intrinsic than extrinsic rewards.[17] Similarly, research into proactive behavior at work suggests that older workers do not generally show lower levels of proactive behavior at work but instead may engage in proactivity differently from their younger colleagues.[18] This was reinforced in my study; I observed a desire to engage in proactive goals that would be more likely to create a sense of enjoyment. This aligns with *socio-emotional selectivity* theory in that older adults are more likely to seek out experiences that generate positive feelings. I also got a sense that older workers are more prudent in determining their proactive goals. Several participants shared their thought processes when deciding whether to take proactive action, often weighing up whether it was "worth it." If they doubted their efforts would lead to a positive change, they considered it not worth pursuing. Some participants' *reason-to* be proactive was associated with a desire for a greater purpose and wanting to give back, which links to *generativity* theory. Whereas for others, financial security became less of a priority compared to their younger years, which changed their approach to being proactive. I got a sense that these individuals were more willing to take interpersonal risks associated with speaking up or taking charge than they might have earlier in their careers. This change in attitude seemed to stem from a "what have I got to lose" mindset. These insights certainly challenge the notion that older workers are less proactive. I'd suggest they illustrate that older workers may be applying the principles of *wise proactivity*, which I introduced in Chapter 2, to an even greater extent. This reinforces the importance of not making assumptions; by truly understanding an individual's values and motivational drivers, leaders and managers are more able to more tailored approaches to support their team members.

Practical Recommendations

The organizations most likely to fare well in the Super Age are those that value all workers, create collaborative, generationally diverse teams, and nurture the creativity and innovation they can bring. Despite the widely held stereotypes, older workers are just as inclined to be proactive and initiate change as their younger peers, but it hinges on a supportive organizational climate and empowering leadership. I feel optimistic about the possibilities the Super Age can provide, but it does require addressing some of the shortcomings in current practices. Here are just a few ideas to spark your thinking as to what you could do differently in your organization.

Intergenerational Contact

When interviewing research participants for my study, I asked, "What advice would you give to an organization looking to help older workers feel more confident in being proactive at work?" The overwhelming response was that bringing together employees of all ages would be key. They emphasized the importance of collaboration across the generations to drive innovation and engagement, recognizing that there is much we can learn from one another. Promoting intergenerational teamwork offers multiple benefits. One of the most effective ways to challenge stereotypical assumptions is to provide opportunities to experience counter-stereotypes. When people from different backgrounds and perspectives collaborate, it breaks down pre-conceived ideas, leading to stronger, more inclusive teams. I've experienced this firsthand, serving as a Non-Executive Director on a board with members ranging in age from their 40s to their 80s has been incredibly insightful. The diversity of experiences and perspectives that come with such a wide age range adds immense value to our discussions and decision-making. Intergenerational contact could also take the form of peer buddying programs to encourage skills exchange between early career and twilight career workers. I must stress that when encouraging inter-generational contact, there needs to be high levels of trust and psychological safety, to create positive interactions and experiences among the group. Without it, there is a risk that negative stereotypes will be further reinforced.

Rethinking Rewards

There is often an assumption in organizations that pay, and bonuses are universally motivating, but this is overly simplistic when applying it to proactivity among older workers. Findings from my study highlighted that for many older workers, their motivation to be proactive was not related to financial reward, but driven by intrinsic motives, e.g. doing something they cared about. Being proactive typically means taking an initiative of your own volition, which puts into question the idea of motivating proactivity through financial rewards. That said, this does not negate the need to recognize the contributions of proactive employees, who are making a difference to the organization. Alternative approaches to motivating proactivity may include providing flexible working arrangements, job enrichment (e.g., development opportunities), and enabling job crafting opportunities.

Calling Out Microaggressions

At the beginning of this chapter, I suggested ageism is the most permissible "ism" at work. I believe it's time to call it out. Tackling ageist microaggressions within the workplace is critical. My study defies the stereotype that older workers are less proactive, to the contrary, it suggests that certain proactive behaviors are dialled up with age. Proactive behavior is more likely to flourish in a psychologically safe, age-inclusive environment, where older people are valued for their experience rather than being judged as being resistant to change. Calling out discrimination is not always easy, but if nothing is said, nothing will change. In my experience, most people don't realize their comments are ageist, and they are certainly not coming from a place of malice, that's just how stereotypes work. I often respond in a way that aims to educate rather than judge, whether that be by sharing some of the lifespan theory insights or bringing in personal experiences that don't support the ageist remark. For example, if someone says, "I'm too old to learn," I'd reply with, "Age should be no barrier to learning, plenty of my students are over the age of 40." Leaders and managers must also role model age-inclusive behaviors. Creating spaces where everyone feels welcome to share ideas and encouraging a culture of curiosity, where employees can learn from one another, regardless of age. This also means being mindful of the language they use. For example, avoiding generational labels and phrases like "digital native" for younger employees or "Luddites" for older workers, which are inaccurate and unhelpful. Everyone has a responsibility to challenge misconceptions, but the tone from the top is vitally important.

One thing we all have in common is that we will age, as our working lives continue to lengthen, we must create workplaces where people of all ages feel valued and included. Let's be proactive in addressing age inclusivity, ensuring that everyone can contribute and thrive, no matter their stage in life.

References

1. AARP International. (n.d.). *Older women*. AARP International. www.aarpinternational.org/resources/older-women-resources
2. Totaljobs. (2024). *The age advantage: Overcoming age bias to hire experienced talent*. www.totaljobs.com/recruiters/file/general/TJ-The-Age-Advantage-Report.pdf
3. Gendron, T., Marrs, S., Inker, J., & Palmarini, N. (2024). Generational bias: Another form of ageism. *The International Journal of Aging and Human Development*, 98(3), 284–299.
4. Rudolph, C. W., Rauvola, R. S., Costanza, D. P., & Zacher, H. (2021). Generations and generational differences: Debunking myths in organizational science and practice and paving new paths forward. *Journal of Business and Psychology*, 36, 945–967.
5. Baltes, P. B. (1987). Theoretical propositions of life-span developmental psychology: On the dynamics between growth and decline. *Developmental Psychology*, 23(5), 611.
6. Baltes, P. B., & Baltes, M. M. (1990). Psychological perspectives on successful aging: The model of selective optimization with compensation. *Successful Aging: Perspectives from the Behavioral Sciences*, 1(1), 1–34.
7. Carstensen, L. L. (1995). Evidence for a life-span theory of socioemotional selectivity. *Current Directions in Psychological Science*, 4(5), 151–156.
8. Erikson, E. H. (1963). *Childhood and society*. WW Norton & Company.
9. Pasupathi, M. (1999). Age differences in response to conformity pressure for emotional and nonemotional material. *Psychology and Aging*, 14(1), 170.
10. Kanfer, R., & Ackerman, P. L. (2004). Aging, adult development, and work motivation. *Academy of Management Review*, 29(3), 440–458.
11. Canduela, J., Dutton, M., Johnson, S., Lindsay, C., McQuaid, R. W., & Raeside, R. (2012). Ageing, skills and participation in work-related training in Britain: Assessing the position of older workers. *Work, Employment and Society*, 26(1), 42–60.
12. Parker, S. K., & Knight, C. (2024). The SMART model of work design: A higher order structure to help see the wood from the trees. *Human Resource Management*, 63(2), 265–291.

13. Bakker, A. B., & Hakanen, J. J. (2019). Engaging aging: A model of proactive work behavior and engagement with increasing age. In T. Taris, M. Peeters, & H. De Witte (Eds.), *The fun and frustration of modern working life: Contributions from an occupational health psychology perspective* (pp. 153–163). Pelckmans Pro.
14. Totaljobs. (2024). *The age advantage: Overcoming age bias to hire experienced talent.* www.totaljobs.com/recruiters/file/general/TJ-The-Age-Advantage-Report.pdf
15. Mental Health America. (2024). *Caregiving and the sandwich generation.* Mental Health America. https://mhanational.org/caregiving-and-sandwich-generation
16. Horowitz, J. M. (2022, April 8). More than half of Americans in their 40s are 'sandwiched' between an aging parent and their own children. Pew Research Center. www.pewresearch.org/short-reads/2022/04/08/more-than-half-of-americans-in-their-40s-are-sandwiched-between-an-aging-parent-and-their-own-children/
17. Inceoglu, I., Segers, J., & Bartram, D. (2012). Age-related differences in work motivation. *Journal of Occupational and Organizational Psychology, 85*(2), 300–329.
18. Zacher, H., & Kooij, D. T. (2016). Aging and proactivity. *In Proactivity at work* (pp. 276–312). Routledge.

Chapter 15

The Neurodivergent Lens

Neurodiversity – Challenging Conventional Approaches

The term neurodiversity has been around since the late 1990s. It came out of autism advocacy movements and is now applied and understood more broadly to reflect how our brains process information differently, recognizing that we all experience and interact with the world around us in different ways.[1] Neurodivergent, neurominority, and neurodistinct are often used to describe individuals who deviate from neurotypical norms, presenting with conditions such as ADHD, autism, dyslexia, dyscalculia, dyspraxia, and Tourette's. Modern research tells us that there are high levels of co-occurrence, and it is estimated that between 15 and 20% of the global population is neurodivergent.[2] Neurodiversity is increasingly recognized at work as a feature of diversity that needs to be supported. Neurodivergent people can also be considered disabled and thus have the right to accommodations, so different ways of working. Despite the fact accommodations can be beneficial to the whole workforce, much organizational practice stereotypes neurodivergent people and has ableist stereotypes about what good work looks like.

This topic is close to my heart, as neurodivergence is prevalent among my family and friends, and expanding my understanding has helped me become more empathetic to their needs and my own. When developing the PROACTIVE work design model, I recognized that some of the dimensions of the model might pose more challenges for some individuals than others. The connection between proactivity and neurodiversity can be considered from two perspectives. Firstly, how neurodivergent individuals observe and interpret proactivity in others. Secondly, how they experience and engage in proactivity themselves. This chapter aims to bring your attention to some aspects of the model from both perspectives, to highlight how proactivity may be more nuanced for neurodivergent employees. While this chapter does not provide an exhaustive exploration, I will focus on a few

DOI: 10.4324/9781003480693-19

key aspects of the model and signpost to further resources where necessary. The focal topics relate to Organizational Fairness, Communication, Time, and Energy. To conclude, I offer an evidence-based coaching resource that may prove useful in addressing some of the areas discussed throughout this chapter.

Organizational Fairness

Let's start with fairness at work. In Chapter 6, I provided detailed insights into the importance of Organizational Fairness to create a positive working environment for proactivity, yet individuals experience fairness differently. Autistic and ADHD individuals, in particular, tend to have a strong sense of justice, which can impact how they respond to perceived unfairness. They may, therefore, be more willing to fight for fairness and have lower perceptions of the associated interpersonal risks.[3] In other words, they may be more likely to proactively speak up, without considering the potential consequences. People motivated by fairness often spring into action when they perceive injustice, yet emotions can take over which makes it hard to regulate one's reactions and influence others effectively. During my career, I have found myself in situations that have truly tested my personal "fairness barometer" and, in some situations, have led me to act impulsively and emotionally, which I have gone on to regret. In Chapter 6, I provided practical recommendations for instilling a sense of fairness across various aspects of the employee experience. From a neuroinclusion perspective, managers need to recognize that neurodivergent employees may perceive situations differently and may speak up about issues more readily. Managers should actively listen to their concerns without disregarding or trivializing them, dismissing them will only add to further frustration and demotivation while undermining trust. If emotions become heightened, it's important to provide a nonjudgmental space to validate the individual's feelings without making assumptions and jumping to conclusions. By responding with empathy, understanding, and support, managers can help neurodivergent employees feel valued and respected. Alongside fairness considerations, this also highlights the importance of creating a psychologically safe environment for proactivity, which is discussed in Chapter 4.

Communication and Influence

The Potential for Misunderstanding and Misattribution

In Chapter 8, I highlighted the importance of good communication. Reiterating that when communication is poor or breaks down, the cohesiveness and effectiveness of the organization will suffer. I highlighted issues around interpreting proactive individuals' behavior, which can become more nuanced when considering neurodivergent experiences. In this section, I focus on rejection sensitivity and hostile attribution, which can impact how employees engage in workplace interactions and their experiences of proactivity at work. Before doing so, it is important to introduce the concept of *double empathy*,[4] which challenges the common misconception that neurodivergent individuals lack empathy, particularly those identifying as autistic. Traditionally, autism has been viewed through a lens of deficiency, often focused on reduced social interactions or an inability to understand others' perspectives. Milton's theory of *double empathy* presents an alternative perspective, arguing that the disconnect between autistic and non-autistic individuals is not a one-sided failure of empathy but a mutual misunderstanding on both sides. It's not that autistic people lack empathy, rather, they experience and express emotions differently than non-autistic individuals. As such, both groups struggle to fully empathize with each other because their ways of perceiving the world and communicating are fundamentally different. Understanding the double empathy problem encourages us to approach communication challenges with greater openness. It reminds us that difficulties in understanding can stem from both sides. With this in mind, we can better navigate some of the specific communication challenges that I will now outline.

Rejection sensitivity dysphoria (RSD) *Rejection sensitivity dysphoria (RSD)* refers to emotional sensitivity due to a perception of being criticized, dismissed, or rejected by others. It is a strong, but transient, reaction that is not under the individual's control. RSD is a common but underresearched symptom of ADHD and other neurodivergent conditions.[5] Individuals experiencing RSD may respond to perceived criticism or rejection with typical fight or flight responses, so having an emotional outburst, or withdrawing from social situations. Bringing this back to proactivity at work, imagine a colleague who experiences RSD proposing what they perceive as a great idea to improve the organization, but other colleagues react negatively by dismissing or criticizing the idea. There is a distinct possibility it will leave the proactive person feeling frustrated and dejected, which has potential implications for relationships at work and engagement in being proactive in the future. Another situation that might arise is when a neurodivergent colleague shares a stream of consciousness, offering an array of proactive, yet unfiltered ideas. While this can be valuable for creativity and innovation, it may also present challenges for managers and co-workers who need to manage the conversation thoughtfully, to minimize the risk of perceived rejection. The practical resources offered in Chapter 8 related to connecting with emotions and perspective-taking might be particularly helpful for individuals navigating challenges associated with RSD. As a manager, showing support and offering reassurance to a colleague experiencing such extreme emotional responses, listening without judgment, and acknowledging their valid emotions, will go a long way.

Hostile attribution

I spoke at length in Chapter 8 about the consequences of proactivity associated with misattribution of intent. I introduced the concept of *hostile attribution*, a cognitive tendency where individuals interpret social cues as intentionally hostile. Past negative social experiences (e.g., at school) can influence how neurodivergent individuals perceive and interpret social situations. Holding onto unpleasant memories of negative interactions with others may lead to a heightened sense of vigilance and being more attuned to potential threats.[6] For example, suppose a proactive co-worker proposes a new process improvement idea. One interpretation is to positively acknowledge the benefits of the idea and provide support for it. Whereas, through a *hostile attribution* lens, it may be interpreted as a way to control or dictate the work of others and may be associated with past experiences of feeling powerless or undermined. In turn, this can lead to feelings of resentment, which can disrupt team dynamics. Managers should be mindful of how past experiences can influence their team members' current behavior and their responses to proactivity in others. Again, this requires a focus on creating a supportive environment that values open two-way communication. From a team perspective, it's important to facilitate open team conversations. For example, after meetings or discussions, take time to reflect as a team on *"what did we hear versus what was actually said?"* Encourage team members to clarify assumptions and interpretations, ensuring everyone is on the same page.

The Problem with Small Talk and Social Cues

Small talk is a common social norm in many cultures. It serves to build rapport and establish connections, which helps build networks and strong alliances. Similarly, we are often judged by others based on our use of non-verbal communication cues, such as eye contact and tone of voice. As described in Chapter 10, influencing others to support our proactive endeavors often requires rapport-building tactics using interpersonal skills that are based on neuronormative assumptions. Many neurodivergents take a more literal approach to work. When the job description outlines certain responsibilities, it can feel confusing or frustrating to be asked to do something that seems unrelated, like making small talk such as discussing weekend plans. This, again, reinforces the double-empathy problem. It's important to note that while social norms exist around communication styles, we should resist judging others based on neurotypical, ableist standards.

Many of the interventions to develop political skill and situational judgment effectiveness, as described in Chapter 10, remain relevant and useful across different neurotypes but may need to be tailored and adapted to individual needs. We must remain alert to different styles of communication and be mindful of the double empathy issue. Neurodivergent individuals often experience distress that stems from a heightened awareness of potential challenges in social interactions, such as uncertainty about what to say, fear of being misunderstood, or concerns about negative evaluations – whether being perceived as awkward or incompetent and resulting in social consequences, like not being taken seriously.[7] Coaching and mentoring can be powerful in supporting neurodivergent employees in navigating social demands at work. Still, I cannot overstate the importance of utilizing qualified coaches and mentors who have a good understanding of neurodiversity and neurodivergence.

Time

Time is a slippery concept among neurodivergents, this in part can be explained by differences in *prospective memory,* that is the ability to remember both future tasks and maintain an awareness of the present moment.[8] This awareness also helps us track where we are in time. The underlying issue often lies in *working memory*, the cognitive function responsible for holding and processing information in real time. Differences in working memory make it harder to keep track of tasks, deadlines, or the sequence of steps involved in completing complex activities. One common trait that complicates prospective memory is *hyperfocus*.[9] This is when you become deeply immersed in tasks or topics of interest, sometimes for hours, to the point where you lose all sense of time. While this intense concentration can lead to high levels of productivity in specific areas, it can also impact other tasks or deadlines which simply get forgotten. This phenomenon is often referred to as *time blindness*. Because working memory plays a key role in processing and sequencing information, neurominorities often find it hard to stay on top of deadlines, appointments, or future tasks. The challenge of remembering what needs to be done next while also keeping track of where they are in time creates a significant hurdle in managing both daily life and professional responsibilities. Without a clear sense of time, prioritizing tasks becomes difficult, and transitions between activities can feel disorienting. Neurodivergent employees may get stuck in one task due to hyperfocus or, conversely, find it hard to pull themselves away to begin the next task. This can lead to feelings of falling behind or being overwhelmed by unfinished work, further exacerbating issues with time management and task completion. In Chapter 9, I outlined several tactics for mitigating *Time Traps,* which have broad applicability. In addition, it's essential to accept that time management challenges can be particularly difficult among neurodivergents. Rather than criticizing them for being disorganized, it's important to offer support in developing personalized strategies for managing time, tasks and transitions more effectively. Again, coaching and mentoring can be powerful developmental tools to offer by way of support in this area. By doing a simple search online, resources and blogs are abundant with ideas for taking better control of time. I recommend ADDitudemag.com as a useful starting point.

Energy

In Chapter 2, I emphasized the state of being *energized-to* as a critical feature of the proactive motivation process. In Chapter 12, I described how being proactive at work can be vitalizing and depleting, highlighting the importance of restoring energy to sustain proactivity. In this section, I want to emphasize how this can pose an additional challenge for neurominorities. Exhaustion is a common concern among the neurodivergent community. This is explained by the fact that in addition to managing daily demands, they may also experience challenges relating to sensory overwhelm and a pressure to conform and fit in, which often means masking out traits to adhere to the expectations of others. This can lead to what is called "autistic burnout" (although it is not limited to autism), which is described as long-term exhaustion, reduced tolerance to stimulus, and loss of function.[10]

Sensory Sensitivity and Overwhelm

Sensory processing differences are common in neurodivergent people. The sensory systems that can be challenged run across all of our senses, from sights, sounds, and smells to textures, but also include bodily sensations. This can be experienced through *hypersensitivity* (over-responsiveness) and *hyposensitivity* (under-responsiveness) to a variety of stimuli.[11] For those experiencing hypersensitivity, challenges in work settings, such as enduring bright lights, strong smells, and background noise, can be physically and emotionally exhausting. This can result in sensory avoidance, e.g., trying to get away from the stimulus by tuning out, which can have implications on how the individual is perceived by others. Whereas people who are hyposensitive may engage in sensory seeking to get more sensory input from their environment, for example, by making loud noises or moving around. However, such sensory-seeking activities are often frowned upon at work, so this can lead to hyposensitive people suppressing the activities that can help them self-regulate, leading to sensory overload and exhaustion. By understanding and accommodating sensory sensitivities, we can help neurodivergent employees conserve the energy needed to actively engage and contribute proactively at work.

Navigating the Complex World of Work

Neurodivergent *masking* is the practice of suppressing or concealing aspects of one's neurodivergent traits; to appear neurotypical in order to fit in.[12] Masking at work typically involves mimicking or mirroring the behaviors of neurotypical peers or colleagues and may include behaviors like forcing eye contact even though it feels uncomfortable or developing social scripts to get by in social situations. Masking is frequently discussed within neurodivergent communities, highlighting the anxiety and exhaustion that come from navigating the complexities of our social world. Sadly, the social obligation to mask and the anxiety associated with fitting in is heightened among historically underrepresented groups, namely female, nonbinary, and neurodivergents of color.[13] This, again, reinforces the additional energy demands for neurodivergent employees, which potentially makes being proactive at work even more challenging, given the energy that is required.

Besides depletion linked to masking, certain ways of working can also impact energy levels. For example, while hybrid and remote work can be beneficial in many ways to well-being, it can blur the boundaries of work and home. This can be problematic for neurodivergent employees who may struggle to manage transitions and know when to stop working. A recent study showed how deleterious effects of remote working were exacerbated for ADHDers, explained by time blindness.[14] Neurodiversity comes with strengths and challenges, hyperfocus is often described as a neurodivergent strength, as it allows you to be super productive and focused. But it is double-edged, while this flow-like state can be beneficial for well-being and happiness, it can consume cognitive energy, leaving you feeling depleted. What's more, it is not uncommon for hyper-focusers to lose track of time to the point of forgetting to eat or working late into the night, which is, of course not a healthy pattern of behavior and has consequences for well-being.

Knowing that energy depletion poses a genuine risk to neurodivergent employees is critical. Managers should be keenly aware of the heightened risks of exhaustion and burnout, which impact individual well-being, team dynamics, and performance. It's critical for managers to actively safeguard against this by promoting an environment where rest and recuperation are openly discussed and prioritized. Open conversations about boundaries and expectations around working and not working are essential, along with role modeling a healthy work–life balance. It's also vital that managers acknowledge how energy-consuming being proactive is, and their crucial role in providing adequate resources and finding ways to remove internal barriers and frustrations, which can be depleting.

Practical Resources

Feedforward Coaching

In addition to the practical resources provided in each chapter, the *Feedforward* approach to coaching conversations is a powerful tool for working with neurodivergent employees.[15] Defined as a structured discussion where individuals are encouraged to reflect on their strengths by sharing a specific positive experience and examining the factors that contributed to its success, before moving on to goal setting and action planning.[16] A key benefit of feedforward coaching is its ability to emphasize a positive, forward-looking approach to development by attending to individual strengths and potential, rather than their weaknesses or past mistakes. This approach is especially beneficial for neurominorities, whose unique abilities are often overlooked or misunderstood. Feedforward conversations tend to feel more authentic and affirming, creating a safe space where neurodivergent employees can explore their capabilities and areas for growth without feeling a sense of judgment. By helping identify, articulate, and contextualize their strengths, it becomes easier to encourage perspective-taking and create accountability. It also provides an opportunity to explore the potential "dark sides" of strengths, that is where they may be overplayed and not serve them well. For example, an employee who excels at quickly understanding complex issues might become frustrated with colleagues who need more time to process information, or they might rush through tasks and overlook important details in the eagerness to find a solution. Knowing that strengths can be overplayed can help individuals strike a balance and create strategies to manage how their strengths are expressed in various contexts. Here are some top tips to maximize feedforward conversations:

i **Provide a Light Structure:** While some neurodivergent employees may find highly structured formats overwhelming, a light structure can guide the conversation without making it feel restrictive. Balance flexibility with a clear direction to ensure the conversation remains focused and productive.

ii **Create the Right Environment:** Start by focusing on past successes and strengths, rather than problems or deficits. This positive framing sets a tone of trust and encouragement, which is critical when coaching neurodivergent employees who may have experienced more negative feedback in school and work settings.

iii **Emphasize Strengths in Context:** Encourage reflection on situations where they've successfully utilized their strengths. This contextualization not only reinforces the relevance of their capabilities but also helps them understand how their unique attributes may shape their experiences at work.

iv **Acknowledge Over-played Strengths:** Acknowledge and accept the potential downsides of their strengths when overplayed. For example, an ADHDer may have an abundance of energy and enthusiasm for proactive endeavors but risk burnout if they do not sufficiently recuperate. Discuss strategies for effectively managing these overplayed strengths.

v **Encourage Reflection:** Encourage engagement in developing greater self-awareness, which in turn helps gain clarity and insight into how best to apply these abilities at work.

Top Picks: Books and Websites

In addition to the resources signposted within this chapter, here is a short collection of personal recommendations designed to help you build knowledge in supporting neurodivergent colleagues. The more we know, the better we can understand and provide meaningful support. While these are just a few suggestions, I encourage you to explore further, there is a wealth of information out there.

Birkbeck University of London's Centre for Neurodiversity at Work undertakes research to enhance workplace practices for neurodiverse employees. Visit their website to access cutting-edge research outputs and resources:

www.bbk.ac.uk/research/centres/neurodiversity-at-work

City & Guilds is a UK-based charitable organization offering vocational qualifications and training to enhance workplace skills. They publish an annual Neurodiversity Index report to provide insights into making workplaces more neuroinclusive: https://cityandguildsfoundation.org/what-we-offer/campaigning/neurodiversity-index/#report

Genius Within is a UK-based Community Interest Company specializing in supporting neurodivergent adults and employers. They offer a range of services, research, and helpful resources: https://geniuswithin.org/

Neurodiversity in the Workplace – Interests, Issues, and Opportunities, edited by Susanne M. Bruyère, Adrienne Colella. This book provides a perspective on the role and responsibility of employers, as well as those working to enhance workplace practices, in addressing barriers to neuroinclusion.

Neurodiversity Coaching – A Psychological Approach to Supporting Neurodivergent Talent and Career Perspective, by Nancy Doyle and Almuth McDowall. This book provides a comprehensive and insightful overview of key concepts and considerations for coaching neurodivergent talent.

Neurodiversity in Business – The Neurodiversity Charity is a UK industry group for organizations to share industry good practices on recruitment, retention, and empowering neurodiverse workforces. Visit their website to access research and resources: https://neurodiversityinbusiness.org/

References

1. Walker, N. (2014). *Neurodiversity: Some basic terms & definitions.* Neuroqueer. https://neuroqueer.com/neurodiversity-terms-and-definitions/
2. Doyle, N. (2020). Neurodiversity at work: A biopsychosocial model and the impact on working adults. *British Medical Bulletin, 135*(1), 108.
3. Schäfer, T., & Kraneburg, T. (2015). The kind nature behind the unsocial semblance: ADHD and justice sensitivity – A pilot study. *Journal of Attention Disorders, 19*(8), 715–727.
4. Milton, D. E. M. (2012). On the ontological status of autism: The 'double empathy problem'. *Disability & Society, 27*(6), 883–887.
5. Dodson, W. (2024). *New insights into rejection sensitive dysphoria.* ADDitude.
6. Russo, P. N. M., McKown, C., Johnson, J. K., Allen, A. W., Evans, S. B., & Fogg, L. (2015). Social-emotional correlates of early stage social information processing skills in children with and without autism spectrum disorder. *Autism Research, 8*(5), 486–496
7. Wilson, A. C., & Gullon-Scott, F. (2024). 'It's not always textbook social anxiety': A survey-based study investigating the nature of social anxiety and experiences of therapy in autistic people. *Autism, 28*(11), 13623613241251513.
8. Sheppard, L. (2022). A systematic review of prospective memory in children and adults with attention deficit hyperactivity disorder (ADHD). Doctoral dissertation, University of Edinburgh. Edinburgh Research Archive.
9. Nicholson, R. M. (2022). *Hyperfocus in autism: An exploration inspired by the principles of neurodiversity.* Immaculata University.
10. Raymaker, D. M., Teo, A. R., Steckler, N. A., Lentz, B., Scharer, M., Delos Santos, A., & Nicolaidis, C. (2020). "Having all of your internal resources exhausted beyond measure and being left with no clean-up crew": Defining autistic burnout. *Autism in Adulthood, 2*(2), 132–143.
11. Autism Speaks. (n.d.). Sensory issues. Autism Speaks. www.autismspeaks.org/sensory-issues
12. The Brain Charity. (n.d.). What is masking? The Brain Charity. www.thebraincharity.org.uk/what-is-masking/

13. Doyle, N., McDowall, A., & Waseem, U. (2022). Intersectional stigma for autistic people at work: A compound adverse impact effect on labor force participation and experiences of belonging. *Autism in Adulthood*, 4(4), 340–356.
14. Das, M., Tang, J., Ringland, K. E., & Piper, A. M. (2021). Towards accessible remote work: Understanding work-from-home practices of neurodivergent professionals. *Proceedings of the ACM on Human-Computer Interaction*, 5(CSCW1), 1–30.
15. Crook, T., & McDowall, A. (2023). Paradoxical career strengths and successes of ADHD adults: An evolving narrative. *Journal of Work-Applied Management*, 16(1), 112–126.
16. McDowall, A., Freeman, K., & Marshall, S. (2014). Is feedforward the way forward? *International Coaching Psychology Review*, 9(2), 135–146.

Index

For Product Safety Concerns and Information please contact our EU
representative GPSR@taylorandfrancis.com
Taylor & Francis Verlag GmbH, Kaufingerstraße 24, 80331 München, Germany

www.ingramcontent.com/pod-product-compliance
Lightning Source LLC
Chambersburg PA
CBHW050648280326
41932CB00015B/2825